THE COLONIAL EMPIRE
AND ITS
CIVIL SERVICE

THE COLONIAL EMPIRE
AND ITS
CIVIL SERVICE

by

CHARLES JEFFRIES, C.M.G., O.B.E.

Assistant Secretary in the Colonial Office

With a Foreword by the

RT. HON. LORD HARLECH

Secretary of State for the Colonies, 1936–1938

✤

CAMBRIDGE

AT THE UNIVERSITY PRESS

1938

CAMBRIDGE
UNIVERSITY PRESS

University Printing House, Cambridge CB2 8BS, United Kingdom

Cambridge University Press is part of the University of Cambridge.

It furthers the University's mission by disseminating knowledge in the pursuit of
education, learning and research at the highest international levels of excellence.

www.cambridge.org
Information on this title: www.cambridge.org/9781107475021

© Cambridge University Press 1938

First published 1938
First paperback edition 2014

A catalogue record for this publication is available from the British Library

ISBN 978-1-107-47502-1 Paperback

ACKNOWLEDGEMENTS

I WISH to thank, in the first place, the Rt. Hon. Lord Harlech for not only permitting but encouraging the production of this book, and for his kindness in contributing a foreword; the authorities of the Colonial Office, and especially Sir George Tomlinson, for encouragement, advice and help; the Librarian and staff of the Colonial Office Library; the Editor of *The Crown Colonist*, for assistance in connection with the map, and for permission to include some material which has already appeared in that journal; and, finally, all those members of the Colonial Office staff and of the Colonial Service who have, directly or indirectly, helped to supply the information upon which this book is based, and have assisted me with their criticisms and suggestions.

Since the book had reached an advanced stage of preparation at the time of Lord Harlech's succession to the peerage, references to him in the text as Mr Ormsby Gore have been retained.

C. J. J.

FOREWORD

by the

SECRETARY OF STATE FOR THE COLONIES

I AM glad that this book has been written. The moment of its appearance is singularly opportune, for at no time have the problems of the Colonial Empire been subjected, and rightly subjected, to closer scrutiny. As trustees for its peoples and territories we have at all times to be ready to render an account of our stewardship, but no such account can be complete unless it also takes notice of the agents employed by the trustees, the manner in which they are recruited, the conditions under which they serve, the rewards to which they may aspire, and the training which they undergo in order to fit them for the diverse duties which they have to perform. Of their duties it is difficult to speak succinctly or comprehensively, so varying is their scope. Complex indeed must be the composition of a Service whose members must be as ready to adapt themselves to the wind-swept heaths of the Falklands as to the luxuriant jungle of Malaya; to the islands of the Western Pacific and the Caribbean Sea as to the great spaces of the African Tropics; to Cyprus and Hong Kong as to Bermuda and Mauritius. These names, chosen almost at random, may serve to indicate the range of the theatres in which members of the Colonial Service have to play their parts and the diversity of peoples and problems with which they are confronted.

Adaptability is an attribute of youth and the Service is still young. In the early part of the present century recruitment for the Eastern Cadet Services was securely established, but the staffing of the great African dependencies was small and even haphazard. It was indeed only in the three or four years before the Great War that as a result of the reduction of the minimum age limit it was possible to include the Colonial Service among the careers open to young men as soon as they came down from the Universities. But the stream of recruits of the new type was at once stopped by the outbreak of the War and by the end of 1918 the staff of every Colony was reduced to a mere shadow of its former self.

Progress since the War has been achieved in typically British fashion by a process of trial and error. There have been many difficulties, due in part to uncontrollable world causes. Whereas those responsible for recruitment have prayed before everything else for steadiness in numbers, successive periods of economic prosperity and depression have been accompanied by violent fluctuations in the demand for staff. Nevertheless progress has been marked and sustained. It discloses two outstanding features to which I would draw attention.

In the first place nothing has been more important and significant than the provision of special training for men selected for various branches of the Colonial Service. This development is essentially modern. Even so recently as the beginning of the present century, current conceptions of Colonial policy were so far from being defined that, even if the need for training had been expressed, it would have been difficult to say what should be taught and who should teach it. Colonial administration was still in the stage of tentative endeavour, if not of rule of thumb.

But now all that has been changed. The growing realisation of the implications of our trusteeship has given rise to the belief that the profession of Colonial Administration is one which calls not only for personal and educational qualifications of a high order, but also for a special preparatory study of the political, social, economic and scientific problems arising from our obligations to dependent peoples and territories. Thus from small beginnings the training of Cadets of the Colonial Administrative Service has been expanded into a carefully balanced course which occupies an academic year at both Oxford and Cambridge. It embraces not only law and languages, but is designed to provide a general introduction—historical, geographical, anthropological and economic—to the particular tasks on which the Cadets will later be engaged.

The development of the technical and scientific branches of the Colonial Service has also given rise to special problems in the matter of training. In the years following the War the need for staff was plain and insistent, but the supply of persons possessing the required qualifications was wholly insufficient. The problem was therefore to create a supply to meet a highly specialised demand. The solution has been found in the recruitment of men possessing a good general scientific education, and in giving them the additional training required for the special nature of the work that they are required to do. For the means by which this object has been achieved, in particular by the institution of scholarships to cover the period of training, I must refer the reader to Mr Jeffries' book, but I cannot refrain from expressing my gratitude to the Committees over which Lord Lovat and Sir James Irvine presided as well as to the authorities of the Imperial College of Tropical Agriculture in Trinidad and the Imperial Forestry Institute at Oxford for their invaluable contributions to the solution of these important and intricate problems.

The second important development in the modern conception of the Colonial Service is all that is implied in the term "Unification" as first formulated in the report of the Warren Fisher Committee in 1930. While the Committee dwelt on the essential unity of the Colonial Service, they insisted no less on the practical distinction between local branches the members of which were of local origin, locally recruited and appointed, and those other branches (recruited mainly in this country) which discharged the higher tasks of Colonial administration. No rigid or insuperable bar was to be placed between the two classes of officers; but it was made plain that in regard to the second class of appointments the Secretary of State must retain control of conditions of entry and, in so far as might be practicable, of terms of service, as well as of the posting of individual officers so as to ensure the best use of the talents and experience of each.

This, then, is the essential significance of "unification". From the point of view of whoever is Secretary of State for the Colonies it gives him a body of chosen agents for whose selection and welfare he takes full responsibility. From the point of view of the officer it opens up a wide variety of prospects. Finally from the point of view of individual Colonial Governments the policy of unification ensures that for the filling of certain "key" posts they can draw on a body of men whose collective experience far outsteps the bounds of any single Dependency.

In speaking of the variety of avenues along which officers of the Unified Services may advance I do not wish to create the impression that the Colonial Service lives in a state of perpetual flux. There must always be a number of highly important duties which for their successful discharge require before everything else a close knowledge of local conditions, people and languages. Many of the men who fill such posts spend the whole of their service in the Colony in which they started and are well content to devote themselves to the promotion of the welfare of the people whom they have come to know so well. They are indeed the backbone of Colonial administration and they do not go unrewarded. Other posts there are, however, which call for a greater variety of experience. A glance at the records of Governors, Colonial Secretaries and the Heads of technical departments is sufficient to show that many, if not most, of them have served in several Colonies, thus bringing at each stage in their careers ever widening experience to bear on the problems placed before them. Such records and the wide range of opportunities which they disclose cannot fail to be a lively stimulus to the imagination and ambition of even the last joined recruit. In particular I would stress the policy, already proclaimed to the world, that in selecting Colonial Governors the Secretary of State looks first and foremost to the Colonial Service. It is now quite exceptional for the higher posts in the Colonial Empire to be filled from outside the Colonial Service, except in the three fortress Colonies of Bermuda, Gibraltar, and Malta, where the practice is to appoint as Governor a soldier of distinction; and indeed it would be a poor compliment to the Service if it were deemed incapable of producing from within its ranks men fit to rise to the highest responsibilities.

I warmly commend Mr Jeffries' book both to those who are looking to the Colonies as a field for their life work and to those who wish to know more of the intricate and absorbing problems involved in the organisation of a great Public Service.

W. ORMSBY GORE

COLONIAL OFFICE
February 1938

CONTENTS

Introduction. THE COLONIAL EMPIRE   *page* xv

PART I

THE DEVELOPMENT OF THE COLONIAL SERVICE

Chap. I THE EARLY HISTORY OF THE COLONIAL
SERVICE   3

II EXPANSION IN AFRICA   15

III THE GREAT WAR AND THE PERIOD OF
RECONSTRUCTION   30

IV THE PROBLEM OF THE SCIENTIFIC
SERVICES   42

V THE WARREN FISHER COMMITTEE   53

VI THE UNIFICATION OF THE SERVICE   63

VII PROGRESS OF THE POLICY OF UNIFICA-
TION   76

PART II

THE COLONIAL SERVICE TO-DAY

VIII GENERAL STRUCTURE OF THE SERVICE   93

IX CONDITIONS OF EMPLOYMENT   105

X THE COLONIAL ADMINISTRATIVE SER-
VICE   128

XI THE COLONIAL LEGAL SERVICE   143

XII THE COLONIAL MEDICAL SERVICE   149

CONTENTS

Chapter   *page*

XIII THE COLONIAL FOREST SERVICE, THE
      COLONIAL AGRICULTURAL SERVICE,
      AND THE COLONIAL VETERINARY
      SERVICE   162

XIV   OTHER UNIFIED BRANCHES OF THE COLO-
      NIAL SERVICE   175

XV   BRANCHES NOT AS YET UNIFIED   186

XVI   GOVERNORS   198

XVII THE COLONIAL OFFICE   206

XVIII RETROSPECT AND PROSPECT   224

Appendices I THE FINANCIAL ORGANISATION OF
                COLONIAL GOVERNMENTS   243

          II SUMMARY OF APPOINTMENTS IN
              THE YEARS 1921 TO 1936   248

          III IMPORTANT DATES IN THE HISTORY
              OF THE COLONIAL SERVICE   250

          IV NOTE ON BOOKS   252

          V   LIST OF GOVERNORSHIPS   254

Index   255

Map of the Colonial Empire   *at end*

INTRODUCTION

THIS book is an attempt to tell, as straightforwardly and simply as possible, the story of the development of the British Colonial Service, and to describe the Service as it is to-day. It is written frankly from the point of view of an outside observer. Of the immense variety of life and work in the Service, of the alternations of excitement and of humdrum toil, of hope and perhaps of disappointment, it would be an impertinence for any but those who have actually experienced them to speak. But this is a study of history and organisation; and it may be that it is easier for an onlooker than for an active member of the Service to present a general conspectus of the whole.

While this account is based partly on official documents, and partly on information gained in the course of practical work at the Colonial Office, it must not be taken as in any sense an official pronouncement, or as expressing the official point of view. The responsibility for the accuracy of my statements is my own, and any comments or opinions expressed are similarly of a purely personal character. I hope, however, that they will not be found misleading, or of such a kind as to give offence.

The Colonial Service already has its chroniclers. Many able and distinguished pens have given us first-hand accounts and impressions of experiences in different parts of the Colonial Empire; while the functions of the Service have been described and discussed in such works as the late Sir George Fiddes's book on the Dominions and Colonial Offices, in the "Whitehall" series, and Sir Anton Bertram's book on the Colonial Service.[1] It will, however, appear from the following pages that the Colonial Service has undergone radical changes within the last few years, and there is as yet no comprehensive published record of these important developments. The chief purpose of this book is to interpret the recent changes in relation to the historical and geographical background, to show how and why they came

[1] See Appendix IV, "Note on Books".

about, and what has been their practical effect. It is my hope that such an account may be of some value to those who may seek to know more than has hitherto been conveniently accessible of the development of the Service, and especially to those who may be interested in the Service as a possible career for themselves, their children or their pupils.

The difficulty of the task to be attempted lies in the fact that we have to deal with no cut-and-dried system, but with a living growth. The Colonial Service is not a machine. It is an organism which must adapt itself to an almost infinite variety of conditions. There is no sealed pattern of official organisation which can be imposed upon each Colony irrespective of local circumstances. The members of the Service are not a set of chessmen moved by invisible hands in Downing Street, nor is the Colonial Empire a board upon which pieces can be disposed at will. The Service is a Service of men and women, and its work relates to the welfare and happiness of men and women; its problems, then, are human problems, calling for individual rather than routine treatment. At the same time, the march of events has broken down the isolation of the Colonial Dependencies from each other and from the rest of the world, and has called forth a spirit of combination. The story of the Colonial Service is the story of the attempt to strike a balance between the forces making for a closer and more coherent organisation and those making for the growth of separate and individual institutions in the component parts of the Colonial Empire.

In the interests of clarity, we must commence with a definition of terms, but it is necessary to emphasise that the definitions which we shall employ are arbitrary and directed to the purpose of our present study. For other purposes and in other connections the same terms might be used with a different connotation.

His Majesty's Colonial Service consists of the aggregate of the public services of the Colonies, Protectorates and Mandated Territories for the government of which the Secretary of State for the Colonies is responsible. All members of the Government Services of these territories are entitled to regard themselves as members of the Colonial Service. But the Colonial Service, at any rate as we shall use the term, does not include officers of municipal or other public authorities in the territories mentioned, unless those authorities are directly controlled by the Government or unless the officers' appointments are subject to the approval of the Secretary of State. Nor does it include officers of territories not administered under the supervision of the Secretary of State for the Colonies (such as, for instance, the South African Protectorates for which the Secretary of State for Dominion Affairs is responsible), unless such officers happen to be members of the Colonial Service detached for duty there. Again, it does not include the staff of the Colonial Office in London, which is a part of the Home Civil Service, or the staff of the Crown Agents for the Colonies, or the public services of the Anglo-Egyptian Sudan or of 'Iraq.

The Colonial Service, then, is the Civil Service of a certain group of British Dependencies, of varying constitutional status, with a great variety of local conditions, and having a very wide geographical distribution, but linked together by a common dependence on the British Crown through a single Minister of the Crown. In this book we shall refer to these Dependencies collectively as the Colonial Empire, using the term in this strictly limited sense. The words "Colonies" and "Dependencies" will also be used indifferently to describe the same group without reference to exact constitutional definition, and with a similar limitation.

The Service with which this study is concerned numbers at the present time some 200,000 men and women, divided amongst more than 50 separate administrations, and serving a population of nearly 50,000,000, distributed over an area of nearly 2,000,000 square miles. Figures alone do not convey a very clear impression, and it may therefore be of interest to note that the aggregate area of the Colonial Empire is almost twice the size of British India, while its population is nearly double that of the self-governing Dominions. The greater part of this area and of this population is in the tropics.

It is only within the last few years that it has become natural or customary to speak of the British Colonial Empire as a definite entity. Not so long ago, the word "Colonies" was generally used to denote those countries which are now properly known as the Dominions. The very name of Empire has largely been discarded in favour of a phrase far more suitable to the position of the Dominions, the Commonwealth of Nations. Yet it is well to remember that there remains a British Empire in the true sense of the words; an Empire which neither in size, in manpower nor in economic importance is a negligible factor in world affairs; an Empire to which its constituents are proud to belong and which the Mother Country is no less proud to hold in trust. It is an Empire whose units are to be found in every zone of the earth's surface, save only the Arctic. Within it are produced all manner of primary products and raw materials needed for the manufactures of the world. It numbers amongst its peoples almost every race of mankind. It holds many secrets of man's past; and it is not entirely fanciful to suppose that it may hold the key to some of the problems of his future.

The most obvious characteristic of this Colonial Empire is, without doubt, its variety. No geographical continuity binds together these diverse territories, no similarity of climate or situation. The units vary in size, from vast Continental countries like Nigeria to small oceanic islands; they vary in history, in civilisation, in constitutional development and in form of government. Until fairly recently, in regard to matters affecting the public services as well as in regard to other matters, policy and practice have been dominated by the implications of this variety. But gradually, during the past few years, attention has been increasingly called to an underlying unity. The symbol of this unity is the linking of the various components to the Central Government and to each other through the medium of the Colonial Office; but it is becoming clearer that this link is not merely symbolical nor is it accidental. Scientific and political developments have lessened both geographical and cultural differences. More and more the Dependencies are finding that they have common interests and common problems, that not only is it possible for them to stand together, but by doing so they gain strength which they could scarcely hope to develop in isolation. A notable example of the modern tendency was the appearance for the first time at the Ottawa Conference of 1932 of the Colonial Empire as an economic unit of the British Commonwealth. A not less notable illustration is provided by the unification of the Colonial Service, which furnishes the main theme of this book.

Any attempt to survey the Colonial Empire is attended by difficulty, since the classification of the units must vary according to the basis of classification which is adopted. Geographical situation, climate, racial distribution, constitutional status, social or economic characteristics, would each afford a basis on which the constituent parts of the Colonial Empire would group themselves differently. For the moment, the chief consideration is to obtain a comprehensive list of the territories which form the theatre of the operations of the Colonial Service, and it will be most convenient to enumerate them according to geographical grouping.

The nearest Colony to Britain is Gibraltar, and we may proceed eastwards from this starting-point. Gibraltar and Malta are the two "fortress" Colonies of the Mediterranean; they are under military Governorship, but the Colonial Office is responsible for the civil administration, which is conducted by members of the Colonial Service. The third Mediterranean Colony is Cyprus, which has been under British administration since 1878, but has had the status of a Colony only since 1925. The administration of Palestine under the Mandate is carried out by the Colonial Service, members of which are also employed as advisers in the mandated territory of Trans-Jordan.

The "youngest" Colony is Aden, which, having formerly been part of India, was created a Colony on 1 April 1937. Associated with the Colony is the Aden Protectorate, extending over a considerable area of Southern Arabia. In the Indian Ocean are the island Colonies of Seychelles and Mauritius, over 900 miles apart, both preserving strong traditions of their French colonisation in the eighteenth century. South of India lies

≪ xix ≫

Ceylon, equal in size to Holland and Belgium, and supporting a population of about 5,500,000. Farther east, we reach British Malaya, comprising the Colony of the Straits Settlements; the Federated Malay States of Perak, Selangor, Negri Sembilan and Pahang; the Unfederated States of Johore, Kedah, Kelantan, Trengganu and Perlis; together with the States of Brunei and North Borneo. The last mentioned is administered by the British North Borneo Company. Last of the Eastern group of Colonies to be catalogued is Hong Kong, the great island port off the south-eastern coast of China.

In the Pacific Ocean are a number of Dependencies, of which the principal is the Colony of Fiji. The Governor of the Colony is also High Commissioner for the Western Pacific Dependencies, which include the Gilbert and Ellice Islands Colony, the Solomon Islands Protectorate, Tonga, and the New Hebrides. The last-named group is administered in conjunction with France as a Condominium. In the South Atlantic lies the Colony of the Falkland Islands, with its dependencies of South Georgia, South Orkney and South Shetland.

We pass to the historic Colonies of the West Indian and Central American groups. On the mainland are two Colonies, British Guiana and British Honduras. The island Colonies are seven in number: Bermuda and Bahamas off the coast of the United States; Jamaica (with its dependencies the Cayman Islands and the Turks and Caicos Islands); the Leeward Islands (Antigua, St Christopher-Nevis, Dominica[1], Montserrat and the Virgin Islands); Barbados; the Windward Islands (Grenada, St Lucia, St Vincent); Trinidad and Tobago.

In mid-Atlantic is St Helena, with its dependencies, Ascension and Tristan da Cunha. We now come to Tropical Africa. Here, on the west coast, are four Dependencies, each consisting of a Colony of comparatively ancient foundation, backed by a Protectorate of much larger area and of recent development. The smallest is the Gambia, at the mouth of the great river of that name: the Colony covers 69 square miles, and the Protectorate over 4,000. Next in position and in size is the Sierra Leone

---

[1] Dominica is shortly to be transferred to the Windward Islands.

Colony and Protectorate, with a total area of nearly 28,000 square miles; then the Gold Coast Colony, with Ashanti, the Northern Territories and that part of Togoland which is under British mandate: in all, over 90,000 square miles, which is rather more than the area of Great Britain. Largest of all is Nigeria, which, with the Cameroons under British mandate, is almost as large as the United Kingdom, France and Belgium together, or about one-third the size of British India. Its population is about 20,000,000.

Lastly, on the eastern side of Africa are: the Somaliland Protectorate, larger than England and Wales, but with a population of only 300,000; the Uganda Protectorate; the Kenya Colony and Protectorate; the mandated territory of Tanganyika; the Zanzibar Protectorate; the Nyasaland Protectorate; and Northern Rhodesia. Uganda covers over 90,000 square miles, and supports a population of 3,500,000; the population of Kenya is estimated to be rather less, but its area is about 225,000 square miles, much of this being desert. Unlike the Colonies and Protectorates of West Africa, the Kenya Protectorate is on the coast, and the Colony inland; the reason for this is that the coastal strip forms part of the dominions of the Sultan of Zanzibar. The Zanzibar Protectorate is ruled by its hereditary Sultan, who is advised by a British Resident: it consists of two islands, situated about 20 miles from the mainland, with a combined area of about 1,000 square miles, and a population of rather over 200,000. The Tanganyika Territory is the largest Dependency on the east coast, being about as large as Nigeria, but carrying an estimated population not much exceeding 5,000,000. Nyasaland is a little smaller than England, and has a population of 1,500,000; Northern Rhodesia, on the other hand, distributes about the same number of people over an area of over 280,000 square miles, or nearly five times that of England and Wales.

The countries which have been enumerated form the Colonial Empire, in the sense in which that term will be used for the present purpose. They have come under the British flag at different times during the last three hundred years, in widely differing circumstances. Some have been acquired as spoils of war, others at the spontaneous desire of the inhabitants. Some have become ours as it were by accident, others as a deliberate result of policy, whether for strategic purposes, for settlement, or for commercial development. But, whatever the historical background, the conception of trusteeship is now firmly established as the guiding principle of Imperial policy in relation to the Colonial Empire.

It is not the purpose of this study to deal in any detail with the geographical, political, or economic aspects of the Colonial Empire, except in so far as an understanding of these aspects is necessary for a true comprehension of the history, present structure, and functions of the Colonial Service. But some brief appreciation of the general position must be attempted. It has already been observed that although almost every region of the earth contains some unit of the Colonial Empire, the great mass of the territories lies within the tropical zone. The exceptions are, indeed, not by any means unimportant, but in size and population they are sufficiently in a minority to justify the Colonial Empire being regarded as on the whole homogeneous in point of general climatic conditions. Another important general geographical consideration is that practically all the Dependencies, if not themselves islands, depend upon sea-borne communications. Their main trade frontiers are on the sea coasts. They thus have a common interest in the maintenance of open lines for marine trade.

The political constitutions and conditions of the various Dependencies differ considerably, but here again it is possible to make certain broad generalisations. The principal general characteristic is precisely that implied in the word "Dependencies". Whatever stage of domestic political development any of these countries may have reached, none of them possesses what is termed "responsible" government. All depend on the British Parliament as the ultimate controlling authority. There is nothing derogatory in this dependence. Few, if any, of these territories would wish to expose themselves alone to the strenuous conditions of the contemporary world. The British

Government levies no taxes for its services; it makes no profit out of the Colonial Empire. It is content to regard these lands as a trust.

This political dependence is shown in practice by the presence, at the head of each administration, of a King's representative, usually known as the Governor. (The full title is "Governor and Commander-in-Chief". In Jamaica the historic title of "Captain-General and Governor-in-Chief" is retained. In Palestine the head of the administration is styled "High Commissioner", while the Governors of the Straits Settlements and Fiji are also respectively High Commissioners for the Malay States and the Western Pacific.) The actual powers of the Governor vary according to the constitutional arrangements of the individual Dependencies and to the presence or absence of developed local self-governing institutions; but his position as "the single and supreme authority responsible to and representative of His Majesty" is a fundamental characteristic of the Colonial system.

For political purposes, the Dependencies may be divided into the following classes:

(i) Those in which the Governor is the sole legislator. This group includes Gibraltar, Somaliland, St Helena, Aden, and also, at present, Malta and Cyprus.

(ii) Those in which there is a legislative body, consisting partly of officials and partly of unofficials. This is by far the largest group, but the details of the constitutions vary considerably. In some Colonies the unofficial members are elected; in others they are nominated by the Governor; while in others, again, both methods of appointment exist side by side. In many cases, but not in all, the constitution provides for an official majority.

(iii) Those with legislative bodies which are wholly or mainly elective. This group includes certain of the old-established West Indian Colonies, and also Ceylon.

(iv) Protected States, under their traditional Rulers. The Malay States (Federated and Unfederated), and the Zanzibar Protectorate are the principal representatives of this class, but included in various territories there are many others, such, for example, as the Kingdom of Buganda in the Uganda Protectorate, the Emirates of Northern Nigeria, or the Confederation of Ashanti. In such states, administration is, to a greater or less degree, carried on by local authorities, according to local law and custom, subject to the advice of a British Resident.

While, then, there is no such thing as a typical "Crown Colony" Government, it is possible to trace, in the Colonial Empire, a series of stages in development, from a benevolent autocracy towards a progressive association of the inhabitants of the various Dependencies with the control of their own affairs. Development along these lines will no doubt continue, but it is not likely to follow any uniform pattern. It must be adapted to the needs and circumstances of the various countries; here it may take the form of parliamentary institutions, there that of the independent growth of indigenous States within what is now a single administration. There is a wide field for political experiment, and at all stages the Colonial Service has an important part to play, a part calling for wisdom, for sympathetic understanding of the aspirations of the Colonial peoples, and for clarity of judgment.

Turning to the economic sphere, we find that, once again, attention has been increasingly focussed in recent years upon that paradox of unity within variety which forces itself upon the observer at every point of a survey of the Colonial Empire. Although their circumstances differ widely in many ways, the Dependencies as a whole have very considerable interests in common. Their economic position is, broadly speaking, that of a group of countries concerned with the production and export of raw materials and with the importation of manufactured goods. Their prosperity depends not only on production but on the successful marketing of the products of their industry. In many instances Colonies remote geographically from one another have to sell the same product in the same market: sugar, for example, reaches the world markets from places as far apart as the West Indies, Mauritius and Fiji. Experience has amply shown that the Colonies have far more to gain by pooling their resources and by working in co-operation, than by competing with one another.

Similarly, in matters connected with the public services, the mainspring of the modern developments of which this book has to tell is the growing recognition of a common need, transcending though not eliminating local and special requirements, for co-operation in creating and maintaining a general reservoir of expert staff which shall be at the disposal of the Dependencies as a whole, and which is capable of being distributed amongst the participating Governments in the manner best calculated to serve the interests of all at a particular moment. Here again, experience has proved that the Colonies are interdependent, and that the best prospect of providing each with a strong and efficient public service is afforded by a policy of co-ordinated effort to secure and to retain the best available personnel. The first part of this book describes how and why such a policy has come to be adopted; in the second part I attempt to present a picture of the organisation of the Colonial Service as it exists to-day.

THE COLONIAL EMPIRE & ITS CIVIL SERVICE

⊸⋄⊷

PART I
THE DEVELOPMENT OF THE COLONIAL SERVICE

✳

CHAPTER I

THE EARLY HISTORY OF THE COLONIAL SERVICE

ALTHOUGH its connotation has altered with the passage of time, the expression "His Majesty's Colonial Service" can claim a century of authority. It appears in an explanatory memorandum introducing the first version of the Colonial Regulations, dated 30 March 1837, less than three months before the accession of Queen Victoria. "Lord Glenelg", the memorandum states, "has had frequent occasion to observe, that there are various regulations connected with His Majesty's Colonial Service, which appear to be inaccurately understood, and, on that account, imperfectly observed, in many of His Majesty's Colonies." Accordingly, the document proceeds to explain, in the stately diction of the period, His Lordship had brought together various rules which he found to have been hitherto dispersed through the correspondence of his predecessors.

The Colonial Empire to which these regulations of a hundred years ago relate was, of course, very different from that with which we are concerned to-day. It included some territories —the Canadas, Newfoundland, the Cape of Good Hope, the Australian settlements—which are now Dominions. The West Indian Colonies appear in the list substantially as they are at present, though Barbados and Tobago were then included in the Government of the Windward Islands. Gibraltar, Malta, Sierra Leone and Gambia, St Helena, Ceylon, Mauritius, complete the tale, with the addition of Heligoland. Malaya, Nigeria, the Gold Coast, the Eastern African territories, had not come into existence as parts of the Empire.

The "Rules and Regulations for the Information and Guidance of the Principal Officers and Others in His Majesty's Colonial Possessions", to give them their full title, enable some impression to be gained of the Colonial Service of a century ago. The head of each administration was, as now, the Governor, whose powers and duties the Regulations are to a large extent occupied in setting forth. Governors and other officers were required to pay substantial fees and stamp duties in connection with their appointments. Public officers were appointed by the Governor, subject to confirmation from home; but in some cases (not clearly defined) they were nominated by the Secretary of State or, in the case of revenue officers, by the Lords Commissioners of the Treasury, who appear to have exercised a close degree of financial control over the Colonies at this date.

The principal officers of a Colonial Government are mentioned in the Regulations under the following titles:

The Lieutenant-Governor.
The Chief Justice.
Puisne Judges.
The Colonial Secretary.
The Commissioners or Government Agents of provinces or districts.
The Attorney-General.
The Solicitor-General.
The Treasurer, Paymaster-General, or Collector of Inland Revenue.
The Auditor-General, or Inspector-General of Accounts.
The Commissioner of Crown Lands.
The Collector of Customs.
The Comptroller of Customs.
The Surveyor-General.

Many of these titles continue in use at the present day.

It would seem that some even of the senior officers were felt to be in need of some stimulus to activity, since it is laid down that the Colonial Secretary is not to have his pay issued until he has produced the Blue Book, and the Treasurer is placed under a similar disability until he shall have rendered his accounts.

The conditions of service do not seem to have been very attractive by modern standards. It was to be understood, as a general rule, that "no Colonial officers, of any rank or description, are entitled to retiring pensions"; though cases could be considered on their merits. Passage allowances were granted only to Governors and clergymen. Leave of absence was heavily discouraged, and was to be confined, as far as possible, to cases either of serious indisposition or of urgent private affairs. Possibly the latter was a polite fiction. Half-salary only was paid during leave, except in the case of the higher orders of the clergy; but leave of absence to these dignitaries "must be restricted within the limits of what is absolutely necessary". Free quarters were not to be provided without the special authority of His Majesty's Government. Public offices were to be supplied with such furniture, of a plain but substantive (sic) quality, as might be absolutely requisite for the proper accommodation of the persons belonging to the departments; but it is regrettable to note that "the Lords Commissioners of the Treasury consider carpeting to be quite unnecessary for this purpose, except in climates where a considerable degree of cold is experienced".

I suppose that the popular idea of the Colonial Service a century since is more or less accurately reflected by Thackeray in *Vanity Fair*. It will be recollected that when the infamous Lord Steyne was detected in his intrigue with Becky Sharp, he disposed of her injured husband by the simple process of securing his appointment to a Colonial Governorship. The announcement of the appointment was made in the following terms:

"Governorship of Coventry Island.—H.M.S. *Yellowjack*, Commander Jaunders, has brought letters and papers from Coventry Island. H. E. Sir Thomas Liverseege had fallen a victim to the prevailing fever at Swamptown. His loss is deeply deplored in the flourishing Colony. We hear that the Governorship has been offered to Colonel Rawdon Crawley, C.B., a distinguished Waterloo officer. We need not only men of acknowledged bravery but men of administrative talents, to superintend the affairs of our Colonies; and we have no doubt that the gentleman selected by the Colonial Office to fill the lamented vacancy which has occurred at Coventry Island is admirably calculated for the post which he is about to occupy."

We need not take Thackeray's irony at its face value; but at least we may fairly conclude that the public whom he addressed were not disposed to regard it as entirely fantastic that an important Governorship should be filled by a piece of shameless jobbery, or that the conditions of life in a flourishing Colony should be so bad that no insurance company would do business with the Governor-designate, who, in fact, was destined to be killed off by yellow fever like his lamented predecessor.

I have spared a page or two to look back upon the Colonial Service of a distant past, but I do not propose to attempt any detailed history of the public services of the Colonies during the Victorian era. The main Colonial problems of that period were worked out in what are now the Dominions and in India. In comparison the affairs of the Dependencies which were to form the nucleus of the modern Colonial Empire were on a minor scale. Outside India, the question of administering and developing countries populated by aboriginal non-European peoples hardly arose; in the future Dominions the questions which came up for decision were principally those connected with the establishment and organisation of British settlements overseas; the lesser Colonies were either "garrisons", maintained for strategic purposes, or "plantations", existing for the production of sugar, cotton and other raw materials needed for the manufactures of the Mother Country. The last-mentioned, it is true, presented important problems consequent upon the abolition of slavery; but these problems were mainly of a political and economic character, and did not greatly affect the questions of Civil Service organisation, with which we are here concerned.

In these circumstances, although the Regulations of 1837 were in due course followed by a succession of "Rules and Regulations for Her Majesty's Colonial Service", a Colonial Service, in the sense of a body of officers employed in the service of the Colonial Empire as a whole, could not be said to exist. The Colonies were as a rule self-supporting in the matter of staff, only the highest offices, such as those of Governor, Chief Justice and Colonial Secretary, being filled from outside. These offices were regarded as proper objects for the exercise of "patronage" by the Secretary of State, and while it need not be assumed that this patronage was normally exercised otherwise than in a public spirit; while, also, it is clear that, at any rate towards the close of the century, ability and administrative experience were thought of more importance than other considerations; nevertheless there is evidence of a steadily growing consciousness in responsible quarters that the patronage system was inadequate to meet the needs of the Colonial Empire, and to supply the personnel required to deal with the new and complex problems of administration which the expansion of that Empire was continually presenting. If this were true in respect of the military and trading stations and the plantation Colonies, it was far more so in respect of the newer Colonies and Protectorates in which questions of native administration had to be dealt with. To say this is not to disparage the admirable work done by the Colonial Services as a whole during these difficult years. The noble tradition of public service handed down from father to son in many of the old Colonial families, and persisting to the present day, is evidence of the spirit in which these men laboured. It was the system which was found wanting.

At different times during the nineteenth century the Eastern Dependencies—Ceylon, Malaya and Hong Kong—came under the control of the Secretary of State for the Colonies. Ceylon and the Straits Settlements were previously administered as parts of India, and in any case their proximity to India and a general similarity of conditions naturally pointed to the adoption of Indian organisation as a model, rather than the methods of the West Indian and other territories already dealt with in the Colonial Office. It was natural, too, that Hong Kong should be associated with Malaya. Hence, from the point of view of the subject with which we are here concerned, these Dependencies developed as a group, the principal feature of the organisation of each being the presence of a European "civil service" based on the model of the Indian Civil Service, and charged with the responsibility for carrying on the various departments of government, including, as in India, the work of the judiciary. These "civil services" were recruited on much the same lines as the Indian Civil Service; as long ago as 1869 a competitive examination by the Civil Service Commissioners was introduced for the Straits Settlements, Hong Kong and Ceylon services. In 1882 a combined examination was instituted, successful candidates being given the choice of Colonies; the Malay States, as yet unfederated, however, retained the nomination system. In 1896 the examination was joined to that for the Home and Indian Civil Services, and the Federated Malay States were included; and this arrangement continued in force until 1932.

Here, then, we find for the first time a practical approach towards the conception of a Colonial Administrative Service in which, though its application was restricted to a definite area, the principle of combination for recruiting purposes was recognised. There can be no doubt that the association of the Eastern Dependencies with each other and eventually with the larger Services recruiting in the same field was of great benefit to them. By this means they were enabled to secure for the "Eastern Cadetships" candidates of a higher intellectual standard than they could have attracted by independent recruitment, and the justification of the policy is amply supplied by the remarkable advances made by the Dependencies in question during the last half-century. At the same time, it has to be recognised that one effect of the system was to make the Cadet Services into more or less closed corporations. This was probably of more value in the earlier stages than later, when large and efficient administrative services had developed elsewhere in the Colonial Empire.

The formation of the Eastern Cadet Services satisfactorily disposed, for the time being at least, of the problem of organising the public administrations of the Dependencies with which they were associated. Meanwhile, questions of Service organisation were beginning to demand attention elsewhere.

The modern history of the institution now known officially as the Colonial Service may fairly be said to begin with the advent of Mr Joseph Chamberlain as Secretary of State for the Colonies in 1895. There is always a tendency for practical developments to outstrip their formal recognition, and while, in 1895, the essential differences between Dominions and Dependencies, with which we are all now familiar, were already potentially or actually in being, all these territories were in form Colonies, graded in a single list from the fully self-governing to the completely dependent. All were in common dealt with by the Colonial Office, and no special organisation existed there for handling the problems of the self-governing and the non-self-governing Colonies separately. Both classes were distributed amongst the departments of the Office on a geographical basis. Considering, then, that the main experience of the Office was concerned with the development of self-governing institutions in the more important of the territories with which it dealt, it is only natural that the general tradition should have been in the direction of regarding each geographical unit as a self-contained organisation with its own public service, entirely distinct and separate from the public service of any other. Except in 'the area where, as already indicated, Indian practice had been used as a model, each territory would naturally form its own public service according to its individual needs and from its own resources, supplemented by such persons as the Secretary of State, in the exercise of his right of patronage, should choose to appoint to it.

Although the modern formal distinction between Dominions and Dependencies was not made at this time, it was already settled practice for all appointments in the public services of the Colonies possessing responsible government to be made locally; only the Governors were appointed on the recommendation of the Secretary of State and were in any sense under the control of the Colonial Office. But in the case of the dependent Colonies there was a steadily increasing demand for recruits from home. Mr Chamberlain had not been long in office before he came to the conclusion that this matter of recruitment called for investigation, and he accordingly instructed Lord Selborne, the Parliamentary Under-Secretary of State, to prepare a survey of the various officials who might be held to come under the head of the "Colonial Service", in order that he might inform himself of the dimensions of that Service and consider whether any changes in organisation were needed.

The report[1] presented by Lord Selborne to his chief a year later gave a detailed picture of the Colonial Service as it existed at this time. The bulk of the Service was employed in the West Indian and Eastern groups of Colonies, but West Africa was already coming into prominence. The Gold Coast, for example, employed a substantial staff, although Nigeria was as yet represented only by the small Colony of Lagos. The "Niger Territories" and the "Niger Coast Protectorate" (the climate of which was bluntly stated by the current Colonial Office List to "resemble that of other parts of West Africa in being deadly for Europeans") remained outside the sphere of direct Colonial Office administration until 1900. East Africa, on the other hand, did not appear at all, since the Foreign Office was responsible then for the Protectorates in this region.

The report gave a grand total of 434 higher administrative officers (about 100 of whom were employed in the Eastern Cadet Services), 310 legal officers, 447 medical officers, and rather more than 300 others; but in fact the number of posts filled from home was considerably less than these figures might be supposed to indicate, since many of the officers concerned were locally recruited, although their appointments required the approval of the Secretary of State. By modern standards, therefore, the recruiting problem was hardly a serious one; but there is evidence that it was not being satisfactorily solved by the patronage system, and that even at this stage difficulty was experienced in finding within the Service itself men capable of filling the highest offices. There was no real training ground of Colonial administration from which a supply of officers could be drawn for Governorships and other important posts. The Eastern Services were not generally available, since they offered within themselves so attractive a career that it would ordinarily have required more inducement than the smaller administrations could offer to tempt their members away. On the other hand, though those smaller administrations might, and did on occasion throw up a number of very capable officers, they could not, in the nature of things, be relied upon for a continuous supply.

[1] Not published.

If these considerations were present at the outset of Mr Chamberlain's term of office, they became increasingly insistent as the nineteenth century gave place to the twentieth, and immense new horizons opened up in Africa. The arduous and unfamiliar nature of the work, the risks to health, the discomforts and lack of amenities inseparable from pioneering conditions in the new countries, did not tend to make the African Services, considered by themselves, very attractive. Yet those very circumstances made it essential that candidates of a high quality should be secured.

The questions raised by Mr Chamberlain's inquiry were exhaustively discussed by the Secretary of State and his principal advisers between 1895 and 1900. Various suggestions for remedying the position were examined, amongst these being the possibility of combining or "allying" the Colonial Services with the Indian Civil Service or alternatively with the Colonial Office itself. But the proposal which received the most support and the most careful consideration was that the separate Services should be combined into a unified Colonial Service, the members of which would be recruited by examination, as in the case of the Eastern Cadets, and would be interchangeable amongst the various Colonies. Eventually, however, Mr Chamberlain was obliged to conclude that the objections to such a scheme were insuperable.

The main difficulty was the West African climate. At that time the "White Man's Grave" had not outlived its sinister reputation. It was virtually impossible to send men there who had not reached a fairly mature age, and who were not prepared to sacrifice the prospect of leading a normal family life. The African Services must, therefore, be staffed by volunteers. A scheme of interchange must involve not only the right of members of those Services to be moved away, but an obligation upon others employed in more favoured regions to be compulsorily transferred to West Africa. Such an obligation, it was felt, would react so severely upon the popularity of the Service as a whole that any advantages which the scheme might have would be more than outweighed. Apart from this, it was supposed that the Colonies which customarily provided their own public services from their local populations, would not easily be persuaded to merge those services in a common service largely recruited from the United Kingdom, and no doubt thus sacrifice to some extent the prospects of their own sons.

Again, experience had shown that it was unlikely that recruitment for West Africa by competitive examination would be successful. Candidates were already difficult enough to secure, and the difficulties would only be increased if they were to be asked to face the immediate horrors of an examination as well as the prospective rigours of the African climate. At the same time, it was not felt that sufficient justification existed for expecting the Eastern Colonies to sacrifice, for the problematic benefit of association with the unpopular Tropical African Services, the advantages which they had secured by associating their recruitment with that for the Home and Indian Civil Services.

It was, however, thought that some progress might be made in the direction of creating a general "staff" service of the Colonial Secretaries and other high administrative officers, and in the direction of facilitating transfers by instituting a general scheme for pensions to officers and their widows. A Committee was to have been set up to go into these questions, but, no doubt owing to the preoccupation of the Colonial Office with the South African War, this project seems to have fallen into abeyance. Nevertheless, these inquiries and discussions served to bring to light the fact that there existed a "Colonial Service" problem distinct from any question relating to the self-governing Colonies; and, while the actual unification of the Colonial Service was not to be accomplished for another thirty years, Mr Chamberlain's régime produced in this field some practical results which in time were to make that unification possible. For example, attention was drawn in the course of the proceedings to the fact that the Colonial Office actually possessed no organised machinery for recording the history and qualifications of the officers of the Service, for the use of the Secretary of State in selecting candidates for promotion. Under the traditional theory of "patronage", not only first appointments (other than those filled by competitive examination) but promotions were the personal concern of the Minister, and as such not within the province of the Office staff. All matters of this kind were accordingly prepared and submitted to him by his Private Secretary, who was not necessarily a permanent official, and might or might not have the time or inclination to devote serious attention to this side of his duties. At best, it inevitably took a new Private Secretary some time to familiarise himself with the necessary information. Fortunately, Mr Chamberlain had, in Lord Ampthill, a Private Secretary who was fully alive to the defects of the system, and on representations from him the Secretary of State laid down that the rendering of annual confidential reports on officers of the Colonial Services, which had fallen into disuse, should be revived and enforced, and that it should in future be the duty of the General Department of the Office to collate and keep these records and to make recommendations for promotions. In this way the foundations of a properly organised Promotions Branch were laid.

First appointments continued to be the personal concern of the Secretary of State, and to be handled by his Private Secretary; but here also certain necessary reforms were introduced. A memorandum was printed for circulation to universities and other likely sources of supply, explaining precisely what openings existed in the Colonies for candidates from this country. At the time of which we are speaking, these opportunities were chiefly in connection with technical or specialist posts, but attempts were already being made (not at first with much success) to recruit administrative cadets for the Gold Coast, and it was realised that West and possibly East Africa would require substantial staff in the near future.

Although Mr Chamberlain was obliged to relinquish the idea of creating a formally unified Colonial Service, he was able, before he left office, to inaugurate an unofficial institution which gave concrete expression to the essential spirit of unity underlying the nominal separation of the public services of the various non-self-governing Dependencies. This institution, which was christened the Corona Club, was designed to provide an annual opportunity for the members of those Services, past and present, and of the Colonial Office staff, to meet the Secretary of State and each other "off parade". The Club, which began in 1900 with a membership of about 300, now has 3,500 on its rolls. It arranges every year a Colonial Service Dinner, at which the Secretary of State for the time being presides, the average attendance being about 350. The character of the Club was prescribed by its founder, and has been carefully preserved: membership is open to all officers of the Colonial Service and the Colonial Office, irrespective of rank, and to no others; the subscriptions are modest, any surplus going to reduce the cost of the dinner; the dinners are as short as possible, and one speech only—that of the Secretary of State—is permitted, the main object of the evening being to enable the members to foregather freely, to meet old friends and to make new ones. The Club has done much to create and to express a spirit of community in the Service, and in recent years its usefulness has been greatly increased by the co-operation of the British Broadcasting Corporation, who, by including the speeches in their Empire programmes, have enabled those members of the Service who are on duty in the Colonies to join in spirit with those who, having retired or being on leave, are able to be physically present at the gathering.

CHAPTER II

EXPANSION IN AFRICA

THE dominating factor of the years from 1900 to the outbreak of the Great War was, so far as the history of the Colonial Services is concerned, the immense expansion of the public services in Tropical Africa. On the west of the continent, the Gambia, Sierra Leone, the Gold Coast and Lagos were old-established Colonies, of no great size, each backed by a considerably larger Protectorate. It was not until the last quarter of the nineteenth century that serious attempts were made to define, explore and administer these Protectorates; but the task, once accepted, rapidly demanded personnel on a scale hitherto unprecedented in the history of the Colonial Empire. At first some of these territories were under the control of the Foreign Office, while a large part of what is now Nigeria was controlled by the Royal Niger Company; but by the end of the century the centralisation of control in the hands of the Colonial Office was accomplished, the last stage being the transfer of the Nigerian territories to that Office on 1 January 1900.

On the eastern coast, the transfer of control from the Foreign Office to the Colonial Office came rather later. Between 1903 and 1905 the British Central Africa Protectorate (Nyasaland), the East Africa Protectorate (Kenya), the Uganda Protectorate, and the Somaliland Protectorate were transferred; Zanzibar remained under the Foreign Office until 1913.

The pioneer work of opening up these vast new territories and of establishing law and order naturally fell to administrators, soldiers and police; but at a very early stage the co-operation of professional and technical staff of many kinds was enlisted. In particular, there was a marked development of the medical services. Mr Chamberlain, when Secretary of State, was greatly impressed by the toll of tropical disease amongst the European staffs working in the African Colonies and Protectorates, and by the urgent necessity for organising research into the causes and cure of tropical diseases, and for providing an adequate supply of specially trained medical officers to look after the health of the Government Services on the spot. The story of the foundation of the London and Liverpool Schools of Tropical Medicine, of the work of Manson, Ross and others, is outside the scope of this narrative. It must suffice to note that in the first years of the present century a great drive against tropical diseases was undertaken, largely at the instance and with the practical support of the Colonial Office, which was actuated primarily by a care for the health and welfare of the officers who were performing difficult and dangerous duties in the tropics in the service of the Empire. But health, as well as trade, has "followed the flag" in the history of British colonisation, and it was not long before the medical services, instituted originally to minister to European officials, extended their beneficent operations to the prevention and treatment of disease amongst the general populations of the countries in which they worked; with the result that they developed into highly organised and efficient State public health services.

The recruitment of medical officers for Tropical Africa was, then, an inseparable concomitant of the increase in the administrative and other services. Already at the beginning of the century over 60 medical officers were employed in the West African Dependencies, and recruitment was proceeding at the rate of about 15 a year. So vital was the necessity of maintaining and expanding the supply of first class men, that special measures were taken to deal with the problem. In 1902 a West African Medical Staff was created as a unified Service, common to all the West African Dependencies. Officers on the Staff were liable to serve anywhere in the group, as the Secretary of State might direct, and were employed on uniform conditions of service. They were also on a common roster for purposes of seniority and promotion within the group. This experiment in unification was so successful that not only was recruitment kept up, but in a short time it was possible to create a West African Medical

Staff Reserve of selected candidates ready to go out at short notice to fill immediate vacancies. When it is considered that the number of officers employed in the West African Medical Staff increased to about 120 in 1905, and 170 in 1909, it is evident that the results of the system were highly satisfactory.

The creation of the West African Medical Staff was an episode of more than local or temporary importance in the history of the Colonial Service. By demonstrating that a Service common to a number of Colonies could be satisfactorily managed without derogation from the independence of the separate Governments, it provided a model for future unification on a larger scale. The experience of its working proved beyond doubt the advantages which the smaller Colonies in particular could gain by co-operation in the recruitment of staff, and by the widening of prospects and the increase of prestige which resulted from co-operation. More important still, the efficiency and devotion of the members of the Staff contributed greatly to the success of the campaign against tropical disease which has transformed the whole aspect of Tropical Africa and other parts of the Colonial Empire. The amazing extent of that success may be judged from the fact that, whereas the death rate of European officials in West Africa was 20·6 per thousand in 1903, it fell to 12·8 per thousand in 1924, 7·7 in 1929, and 5·1 in 1935. Since, as we have seen, it was the unhealthiness of West Africa which was the principal obstacle to the general unification of the Service in the nineteenth century, it may justly be claimed that the West African Medical Staff has not only provided a model for a unified Service, but has very largely helped to create the conditions in which the unification of the Service has become possible during the last few years.

The changes in the general picture of the Colonial Services resulting from the new accessions of territory were revolutionary. The older Colonies for the most part continued along their well-established lines, with little substantial alteration; but alongside them there was coming into being a new Tropical African Empire, organised to a large degree on the traditional Colonial plan, as it had been worked out in the older Colonies, and drawing freely on the wealth of administrative experience which had been acquired; but yet presenting problems of its own, and making demands for staff on a constantly increasing scale. These developments were not without their inevitable repercussions on the older Colonies. The growth of administrative services of high quality and substantial size now began to provide that wide field of experienced staff so necessary for enabling satisfactory selections to be made for Governorships and other senior appointments. Recruiting, again, became a major problem, and the advantages of co-operation amongst the Governments concerned began to be appreciated. This, in its turn, led to consideration of the desirability of assimilating the conditions of employment applicable to officers recruited from the same sources for different Colonies.

The development of the African administrative services during the first ten years of the century was, indeed, remarkable. The most striking increases were in Nigeria. In 1901 the administrative staffs of Northern and Southern Nigeria together amounted to about 50 officers. By 1905 they had increased to over 150, and by 1909 to over 250. In 1910 the total administrative staffs of the Tropical African Dependencies numbered upwards of 470, with a salary bill of close on £200,000. I have already referred to the increases in medical staffs; in other departments also similar developments were proceeding, though not on the same extensive scale. Although the first demand was for administrators and police, to lay the foundations of law and order, and for doctors to look after their health, the rapid organisation of the countries soon gave rise to calls for specialists in continually widening fields: educationists, agriculturists, experts in forestry and veterinary science; engineers to construct and maintain railways, roads and buildings; surveyors to map the land; lawyers and judges; customs and postal officials; treasurers, accountants and auditors; in short, men and women of very varying qualifications, bringing all the resources of the Mother Country to the service of these latest of her children.

It may well be supposed that these demands placed a heavy strain on the Private Secretaries who were still the Secretary of

State's exclusive assistants in disposing of his patronage. In 1910 a step was taken which was to have important results. An additional Assistant Private Secretary was appointed for the specific purpose of dealing with recruitment for the Colonial Services. This officer, who was destined to become, twenty years later, the first Director of Recruitment, was nominally in the same position as other Private Secretaries, holding office at the pleasure of the Minister, and liable to discharge on a change of Minister, or indeed at any other time; but in practice he was employed continuously up to the outbreak of the War, and re-engaged as soon as the War was over, so that he became, in effect, a permanent specialist in the art of selection. He was able to build up a close and continuous liaison with the University Appointments Boards and other sources of prospective candidates, and by discussion with Governors and senior officers to feel the pulse of the Service, gauge its requirements, and test out the results of his work in the light of experience.

The development of the Tropical African Dependencies imposed upon the Colonial Office not only the rôle of a recruiting agency, but that of a central body for co-ordinating the conditions of service. In the older Colonies, where the staffs were for the most part recruited locally, it was primarily the business of the individual Colonial Governments to arrange the conditions of service in the light of local circumstances. The Colonial Regulations contained some general directions as to leave and discipline, but such matters as salaries and pensions were, on the whole, left for each administration to settle for itself. There were no recognised standards, nor, in general, was it conceived as part of the functions of the Colonial Office to lay down such standards. It would have been difficult, if not impossible, to do so in any case, having regard to the diversity of local circumstances, to the differences in cost and standard of living and in wage rates in non-Government employment. But in the Tropical African Dependencies there were growing up large European staffs, in regard to whom these local considerations were not the only ones to be taken into account. It was necessary above all to consider what terms would serve to attract the right type of candidate into the employment of the territories in question, and to provide him with a reasonable career. Conditions of service had to be based not, as in the older Colonies, on the assumption that for the most part officers would be inhabitants of the country, or at any rate would proceed to make their homes there, but on the assumption that they would be non-residents, with homes in the United Kingdom or elsewhere which they would require to visit periodically and to which they would eventually retire. Owing to climatic conditions and the lack of amenities, they would often have to leave their children and probably their wives at home, and incur the expense of keeping up two establishments. These factors were more or less common to employment throughout the Tropical African Dependencies, and were more important than local differences in cost of living. Some co-ordinating authority was evidently needed, and it clearly fell to the Colonial Office to undertake this function.

Accordingly, in 1910, the Secretary of State appointed a Tropical Services Committee, consisting of members of the Office staff, "to consider to what extent the services of the East and West African Colonies and Protectorates could with advantage be assimilated on the lines already adopted for the West African Frontier Force and the West African Medical Staff". Actually, the Committee found little to help them in the organisation of the Frontier Force, and considered that the West African Medical Staff provided the more useful model.

In July 1910, the Committee presented an important interim report, in which they discussed in some detail the organisation of the Administrative services. They found in the existing conditions many of what they termed "meaningless diversities". For instance, the scale for junior administrative officers was £300 by increments of £20 to £400 in Southern Nigeria, and £300 by increments of £15 to £400 in Northern. In Uganda and Nyasaland it was £250 to £350 by increments of £10; in the East Africa Protectorate (Kenya) the salary was £250 fixed. The Committee drew up a series of uniform standard scales:

West Africa

Scale A. £300 by £15 to £400.
Scale B. £400 by £20 to £500, plus £80 "duty pay".
Scale C. £500 by £25 to £700, plus £100 "duty pay",
    or £600 by £25 to £700, plus £120 "duty pay".

East Africa

Scale A. £250 by £15 to £400.
Scale B. £400 by £20 to £500, plus £40 "duty pay".
Scale C. £500 by £25 to £700, plus £80 "duty pay".

"Duty pay", which was attached only to the higher scales, was a non-pensionable emolument drawn during actual residence in Africa. When the officer concerned was on leave, the allowance became available for the person acting for him. The Committee made specific recommendations as to the proportions of posts to be assigned to the three grades in the different Dependencies, roughly on a basis of 4 : 2 : 1.

These scales, and related salaries for other branches of the Services, were brought into force during the next two years. So far, at least, as East Africa was concerned, it was none too soon, for the inadequacy of the existing salaries had been the subject of comment in Parliament, and at the selection of Administrative officers in August 1911, out of the first twelve candidates sounded for East Africa, nine refused offers of appointment. There was also a disturbing number of resignations from the Government Services in East Africa, evidently because the prospects were not sufficiently attractive in comparison with alternative careers.

Not only salaries, but the conditions of employment in general were subjected to careful review at this time. In 1909 a training course was instituted for officers appointed to the African Administrative Services. This was held in London thrice a year, and at first lasted for two months but was later extended to three. The subjects of study included law, tropical hygiene, tropical economic products, surveying and Government accounting procedure. In 1911 the East African leave regulations were revised so as to correspond in principle (though naturally with variations of detail) with those in force on the West Coast. After the necessary actuarial investigations, a scheme for widows' and orphans' pensions was introduced in West Africa in 1914, and a similar scheme was put in hand for East Africa, though, owing to the later start in commencing preparations, the scheme was not actually introduced until 1921.

As for officers' pensions, these have a long story behind them, and the end of the tale has not been reached yet. In 1869 the Secretary of State had sent a circular despatch to the Colonial Governments of the day, proposing a system for the calculation of the pensions of officers transferred from one Colony to another, with the object of securing to them the same pensions as they would have earned if their whole service had been in the public office from which they ultimately retired. This may appear to be a simple and desirable object, but the practical difficulties in realising it are more formidable than may be appreciated at first sight. Each Colony had and has its own pensions law, and none can legislate for another. The traditional basis of pension in British Civil Service practice is a certain fraction—say a sixtieth—of final salary for each year of completed service. Thus, after thirty years' service, an officer might be qualified for a pension of thirty-sixtieths, or half, the salary which he was drawing at the date of his retirement. This is simple and satisfactory when the service has been under a single administration, but when two or more are concerned, complications begin. One possible method is for each administration to pay a pension calculated on the officer's service and final salary under that administration; this, however, is open to the objection that it would normally result in the officer's receiving in total pensions considerably less than he would have received if his service had been under one administration only, and this disadvantage must discourage officers from accepting transfers. A second plan is to calculate the pension as if the whole service had been in the office last held, the earlier employers contributing shares calculated on the service and salary with which they were concerned. Thus, if an officer had served in three successive Colonies A, B and C, Colony A would contribute a pension based on his service there and the salary he last drew there; Colony B would pay one based on his whole service up to the date of his leaving that Colony, minus the pension contributed by Colony A; while Colony C would pay a pension based on his whole service in all three, minus the contributions of A and B. This is substantially the scheme put forward in 1869, but it broke down because of objections pointed out by the Government of Ceylon, the chief of which was that it placed an altogether disproportionate burden on the Colonies with larger services and higher salaries, since it was to these that officers would naturally gravitate on transfer.

Both these systems have behind them the authority of the Imperial Superannuation Acts, and rules made thereunder, but, for the reasons suggested above, they have not been found suitable for the Colonial Service, where it has always been common ground that transfers should be facilitated. After the breakdown of the 1869 proposals, lengthy discussions took place, as a result of which the device was hit upon of dividing pensions in proportion to the aggregate salary drawn from each administration by the officer concerned. That is to say, he would draw a pension calculated as if his whole service had been in one Colony, and each would pay a share bearing the same proportion to the total pension as the aggregate salary drawn by him in the course of his service in that Colony bore to the total aggregate salary drawn by him in the whole of his public service. This arrangement was applied to certain regional groups of Colonies, viz:

(1) Mauritius and Seychelles.
(2) The Straits Settlements, Federated Malay States and Hong Kong.
(3) Certain West Indian Colonies.
(4) The West African Dependencies.

It was limited to internal transfers amongst the respective groups, and did not apply to transfers between one group and another; but in the case of the first three groups there was a further arrangement whereby the pensions in sixtieths were supplemented by a "climatic addition" of five years, and this addition was divided amongst any of the administrations in question, whether in the same group or another, in which an officer might have served. In the case of the fourth group (West Africa), pensions were calculated not in sixtieths but in fortieths.

East Africa has not hitherto been mentioned in this connection. The position there was different from that in the older Colonies, as there were no local pension laws, the principles of the Imperial Superannuation Acts being applied by regulation. These principles were, briefly, calculation of pensions in sixtieths, two years' service being reckoned as three in accordance with the "unhealthy climate" provisions of the Act of 1876. For practical purposes this had the same effect as the West African calculation in fortieths. The East African Dependencies were treated as a group, pensions for mixed service within the group being allocated according to the second of the systems described in the last paragraph but one, and pensions for service both within and without the group according to the first of those systems. (In the case of East and West Africa the rates quoted above are those for European officers; the pensions of non-European officers were calculated in sixtieths without any climatic allowance. But in all other Colonies the rates for Europeans and non-Europeans were the same.)

It will readily be appreciated that this matter of pensions provided an admirable crop of "meaningless diversities", and it is not surprising that it received continuous attention from the Colonial Office. During the period with which we are here concerned, more than one attempt was made to deal with the problem. In 1907–8 an Inter-Departmental Committee, including representatives of the Treasury and Foreign Office, considered the question of "mixed" pensions. Their work was carried on by another Committee, which sat from 1909 to 1914, when the outbreak of War caused the discussions to be adjourned without any appreciable practical result having been achieved; though in the meantime there had been some extension of group co-ordination, the first and third of the four groups above mentioned having been combined, with the addition of Fiji and the Falkland Islands, while Ceylon was now included in the second group.

This somewhat lengthy digression on the subject of pensions

is not entirely irrelevant to the theme of this chapter, since it does not appear unlikely that a satisfactory reconciliation of the divergencies of practice in the older Colonies could have been reached, had it not been for the fact that the balance of the Service was shifting in the direction of Africa, where pension systems existed differing more widely from those in force elsewhere than the latter differed from each other. In any case, it is now time to consider generally the effect of the rise of the Tropical African Empire on the Colonial Services as a whole, and to estimate the position reached by the beginning of the Great War.

As we have seen, one striking result of the development of the Tropical African Dependencies was a great increase in the numerical size of the Colonial Services. In some branches the staff employed in Nigeria alone exceeded the total of the corresponding staffs employed in the non-African Colonies. At the same time, those older Colonies too were in many instances developing their administrative and technical machinery. While, on the whole, few important changes were to be discerned in the smaller island Colonies, Ceylon and Malaya were yearly increasing not only the strength of their public services but the range of governmental activity. Thus, in Ceylon, we find at the commencement of the War not merely the usual administrative organisation of civil service, judiciary and police, but large and well-organised departments dealing with survey, education, agriculture and forestry, all staffed by professional experts. The staff list includes specialists of varied kinds, such as astronomers, mineralogical surveyors, inspectors of mines and factories, botanists and mycologists, analysts, professors of physics and chemistry. It is noteworthy that, while at this time the higher ranks of the Service in Ceylon were predominantly European in personnel, there were already considerable numbers of Ceylonese officers in the junior grades, who would in due course receive promotion and take over duties formerly entrusted to European officials.

It will hardly be felt as an injustice to any other Dependency if the administration of Ceylon be described as the most advanced and highly organised to be found in the Colonial Empire before the War. In proportion, however, to their individual needs and resources, the other Colonies were similarly engaged in developing modern administrative machinery, and over the whole field we may discern a firm tendency towards a scientific conception of the functions of Government and towards the promotion of the social and economic advancement of the people.

The success of the Colonial Services in meeting the new calls made upon them depended, in the last resort, on recruitment. The demand was not only for more and more recruits, but for a continually expanding range of professional qualification. In point of size, the most important recruiting problem was that presented by the Tropical African administrative services, which, in the years immediately preceding the War, were taking on an average from 50 to 70 officers annually; but there were steady demands, though on a lower scale, for doctors, nurses, surveyors, barristers, solicitors, police officers, engineers of various kinds, marine officers, accountants, agricultural and veterinary specialists. And it must be remembered that these demands, formidable as they were, did not emanate from a homogeneous and organised Service, but from an assortment of separate administrations, each with its own peculiar requirements and its own conditions of employment. The occurrence of vacancies was necessarily fortuitous and the terms which might be offered subject to considerable variation. Again, the prospects open to the selected officer might differ very widely according to the Colony to which he should chance to be allotted. The public service of each Colony being distinct and separate, he might find himself a member of a large department with a well-defined avenue of substantial promotion, or an isolated representative of his profession in a Dependency too small and too poor to offer any prospects of advancement at all.

Such an atmosphere was obviously one in which successful recruitment could only with difficulty flourish; and the advantages, indeed the virtual necessity of combination and assimilation were recognised by the formation of the West African

Medical Staff and by the co-ordinated measures taken in connection with the Far Eastern and the Tropical African administrative services. Thus, while it must be a matter of speculation what the ultimate outcome would have been if the War had not intervened, it is a fair inference from the prevailing tendencies that the general line of advance might have been in the direction of constituting a series of regional services, probably with an African Civil Service as the central and largest unit. But such an arrangement would have been under the grave disadvantage that it would inevitably have left without provision many of the smaller and more isolated Colonies, which did not lend themselves conveniently to geographical grouping. For it must be remembered that a regional service is of necessity not only inclusive of the Colonies covered but exclusive of the rest. Whatever disadvantages the traditional arrangements had, they at least possessed the great merit of elasticity. In exercising his control over appointments, the Secretary of State had in theory, and to a large extent in practice, a free hand to approve the promotion of a local candidate or to prefer a candidate from outside, without regard to seniority or to any other consideration than the broad interests of the public service. But the creation of a regional service implied that its members should have prior or even exclusive consideration for promotion within the region; and, while the range of selection and of opportunity was considerably broadened as compared with that afforded by any one of the participating Colonies, it was limited as compared with that afforded by the Colonial Empire as a whole. To take a concrete example: the creation of the West African Medical Staff gave to all medical officers serving in West Africa the prospect of consideration for higher posts in any of the West African Colonies, and virtually excluded from such consideration officers serving in other Colonies. Thus a medical officer employed in Fiji might have a chance of being considered for a senior appointment in Ceylon, but he would have very little chance of being considered for a senior appointment in Nigeria. Conversely, in the absence of reciprocity, it would only be in exceptional circumstances that an officer serving in West Africa would have been considered for an appointment in any other part of the world.

The general effect of creating regional services was, then, at least as much restrictive as emancipatory, and it must be doubtful whether the policy could have been pressed to a logical conclusion. In any event, there were certain solvent processes at work alongside the tendency to which we have drawn attention. Outside the formally constituted regional services, that is to say the Eastern Cadet Services and the West African Medical Staff, successive Secretaries of State firmly maintained their traditional right of "patronage", making use of that right not, as in the olden days, to provide employment for their personal protégés, but as a means to secure selection from the widest possible field. Thus, with the exceptions noted, the Colonial Services were in practice to a large extent treated for the purpose of promotions as one Service; and transfers were sufficiently a matter of course to prevent the serious development of vested interests and to secure to every officer at least the chance of rising to the top of his profession, however unpromising might be the prospects offered by the Colony to which he might be allocated in the first instance. Amongst those who were serving as Colonial Governors at the beginning of the War there were many distinguished officers who had started their careers in minor posts in Colonies with quite small administrative staffs, such as Cyprus, Barbados, British Guiana and Fiji, and who had perhaps graduated through two or three Colonies before reaching the ultimate goal. One remarkable case is that of Sir Hesketh Bell, G.C.M.G., who between 1882 and 1906 held Civil Service appointments successively in Barbados, Grenada, the Gold Coast, Bahamas and Dominica; subsequently serving as Governor of Uganda, of Northern Nigeria, of the Leeward Islands and finally of Mauritius. While such careers naturally came to the few rather than to the many, their existence shows that the loose organisation of the Services did in fact provide openings for talent such as are less likely to be provided in a more highly organised system where it is not so easy to set aside the claims of pure seniority.

The obvious desirability of preserving the advantages of a free and unrestricted flow of promotion and transfer might have seemed to point in the direction of a general unification of the Colonial Service rather than towards the extension of the group system; but at the beginning of the War the conflict between the two opposing tendencies remained unresolved. We have already noted that, in the important matter of pensions, the pressure of facts had led to something not markedly distinguishable from a formulated policy of recognising the essential unity of the Service, and of giving practical effect to that recognition by securing that an officer's pension should be as little as possible affected adversely by the accidents of transfer from Colony to Colony. Formidable as the difficulties were, the trouble taken to deal with them implied an admission that basically the Service was one. There was, however, at this time, little indication of any inclination on the part of the authorities to attempt (outside the regional groups) to apply to such matters as salaries, leave and passage conditions, a similar principle to that accepted in the sphere of pensions.

CHAPTER III

THE GREAT WAR AND THE PERIOD
OF RECONSTRUCTION

THE War found the Colonial Services in a state of transition, but towards a goal not, as yet, clearly defined. On the one hand, the older Colonies were very much as they had been for many years, providing for the most part their public services from their own populations, and only in regard to the higher appointments making contact with other parts of the Colonial Empire as a recruiting ground. In the Far Eastern Dependencies, the administrative staffs were obtained by competitive examination, in association with the Home and Indian Civil Services, and not under any system of pooling with the other Colonies employing officers of a similar type. These Dependencies did, however, share with others a common recruiting organisation for the growing body of professional and technical appointments. The newer Dependencies in Africa were still in the initial stages of finding themselves, and had as yet but little in the way of settled tradition behind them.

Naturally, very little progress in Service matters was possible during the War years. A sufficiency of staff had to be retained to carry on the administration of the Colonial Empire, but all who could be spared were released for duty with the forces. Practically nothing could be done to fill vacancies. Many officers served their country in the best way they could, by remaining at their posts for periods greatly in excess of the normal tours of service, often at considerable sacrifice not only of comfort but of health. The loyalty and devotion of the Colonial Service were fully tried, and not found wanting, during that difficult time.

After the War, the immediate problem was to fill up the vast gaps made in the Service by casualties and by the virtual cessation of recruitment over a period of more than four years. The extent of the necessity may be judged from the fact that 287 vacancies for administrative officers were filled by the Private Secretary for appointments in the two years 1919 and 1920. The annual intake in the immediately pre-War period had been about 70. Fortunately, there was the field of demobilised officers upon which to draw. In the case of the technical departments the shortage was no less serious, and more difficult to cope with, for few trained candidates existed. Thus 25 agricultural officers were appointed in 1920, and 29 in 1921, as compared with 11 in 1913. The corresponding figures for forestry officers were 33, 26 and 1; for surveyors, including geologists, 30, 32 and 2.

At the same time, the War had dislocated financial and economic arrangements in varying degrees throughout the Colonial Empire. Costs of living were fluctuating capriciously, currency in many places was disorganised. Again, the map was suffering bewildering alterations. In Eastern Africa a new territory as large as Nigeria had been taken over, and Palestine, Trans-Jordan and 'Iraq were bringing novel and urgent problems before the Colonial Office. Northern Rhodesia, too, was included in the responsibilities of the Office from 1924 onwards.

In such conditions of disturbance and abnormality, it was manifestly the primary duty of those responsible for the government of the Colonies to deal with the problems of each individual Dependency, as they arose, in the light of the particular circumstances. Until the Colonies had individually found some degree of stability in the new conditions, there was little opportunity for dealing with Service questions on any broad basis. Inevitably, some of the ground gained before the War had to be sacrificed. The difficulty of straightening out the affairs of each Colony was sufficient to tax the ingenuity of the administration without its being further complicated by the necessity of keeping in line with what others might be doing to deal with their own tangles. Perhaps, also, it may be suggested that "self-determination" was in the air, and that there was a consequent tendency for each Colony to wish as far as possible to order its affairs on individual lines.

As it turned out, only in the East and West African groups was there any definite attempt to preserve a measure of co-ordination in the process of reconstruction, and even here the relationship which, before the War, had been maintained between the two groups had to be for the most part abandoned. The West African Colonies were at this time relatively prosperous; their recruiting needs were great; the cost of living had risen considerably; and service in that region was not particularly popular, owing to the climate and the inevitable interference with family life which those working in West Africa must face. In these circumstances, generous terms of employment were clearly indicated as desirable, irrespective of what might be judged suitable in the different conditions of other Colonies. Accordingly, a complete new scheme of service conditions for European officers was drawn up by the local Governments in consultation with the Colonial Office. This scheme was largely based upon the recommendations of local committees, especially one which sat in Nigeria, and contained several novel features. As regards salaries, the "long-scale" system was introduced for the administrative and other superior branches of the Service. Under this system officers, after completing the usual three years of probation, entered upon a salary scale covering some fifteen to twenty years, in the course of which they would proceed by regular annual increments to a maximum of a reasonably high standard. Advancement was to be subject to the passing of "efficiency bars" at fixed points in the scale, but not, as under the old system, upon the occurrence of vacancies. By this means, blocks in promotion would be avoided, and every officer could look forward with certainty to the prospect of reaching the maximum, provided that he maintained his efficiency.

The actual scales adopted in West Africa were, for the administrative service, £500 for three years, then £570 by increments of £30 and £40 to a maximum of £960; and for the technical branches, £480 rising to a maximum of £920. There were also special scales for certain departments; for example the scale for medical officers was £660 to £960, with an arrangement whereby an officer who should remain for three years on the maximum without promotion went on to a higher scale of £1,000 to £1,150.

It should be mentioned that all officers to whom these scales were applicable were provided with free quarters, the value of which was reckoned as an emolument for the purpose of calculating pensions. Further, on reaching £720 in his scale, every officer became entitled to a "seniority allowance" at the rate of £72 a year, payable during resident service in the Colony. The object of this allowance was to compensate in some degree the married officers, the proportion of whom in the service was increasing, for the extra cost of maintaining two establishments during the period of children's education.

While these scales were designed to afford a reasonable prospect to the average officer, there remained, of course, the higher ranges of appointments which still had to be reached by promotion. Thus, administrative officers in Nigeria might be promoted to posts of Resident and Senior Resident; those in the Gold Coast to Provincial Commissionerships. In other departments there were similar "super-scale" posts to which some, if not all, officers might aspire. The salaries of these higher posts were naturally fixed according to the importance and responsibilities of the posts, and not according to any general rule; but in regard to all of them the "duty allowance" arrangement was maintained, the rate of allowance being 20 per cent. of the salary; so that an officer whose post carried a salary of £1,200 received in addition, while on duty in the Colony, an allowance of £240. When he went on leave, the allowance was paid to the officer acting for him.

A further improvement in the conditions of service was effected in the matter of wives' passages. Officers had always been allowed free passages for themselves between the United Kingdom and West Africa on first appointment and on leave; they were now to be granted assistance, amounting to half the cost, towards the passages of their wives, provided that the wife was certified to be physically fit to reside in West Africa for six months, and did actually reside there for at least that portion of the husband's tour of service.

As some make-weight to these important concessions, the conditions of service were amended in certain particulars to the advantage of the Governments. New entrants were required to accept fresh leave regulations, under which the normal tour of service was increased from 12 to 18 months; these regulations were, however, in certain respects more favourable than the old, and serving officers were given the option of accepting them if they so desired. Also, in the case of new entrants, the privilege enjoyed by the existing staff of retiring on pension after eighteen years' West African service was abolished, and the normal re-tiring age was fixed at 55, with a proviso that an officer might, if he wished, retire at any time after attaining the age of 50. Thus, in return for better pay and conditions, the Governments expected to receive more service from their officers.

In West Africa, as elsewhere, the prosperity of the immediately post-War period was soon succeeded by a wave of financial difficulty, and in 1923 the scales adopted three years previously were somewhat modified, in the interests of economy. The principal alterations were at the lower end of the scales, and took the form either of a reduction of the initial salary, as for instance in the case of administrative officers, who henceforth were to start at £450, instead of £500; or of a stoppage of incre-ments during the probationary three years. The scales as finally settled in 1923 remained in force throughout the West African services until 1936, when new salary schemes, based on a different plan, were adopted for new entrants, as will be recorded in due course.

We turn now to the East African Dependencies, to which there had been added the new mandated territory of Tanganyika. Circumstances on the East Coast were very different from those on the West. The East African Dependencies had been more directly affected by the War, and their financial position was far from prosperous. Indeed, all save the East Africa Protectorate[1] and Zanzibar either were, or had recently been, in receipt of grants in aid from the Imperial Exchequer, and were, in con-sequence, under the financial control of the Treasury. At the same time, service in these Dependencies was more popular

[1] The East Africa Protectorate became the Colony and Protectorate of Kenya in 1920.

than service in West Africa, and it did not seem necessary to offer such generous terms as those adopted on the West Coast, even if the Governments could have afforded them.

The East African Governments, like several others, had had recourse to a system of "war bonus" to meet the increased cost of living which began to reach oppressive dimensions towards the end of the War, but there was some local dissatisfaction with the arrangements, and a special Commissioner (Sir Alfred Lascelles) was sent out by the Secretary of State to investigate the question on the spot and to make recommendations in the first place for a temporary adjustment of the difficulties, but also for such permanent revision of the conditions of employment as he might consider reasonable in the light of his inquiries. It was largely on the basis of his report that the salary scales and other conditions adopted in 1920 were constructed.

In the circumstances, these bore little resemblance to those being introduced at the same time in West Africa. For example, the "long-scale" system was not adopted, though in certain branches a somewhat similar effect resulted from an arrangement whereby an officer who reached the maximum salary of a junior grade could be promoted to the grade above, irrespective of the existence of a vacancy in the approved establishment of that grade. Duty allowances were for the most part abolished. In contrast to the decision arrived at in the case of West Africa, where the privilege of retirement on pension irrespective of age, provided that a minimum period of service had been put in, was being abandoned, a similar privilege, which had not existed before, was now introduced in East Africa, the stipulated period being twenty years' East African service. An officer who entered the Service at 22 might therefore retire, or be called on to retire, at the early age of 42, with a life pension equivalent to half his emoluments at the date of retirement.

The revision of salaries in East Africa was much complicated by currency difficulties. In the three largest Dependencies, Kenya, Uganda and the Tanganyika Territory, the traditional unit of currency was the rupee; in the first two countries the Indian rupee, and in the third a German rupee of the same value. At the same time, the British sovereign was legal tender in Kenya and Uganda at the rate of £1 to fifteen rupees. At the end of the War, the exchange value of the Indian rupee in terms of sterling was subjected to violent fluctuations, and, after discussions outside the scope of the present work, the problem created in East Africa by these fluctuations was solved by the transfer of the three territories mentioned to a sterling currency, the rupee being redeemed at two shillings. The immediate effect of this on salaries in the public services was that £1 of salary became worth ten local purchasing units instead of fifteen, and a transitional period had to be envisaged before local prices could be adjusted to the new sterling value of the local coin. It was therefore decided that the new salaries should be supplemented by a local allowance of 50 per cent. in the three territories. In Zanzibar and Somaliland, however, the rupee was retained, and payments of salary locally continued to be made at fifteen rupees to the pound; in Nyasaland sterling currency was already in use, and no question of a local allowance arose.

Another complicating factor was the war bonus, which not only had been at different rates in the various Dependencies, but had been larger in the case of married than of single officers. At first it was arranged to bring officers on to the new scales at the point next above their existing salaries plus bonus, but this gave rise to so many inequalities and anomalies that eventually the salaries of the single officers had to be levelled up to those of the married.

Despite these difficulties, a scheme of more or less uniform scales was brought into force throughout the East African Dependencies. The general level was considerably below that of the new West African scales: for instance, the maximum to which an administrative officer could rise without special promotion was £700 a year, as compared with £960 plus £72 in West Africa; while the posts of Provincial Commissioner were on a scale of £800 to £1,000, as compared with £1,200 plus £240 in the Gold Coast. For a time, the addition of local allowance in the three principal Dependencies obscured the differentiation, although it was not pensionable or paid during leave; but in the course of two or three years the Governments were obliged to cut these allowances drastically as a measure of economy, and it then became clear that if recruitment was to be maintained, and if the services were to be established on a satisfactory basis, the 1920 scheme would have to be reconsidered. Accordingly, in 1926, on the recommendation of a conference of Governors, the remnant of the local allowances was merged in an entirely new set of salary scales based on an adaptation of the West African model. For the administrative services a long scale rising from £400 to £920 was introduced, and the salaries of Provincial Commissioners were raised to £1,200 and £1,350. Similar adjustments were made in respect of other branches, though the long-scale system was not applied universally, as on the West Coast; the general principle was to introduce a definite promotion bar at some convenient point in the scale, such as £720 or £840, and to make progress above that point depend on promotion to a vacancy in an approved establishment of higher posts. This scheme of 1926 still applies to most of the officers serving in East Africa, though for new entrants to the Service it has been somewhat modified in the last year or two in consequence of certain changes in pension arrangements and of the unification of the Colonial Service.

Meanwhile, similar processes were at work in other parts of the Colonial Empire, each Dependency endeavouring in its own way to adjust its public service arrangements to the new conditions as they presented themselves in relation to the special circumstances and requirements of the administration. The problems were so immediate and so various that there was little scope or opportunity for studying the Colonial field as a whole and attempting to construct any general scheme, which might well, at such a time, have proved nothing but a bed of Procrustes. The upshot of the deliberations and decisions taking place everywhere was, however, an appreciable all-round improvement in the standards of remuneration and conditions of employment as compared with the pre-War period. In Malaya, for example, a local Committee, under the presidency of Sir John Bucknill, Chief Justice of the Straits Settlements, devised a scheme of salaries which represented a considerable advance on any previous conception of remuneration in the Colonial Services. The Malayan Civil Service was placed on what was in effect a long scale, with efficiency bars, ranging from £490 to £1,400 a year, with higher posts, filled by promotion, on proportionate rates: for the professional branches the general scale was £560 to £1,120. (In comparing these scales with those adopted for Africa, it should be understood that officers in Malaya, unlike those serving in Africa, were not provided with free quarters.) In addition to these basic salaries, a "War allowance" was to be paid at the rate of 10 per cent. This allowance, afterwards called a "temporary allowance", underwent various fluctuations, but eventually settled down in 1923 to a rate of 20 per cent. for married officers and 10 per cent. for single officers; in this form it survived until 1931, when it was first halved and then abolished altogether.

Somewhat similar schemes were adopted in Ceylon and Hong Kong; but outside the African and Eastern groups the local variations were so numerous that there would be a danger of overburdening this narrative with detail were I to attempt to deal with them. In the Dependencies where the public services were already for the most part of local origin, local circumstances were necessarily the determining factors in the construction of salary schemes. The schemes which have been very briefly described in the last few pages were designed primarily for European officers recruited from outside the Colonies themselves, and the common considerations applicable to such officers as a class enabled and even required some measure of uniformity in conditions of service to be achieved, if only throughout certain well-defined regional areas. Even in this field, as we have seen, the period was one of experiment and adaptation; no set principles had been laid down, and schemes which were intended to be permanent had to be reconsidered in the light of changing events. Though no one would claim that a state of unsettlement is a desirable feature of a public service organisation, yet the freedom of the Colonial Services at this time from a rigid adherence to preconceived ideas and precedents at least had the advantage that it enabled various methods and expedients to be tried out in practice, and the validity of theories to be tested by results.

On one important aspect of conditions of service, namely pensions, some development of general policy was found possible. With the increasing tendency to interchange of officers amongst the Colonies, the question of "mixed service" pensions, which, as has been seen, had already come into prominence before the War, was ever more insistently calling for a practical solution. In 1922 the Secretary of State appointed a Committee, under the Chairmanship of his Financial Adviser, Sir James (afterwards Lord) Stevenson, to consider what could be done to secure greater uniformity in this matter, with special reference to the possibility of instituting a central pensions fund. It may be said at once that the Committee were unable to recommend the establishment of such a fund, to which they saw insuperable practical objections; but, building upon the foundations of the earlier investigations, they succeeded in devising a system by which pensions could be apportioned between two or more Governments under which an officer might have served, without undue prejudice either to his interests or to those of the Governments concerned, and without sacrificing the principle of independent legislation on the part of each administration. In brief, this system was based on the plan of each Colony calculating a hypothetical pension under its own laws, as if the officer's whole service had been under it; it then awarded a pension bearing the same proportion to the hypothetical pension as the aggregate emoluments drawn by the officer from it bore to the aggregate emoluments drawn by him in the course of his whole public service. Thus, if the pension systems of the Colonies in which an officer had served were identical, he would draw a series of pensions, equal in sum to the pension which he would have received if his service had been in one Colony throughout. Even if the pension systems were dissimilar, the method of apportionment was no less workable, and resulted in a material advantage to the officer as compared with any system of calculating pensions separately.

The Committee also made important recommendations for enabling officers to exchange a portion of their pensions for a substantial lump sum, and for the grant of a "death gratuity" of a year's emoluments to the estate of an officer who should die while in the Service.

These recommendations were very largely adopted, as time went on, by the Colonial Governments, but it would no doubt be tedious to enter into a detailed account of the developments of the pensions legislation of the different Colonies. It will be more convenient, in a later chapter, to describe the general position as it exists to-day, without attempting to chronicle the various stages by which that position has been reached.

The general effect, then, on the Colonial Services of the developments of the ten years following the War was a very considerable improvement, in most Colonies, of the conditions of employment, as compared with pre-War standards. The Services were, also, very considerably increased in numbers, in comparison with pre-War establishments, and the work called to an increasing degree for high professional and technical qualifications. Each Colony, according to its needs and its resources, was striving to put its house in order, and to develop its own public services to meet the demands of the time. In many cases these efforts were successful; but the results as a whole were not entirely satisfactory. Those concerned with recruitment for the rapidly expanding Services were conscious of a difficulty in supplying the requirements of the Governments; a difficulty which, it gradually became clear, was not one to be solved merely by an improvement of the terms of employment in those Colonies which were in a position to be generous. Nor could such an expedient help the poorer Colonies which could not compete with the richer if it came to a competition for a limited field of candidates, and yet whose necessities might be as great or even greater.

The reality and magnitude of the problem were not at first apparent. The post-War "boom" was succeeded in the Colonies as elsewhere by a period of depression, and some contraction of the hastily expanded Services took place. This, however, was followed by a time of renewed prosperity and of further expansion, and it was now that the need of some comprehensive solution of the recruiting difficulties was apparent. It became a question of practical urgency whether some fundamental change would not have to be made in the traditional notion of the structure and organisation of the Services, if their efficiency was to be maintained and developed to meet the calls being made upon them in the new conditions.

CHAPTER IV

THE PROBLEM OF THE SCIENTIFIC
SERVICES

THE impression which the last chapter will have given of
a reconstructive effort unattended by any very serious
attempt at co-ordination needs to be qualified in one
important particular. The scientific Services presented a problem
of a special kind. Not only was it a question of replacing war
wastage and of filling vacancies which had perforce remained
unfilled during the War. In the interval between the beginning
and the end of the War, the Colonial Empire, and especially
the African regions which now were becoming a main focus of
interest, had passed from a stage in which the establishment of
the rule of law had been the primary consideration to one in
which the application of science to the economic and cultural
development of the communities was of the first importance.
Yet the time was singularly unpropitious for the necessary expansion of the scientific departments, owing to the absence of a
suitable supply of trained personnel.

This problem was realised to be one which needed to be
tackled on a broad and comprehensive scale, with the aid of the
best advice obtainable. Accordingly, in 1919, Lord Milner as
Secretary of State appointed three authoritative Committees, to
examine and report on the Medical, the Agricultural and the
Veterinary Services respectively in the Colonial Empire as a
whole. The reports of these Committees were rendered in the
course of 1920 and published as Parliamentary papers.[1]

The Committee on the Colonial Medical Services was presided over by Sir Walter Egerton, a distinguished Colonial
administrator, and included such notable representatives of the
medical profession as Sir Humphry Rolleston, Major-General
Sir W. B. Leishman and Sir James Kingston Fowler.

[1] Cmd. 939 (Medical); Cmd. 730 (Agricultural); Cmd. 922 (Veterinary).

In dealing with the problems of the Medical Services, the Committee expressed the opinion that the ideal was that a unified Colonial Medical Service should be set up, the members of which would be liable to serve in any Dependency at the discretion of the Secretary of State. They were forced to conclude, however, that the realisation of this ideal was not practicable in existing circumstances. Amongst the reasons which the Committee cited in support of this conclusion were the differences in salaries, pensions and leave conditions; and, in the specifically medical sphere, the differences in the functions of the medical staffs and in the opportunities for private practice in different Dependencies. Nevertheless, the Committee thought it possible to recommend the formation of a "Colonial Medical Service" divided into regional groups, and considered that even the titular unification of the Service would have a real value in giving it a status in the profession comparable to that of the R.A.M.C. or the Indian Medical Service. The Committee further recommended that unified regional Services on the lines of the West African Medical Staff should be set up in Eastern Africa and in Malaya; and that a Director-General of the whole Service should be appointed. With regard to the question of pay and conditions of employment, the Committee did not feel able to go into much detail, but they observed that a substantial increase in existing salaries would certainly be required, and they expressed the definite opinion that an initial salary of £600 a year would have to be offered in order to secure the right type of recruit.

It was not judged possible to accept all the recommendations of this Committee, but their report had several important practical results. No official recognition was given to the existence of a Colonial Medical Service, but the principle of regional unified Services was adopted for East Africa and Malaya, as the Committee had advised. An initial salary of at least the amount stipulated by the Committee was specified, wherever possible, in the new salary schemes which were being drawn up at this time. No Director-General was appointed, but the recommendation bore fruit some years later when the post of Chief Medical Adviser to the Secretary of State was created.

The Committee on the staffing of the Agricultural departments in the Colonies, under the Chairmanship of Sir Herbert Read, an Assistant Under-Secretary of State, were faced with a situation in which, to quote their words: "it is not generally realised how rich a harvest may be reaped if the agricultural resources of the Colonies and Protectorates are properly developed, nor how small a part of the Empire has been so far subjected to such development." They laid stress on three main points: that a considerable increase in the staffs of the Agricultural departments was inevitable; that the utmost importance must be attached to the quality of the staffs, and to their professional competence, second-rate officers being worse than useless where scientific aid was in question; finally that there was need, in many cases, for substantial increases of salaries if the right type of men were to be attracted and retained in face of commercial competition for their services.

The Committee proceeded to examine in detail the staffs of the Agricultural departments in the various Dependencies, and to make recommendations both as to increases in numbers and as to the salaries to be attached to the various posts. It does not appear that the Committee attempted any very close assimilation of the salaries in different groups, but within such regional groups as the West Indies, East Africa and West Africa, they provided a series of standard scales, which were largely adopted by the local Governments. The Committee hoped that the improvements which they recommended would provide the necessary stimulus to recruitment, provided that it could be brought home to prospective candidates and to their parents that there was the definite prospect of a good career before the young scientist entering the service of a Colonial Government.

The Committee on the staffing of the Veterinary departments was also presided over by Sir Herbert Read. The field covered by this Committee was more restricted, since it was only in certain Dependencies that veterinary matters were of substantial economic importance. It was mainly in Eastern Africa that the

Committee found a need for appreciable increases of staff. But even for the comparatively small Veterinary Services the problem of recruitment was a serious one. There was little hope of more than a very limited number of candidates becoming available until the post-War students had completed their courses at the veterinary colleges. The Committee could only suggest that, by improving salaries and by making provision for such expansion of superior staff as would enable reasonable prospects of advancement to be held out, the Colonies would put themselves in the way of attracting and retaining veterinary surgeons of real ability and scientific interests, as they became available.

So far as the Medical Services were concerned, the policy of providing adequate conditions of employment and relying upon these to attract the requisite supply of candidates was on the whole successful during the ensuing years. It was there a case of recruiting from a large and recognised profession, with a constant flow of new men, a proportion of whom would naturally look to Government service abroad as one of the possible careers open to them, provided that sufficiently attractive terms were offered. It was far otherwise with the Agricultural and other scientific Services. As the Committee on the Agricultural Services had observed, there was no recognised profession of agricultural science; hence a scientific student might often be induced to take up the study of chemistry, engineering or medicine, although he might really be far more fitted by natural inclination for the study of botany or entomology, simply because the latter studies were not looked upon by parents and teachers as likely to lead to any practical career. The same observation might have been applied to forestry, with the added remark that in that department the student's time would be largely wasted if he should not succeed in obtaining a Government appointment, since openings for forestry graduates in the commercial world were very few. Again, while in the case of the Veterinary Services the position might have been supposed to be analogous to that of the Medical Services, in fact the requirements of the Colonies were for veterinarians with a broader scientific training than was provided at the veterinary colleges for those who mainly intended to undertake the practice of veterinary medicine in this country.

As these considerations emerged, it became clear that, if the needs of the Colonies were to be adequately supplied, special training facilities would have to be organised. As early as 1919, the dearth of trained candidates in the profession of forestry had led to an arrangement being made whereby a Government grant was allowed to selected forestry probationers to enable them to complete their university studies. In 1924, when the Imperial Forestry Institute at Oxford was established, this arrangement developed into a definite scheme for sending probationers, after selection, on a year's course at the Institute at the Government's expense. This scheme, which proved of great value in securing the supply of an adequate number of trained men, doubtless pointed the way towards a solution of the problems connected with the Agricultural and Veterinary Services, to which we now turn.

The hopes of the 1920 Committees that their recommendations would suffice to provide for the requirements of the Colonial Governments in these important fields were not realised, and by 1924 the recruiting position of the Agricultural Services had become so unsatisfactory that Mr J. H. Thomas, the Secretary of State at the time, decided to set up a fresh Committee, under the Chairmanship of Lord Milner, to consider the recruitment and training of officers for the agricultural departments of the non-self-governing Dependencies and their conditions of service. The Committee were asked to make suggestions for improving the supply of candidates and for obtaining a higher degree of efficiency in regard to agricultural research and administration. The Committee, which included authoritative representatives of the agricultural sciences, the Colonial Services and the Colonial Office, concluded, at an early stage of their deliberations, that the recruiting problem was one of pressing importance. In March 1925, they presented an interim report[1] dealing with this aspect of their terms of reference. In this

[1] Included in Cmd. 2825 (1927).

report they expressed the definite view that a sufficient number of men of the right personal stamp, and willing to serve in the tropics, were not at that time undergoing appropriate training to fit themselves for service in the Colonial agricultural departments. In other words, ran the report, the supply from which to select did not exist and must be created. Accordingly, the Committee submitted a proposal that a scholarship scheme should be introduced.

Under this scheme, a definite number of scholarships for post-graduate training would be granted annually over a definite number of years. Candidates would be required to possess certain specified academic qualifications, and would be chosen by methods of personal selection. Each candidate would be required to undertake, on the termination of his scholarship, to accept appointment in any Colony to which he might be allotted, and to serve there for at least three years. On the other hand, while it was the expressed intention that vacancies in Colonial agricultural departments should normally be filled by persons who had successfully completed the scholarship course, the Secretary of State would not be bound to offer them appointments. The scholarships were to be of the value of £200 per annum, and to be granted normally for two years, one of which would be spent at the Imperial College of Tropical Agriculture in Trinidad. The scheme would be financed by the participating Colonial Governments, with the assistance of a grant from Imperial funds.

These recommendations were accepted and put into operation with the least possible delay, so that the first batch of scholars was actually selected in 1925.

Lord Milner died shortly after the presentation of the interim report, and the Committee continued their work under the presidency of Lord Lovat, the Vice-Chairman. Their final report, which was presented and published in 1927,[1] contained many important recommendations which are outside the scope of the present study. So far as matters of Service interest are concerned, the Committee, while considering that the current

[1] Cmd. 2825.

salaries, etc., as fixed in the light of the report of the 1920 Committee, were on the whole satisfactory as relating to junior officers in the larger Colonies, laid stress on the importance of providing better avenues for promotion throughout the Services as a whole. They appreciated the difficulties in the way of forming a single Agricultural Service for the Colonies generally, but urged that at least obstacles in the way of a free circulation of staff should be eliminated as far as possible.

This report was one of the most important papers laid before the first Colonial Office Conference, which was convened by Mr L. S. Amery, as Secretary of State, in May 1927. At this Conference, Governors and senior officials of the Colonies came together for the first time to discuss collectively with the Secretary of State and his advisers matters of general interest to the Colonial Empire. In the course of the proceedings, attention was drawn to the widespread feeling in many of the Dependencies, and particularly in the smaller Colonies, that the absence of a unified Colonial Service placed officers, especially those in the scientific and technical branches, under a serious disability in the matter of a career. The Conference set up a Committee, under the Chairmanship of Lord Lovat, to inquire into the possibility of establishing for the whole Colonial Empire a single Scientific and Research Service.

The Committee were naturally unable, in the limited time which could be given to so large a subject, to present any final conclusions; they did, however, produce a valuable report. In this report it was recommended, as an immediate step, that a Colonial Agricultural Research Service should be created, based upon the principle of interchangeability and a common and generous salary scheme. The idea was put forward that the Service should be financed by means of a percentage cess on the revenues of the participating Governments. The question of applying similar principles to medical and veterinary research was to be taken up as opportunity should offer.

The Conference, after considering this report, adopted a resolution approving of the general principles and objects of the scheme, and requesting the Colonial Office to set up a Committee to work out detailed proposals for the consideration of all the Governments concerned.[1]

As a result of these deliberations, two Committees were actually constituted, both under the Chairmanship of Lord Lovat; one to deal specifically with the question of giving effect to the Conference resolution regarding the formation of an Agricultural Research Service, the other to frame proposals for obtaining the highest degree of efficiency in regard to veterinary research and administration that financial considerations would permit. Mr Ormsby Gore, then Parliamentary Under-Secretary of State, was a member of both Committees, which otherwise consisted of official representatives and of specialists in the respective spheres covered by the terms of reference.

The Agricultural Committee found it desirable to depart in some degree from the conclusions of their predecessors. On inquiry, they became convinced that the notion of a unified "research" Service was unsound, and that the true line of progress lay in the direction of creating a unified Colonial Agricultural Service consisting both of agricultural and of specialist officers. They pointed out that it was in practice very difficult to draw a line between the two classes; that it was necessary and even desirable that there should be a measure of fluidity between them; and that any attempt to segregate them might increase the tension and widen the breach which already existed to some extent between the specialist and the general practitioner in this as indeed in most scientific professions.

They proceeded to make detailed recommendations for a general Agricultural Service, divided into two "wings", a Specialist "wing" and an Agricultural "wing". Both "wings" were to have a common salary scale, and while it was contemplated that the "wings" should normally be independent for promotion purposes, provision was made for transfers, in suitable cases, from one to the other. The new Service was not to embrace all the members of Colonial agricultural departments, but was to be filled by the appointment of selected officers who had already served their apprenticeship. In other words, appoint-

[1] See Cmd. 2883 (Summary of Conference Proceedings).

ment to membership would be a form of promotion. On appointment, an officer would be placed on a basic salary scale, running from £750 to £1,000 a year. This salary would be supplemented, if necessary, by local allowances to compensate officers for having to serve in Colonies where the cost of living was high, or the climate bad. Above this "time-scale", the higher posts in the Service, which would be filled by promotion, were graded on salaries ranging from £1,000 to £2,000.

An interesting proposal concerned what the Committee called "brevet administrators". These were to be officers of a few years' service who showed exceptional promise; they were to be admitted to a special group, and watched and encouraged with a view to eventual promotion to Directorships and Deputy Directorships. The Committee attached particular importance to this proposal, as calculated to lead to a higher standard of efficiency in the directing staffs.

The salaries (apart from local allowances) of all members of the unified Service were to be defrayed from a central fund, which was to be financed by a grant from the Empire Marketing Board and by a cess of 1/400th on the revenues of the Colonies. From this fund were also to be met the expenses of a headquarters organisation, consisting of a Chief Agricultural Adviser, with professional and secretarial assistants, and of a standing Colonial Advisory Council of Agriculture and Animal Health.[1]

It has to be recorded that this scheme for the unification of the Service was fated to break down, principally on account of the financial difficulties. The Colonial Governments were prepared to contribute, for limited periods at a time, to the headquarters organisation, and this was in due course set up; but they were not willing to pledge themselves to submit for an indefinite period to a fixed cess on their revenues. However logical the Committee's recommendations might be, the Colonial taxpayer had, and always has, a very natural and understandable desire to spend his money in his own way. The idea of earmarking a proportion of it more or less permanently for disposal

[1] Cmd. 3049.

outside the control of the Colonial legislature was too novel to secure immediate acceptance. Fortunately, however, the question of unification was, as the next chapter will show, being attacked on a wider front, and unification was to be achieved, though not quite on the same lines as the Committee had contemplated, not for the Colonial Agricultural Service in isolation, but for it as part of a wider whole.

The Veterinary Committee were confronted with problems of a rather different kind. Veterinary services had been something of a "Cinderella"; with certain exceptions, the subject of animal health in the Colonies had not received the attention which its economic importance should have justified; the Departments were insufficiently and inadequately staffed and not provided with the necessary funds; little or no attention was paid to the provision of suitable training. This was not entirely the fault of the Colonial Governments; the Committee were not at all impressed with the efficiency of the training facilities available in this country, for here again they found that the teaching staffs were hampered by lack of funds and encouragement.

In these somewhat depressing circumstances, the Committee set themselves to consider what could be done to produce and attract the needed material. Their proposals were, briefly, first to provide for training by means of a scholarship scheme analogous to that in force for the Agricultural Services; secondly to establish a unified Service with more generous conditions than were at that time allowed in most Colonies.

The scholarship scheme which they recommended, and which was put into operation soon after the publication of their report in 1929, was based on the principle of securing for the Colonial Veterinary departments officers who combined professional veterinary qualifications with a sound knowledge of general science. The scholarships were accordingly to be of two classes: (i) for candidates holding a degree in pure science, who would be granted £250 a year for three years to enable them to qualify for the M.R.C.V.S.; (ii) for candidates already holding a veterinary qualification, who would be granted a like sum for two years to enable them to undertake further approved biological training. (The first class was later extended to four years, to correspond to a lengthening of the course for the M.R.C.V.S.)

The proposals for a unified Service were similar in principle to those which the other Committee under the same Chairman were making for the Agricultural Service. A minimum basic salary of £600 a year was prescribed, and the Service was to be divided into grades, with salaries running up to as much as £3,000 a year. As regards finance, it was proposed that the cost of the scholarship scheme should be met partly by a grant from the Empire Marketing Board, and as to two-thirds by contributions from the participating Colonies based on the number of posts in the respective veterinary departments which would normally be filled by officers recruited under the scheme. No proposals analogous to those made for the Agricultural Service were, however, put forward in regard to the establishment of a central fund; it was contemplated that each Colony should be directly responsible for the payment of the staff which it employed.[1]

The reports of these Committees were both available in 1929. Before carrying the story up to the dramatic events of the following year we must turn away from the scientific services to a wider field.

[1] Cmd. 3261.

CHAPTER V

THE "WARREN FISHER" COMMITTEE

A N apology is, perhaps, due to the reader for the necessity of inflicting upon him, in the last chapter, a string of Committees; it was, however, inevitable, for it was by the committee method that developments took place at this time. The Colonial Office as yet possessed little in the way of a permanent organisation for dealing with the problems of the Colonial Empire as a whole. The basis of its organisation was geographical; that is to say, the Office was divided into a number of departments, each of which was responsible for assisting the Secretary of State in dealing with the affairs of a group of Colonies. There was a General Department, but its functions were restricted within definite limits, and it was no part of its duties, for example, to act as a central co-ordinating department with regard to conditions of service in the Colonies. When, therefore, general questions required to be discussed, the most convenient way of proceeding was to set up an *ad hoc* Committee, comprising experienced members of the staff and such outside advisers as could be obtained to give expert assistance with regard to the particular matter in hand.

The geographical organisation of the Office was of long standing. Until 1907 no special distinction was made between Dominions and Colonies; but in that year a separate Dominions Division was set up. The number and respective spheres of the departments on the Colonial side naturally varied from time to time according to the exigencies of the work; the position in 1925 was that there were eight such Geographical departments, each under an Assistant Secretary. A ninth Assistant Secretary was in charge of the General Department, which included in its scope matters affecting the establishment and management of the Office itself, as well as the restricted range of questions affecting the Colonies generally to which reference was made above.

In 1925 a change of great importance took place. The Government decided that the time had come to separate the work connected with the Colonies from that connected with the Dominions, and a new Secretaryship of State for Dominion Affairs was set up. For the time being the two Secretaryships of State were to be held by one Minister (Mr L. S. Amery), but two Permanent Under-Secretaries of State were appointed, Sir Charles Davis for Dominion Affairs, and Brigadier-General Sir Samuel Wilson, then Governor of Jamaica, for the Colonies. Henceforth the Dominions Office and the Colonial Office were separate Departments of State, though they continued to occupy the same building and to share a number of joint services such as the accounts staff and the library. The administrative and clerical staffs of the two Offices, below the rank of Assistant Under-Secretary of State, remained· interchangeable.

As the first Permanent Under-Secretary of State for the Colonies alone, Sir Samuel Wilson naturally turned his attention at an early stage to the question of the organisation of his Office as an instrument for dealing with the special problems which confronted the Colonial Empire in the conditions of the time. He was impressed by the necessity for making better provision for the effective handling of questions which concerned the Colonial Empire as a whole, for the co-ordination of effort, and for the pooling of experience. This consideration led to his decision, after due deliberation and consultation, to effect a reorganisation by which the number of Geographical departments was reduced to seven, while the General department was expanded into two departments and provided with a considerably increased staff. The range of functions of the General Division (as it was now called) was substantially enlarged: so far as the Colonial Services were concerned, it was to deal not only with promotions and transfers but with pensions, discipline and other matters judged to be susceptible to co-ordinated handling.

So far, however, the vital question of recruitment had not been brought under review, the arrangements in force for dealing with this matter being still based on the traditional principle that appointments in the Colonial Services were in the personal gift of the Secretary of State, and not part of the official concerns of the Colonial Office. But, as has been amply illustrated by the last two chapters, recruitment for the Colonial Services had developed into a highly intricate and technical subject; a subject in which all the Colonial Governments were intimately concerned, and one which called for continuity and co-ordination in a very special degree. Mr Amery considered that this question of recruitment called for an investigation of the most authoritative character; he wished also to be advised as to the possibility or desirability of associating recruitment for the Colonial Office itself with that for the Colonial Services. Accordingly, he decided to invite Sir Warren Fisher, the Permanent Secretary to the Treasury and Head of the Home Civil Service, to undertake the Chairmanship of a representative Committee which would be asked "to consider the existing system of appointment in the Colonial Office and in the Public Service of the Dependencies not possessing responsible government, and to make such recommendations as may be considered desirable".

The Committee thus entrusted with the task of drawing together in one comprehensive inquiry the threads of all the previous investigations, included representatives of the House of Commons, of the educational world and of Colonial administration, as well as of the Treasury and the Civil Service Commission. Their deliberations occupied a whole year from their appointment in April 1929. On the change of Ministry in June of that year, the Committee were authorised to continue their work, and their report[1] was presented to Mr Amery's successor, Lord Passfield, in April 1930.

This report, which may without exaggeration be described as the Magna Carta of the modern Colonial Service, is of such outstanding importance to the present study that it is desirable to summarise it in some detail. As will be seen, the Committee, in dealing with their terms of reference, found it necessary to examine not only the systems of appointment to which their attention was specifically directed, but the wider questions of

[1] Cmd. 3554.

organisation, both at home and abroad, with which those systems were inextricably bound up.

So far as the method of appointment to the Colonial Office was concerned, the Committee, while recognising that there might be some weight of opinion in favour of a method which would attach more value to personal qualities than the method of competitive written examination, decided not to advocate any change in the arrangement by which the Office was staffed from the general examination for the Home Civil Service. They were unable to recommend a change either in the direction of selecting all or part of the administrative staff from the Colonial Services, since, as they pointed out, the work of the Colonial Office was in its essentials different from that of Colonial administrations; or in the direction of creating a special form of examination or other system of entry similar, for example, to that in force for the Foreign Office. At the same time, the Committee recommended certain developments of the system of temporary interchange between the Colonial Office staff and the staffs of the Colonial Governments.

But the Committee had a good deal to say about the organisation of the Colonial Office for dealing with matters relating to appointments and staff questions generally in the Colonies. As has been stated, they found no arrangements in being for dealing with such matters comprehensively for the Colonial Empire as a whole. They did not consider this state of affairs satisfactory, and they recommended that a new Personnel Division should be set up, under an Assistant Under-Secretary of State. This Division should be responsible for the co-ordinated handling of Service questions such as recruitment, promotions, pensions and discipline. In it was to be incorporated, on a permanent footing, the existing non-permanent organisation which, nominally as part of the Minister's Private Secretariat, had been charged with the recruitment and selection of personnel for the Colonies. In it, also, was to be merged, suitably strengthened, the existing organisation in the General Division of the Office for dealing with promotions and other staffing questions, in so far as it had developed. The Committee laid great stress upon the necessity of those dealing with such matters at the Colonial Office being given the fullest facilities for maintaining personal touch with Colonial officials, for collecting, by correspondence and by interview, and for recording the completest possible information for the assistance of the Secretary of State in making selections for appointments from the widest available field. Vacancies should be handled not as isolated occurrences, but as part of a general plan, and a sufficient expert staff should be employed on this special work to enable considerably more detailed attention to be given to it than had been possible in the past. The Promotions Committee, which was at this time an advisory Committee of Heads of Departments, meeting informally to submit recommendations to the Secretary of State, was to be reduced in numbers and strengthened in authority. Henceforth, it was to consist of the Permanent Under-Secretary and his immediate Assistants, with such other members of the staff as might be invited to attend in an advisory capacity in connection with particular vacancies.

With regard to the question of first appointments to the Colonial Services, the Committee discussed in much detail the work of the Private Secretaries and its results. They were naturally greatly concerned to reach a right conclusion as to whether the method of personal selection, which was in use for all but a limited number of appointments, should properly be continued in being, or whether it should give place to some other method, such as competitive examination. They could not overlook the fact that the existing system was open to criticism as being, at any rate in theory, a system of patronage. Technically, the Minister for the time being in power had complete control over appointments, and there was no check on his appointing whomsoever he should please to any post. Moreover, the staff employed were his Private Secretaries, and might have their appointments terminated on a change of Minister, or at any time, in which event their experience would be lost to the Colonies. The Committee were unable to escape the conclusion that, if seriously challenged, such a system could not in theory be defended.

≪ 57 ≫

At the same time, the Committee were at pains to make it clear that none of these possible abuses had in fact occurred. Indeed, they were abundantly satisfied that the work of the Appointments staff had been of the greatest value to the Colonial Governments, and that the standard of selected candidates had been maintained at a high, and indeed at a steadily improving level. The evidence of Governors and senior officers left no room for doubt that the selection system, as carried out by this staff, had "delivered the goods". For a variety of reasons, the Committee did not think it advisable in any case to extend the system of competitive examination beyond its existing area (that is to say, the Eastern Cadet and Eastern Police Services). In these circumstances, they concluded that the selection system should be retained, but with certain modifications and safeguards.

In the first place, as has already been observed, they proposed that the selecting staff should cease to be in the position of Private Secretaries, and should be incorporated in the permanent staff of the Colonial Office as part of the new Personnel Division. By this means continuity of policy and of experience would be secured. Secondly, with a view to disposing of the objections to the patronage system, the Committee recommended that a Colonial Service Appointments Board should be set up as a standing independent Board. The duties of the Office staff would be to carry out the necessary liaison work with sources of recruitment, the preliminary sifting of candidates and the preparation for each vacancy of a short list of suitable names, from which it would be for the Board to make the final selection for submission to the Secretary of State, on whose authority the appointments would then be made. The Board was to consist of a Chairman and two other persons, all of whom should be nominated by the Civil Service Commissioners, and one of whom should have had recent experience of service in the Colonies.

It should perhaps be mentioned here that the Private Secretary (Appointments) was not responsible for *all* appointments made from this country. Engineers and other technical staff were recruited by the Crown Agents for the Colonies; certain classes of teachers by the Board of Education; nursing sisters by the Overseas Nursing Association; postal and customs officers in many cases from the home departments. The Committee did not recommend any change in these specialised recruiting arrangements.

So much, then, for the home organisation, and the Committee's far-reaching proposals with regard to it. The Committee did not, however, consider that their task related only to this aspect of the recruiting position. The organisation was but a means to an end; it was necessary to determine what that end was, and how it might best be achieved.

"The Colonial Empire", said the Committee, in a striking passage, "has become a problem of the first magnitude, both on the quantitative and the qualitative side. Its geographical area has been largely extended, its wealth is advancing every year, and the duties of government have been increased in number and immeasurably increased in complexity. On the political side we are labouring to establish a régime which seeks to preserve what is best in the traditional native culture, rather than to provide a cleared ground for the establishment of a ready-made alien polity. Such a purpose demands a high degree of knowledge and understanding on the part of the administrators. On the economic side we have to bring to bear the latest results of scientific research on the development of wealth.... Most of the greater problems of the Colonies to-day are problems of applied science. Obviously, in a field so intricate and so fateful, the organisation of the Government services demands the most scrupulous care."

In other words, the aim must be to place at the disposal of the Colonies, held by us in trust for their inhabitants and for the world, the best material that the home country could supply. The Colonies themselves, many poor and many backward, could not hope to provide from their own resources the necessary trained staff to carry on the business of government. But, to make that material available, it was not enough to provide an efficient recruiting organisation, important as that provision might be. It was not enough to provide better means for mobilising the personnel of the Services for employment in the most productive manner. It was necessary to consider the whole question of the careers offered in the various branches, for without the prospect of a satisfactory career, the attractiveness of the Services to the right type of candidate must inevitably be prejudiced.

The Committee made various recommendations of a general character with regard to the conditions of service which, in their view, were likely to lead to improved attractiveness and efficiency. They referred, for example, to the desirability of providing generous leave and passage conditions; of giving greater facilities for study-leave and courses of instruction; of improving salary scales in certain directions; and of arranging for the accelerated promotion of specially meritorious officers. This did not, however, go far enough. They found themselves brought up at every turn against the difficulties arising out of the independence of each Colony's public service and the lack of a central control securing a reasonable relation between the salary schemes and other terms of employment in the different administrations. They felt obliged, therefore, to embark upon a serious discussion of the problem of the unification of the Services.

As previous chapters of this book have shown, this question was not a new one. It had been put forward, and abandoned, in the last years of the nineteenth century, when the Colonial Empire as we know it to-day was coming into being. The idea had been revived from time to time in connection with the Medical, the Agricultural and the Veterinary Services, but as yet without practical result. The Committee studied the past history of the matter, and analysed the difficulties which had hitherto been regarded as forbidding such a project. They came to the conclusion that these difficulties were capable of solution. Climatic differences, which, as has been seen, were the chief obstacle thirty years before, now need no longer be regarded as a formidable hindrance. The real necessity for important differences in the terms of employment might well be less than was generally assumed. Already there was a considerable degree of assimilation within regional groups, and it was probable that this principle was capable of extension. Already, too, the practice of regarding the Services as a single pool for promotion and transfer was widely established. The fear that unification would unduly interfere with a Colonial Government's control of its staff was, the Committee felt, not well founded; unification would in any event naturally apply principally to the grades normally recruited from outside the Colony by the Secretary of State.

On the other hand, the Committee felt strongly that all Colonies would stand to gain positively from the unification of the Services. Even a merely nominal unification would, in their opinion, have a real value, as giving the Service a prestige comparable to that of the Indian Civil Service, with a consequent effect both on recruitment and on serving officers. In addition, unification would lead to a wider recognition of the principle of inter-Colonial movement of officers, particularly in the professional and technical branches; and to the prospect of a career unlimited to a particular Dependency or group, and of promotion on the ground of merit to the highest appointments. "These", observed the Committee, in a passage which demands quotation, "are not merely attractions in the interest of recruitment, but sound and essential principles to be applied in the interest of the keenness and efficiency of the Public Service. As an ideal, unification has...received at least lip service on many previous occasions. Some of the practical difficulties which years ago loomed so large do not now appear so formidable, while fresh obstacles which now obstruct the road might then have been brushed aside. But the need of efficient service, the penalty of failure, the complexity of the Government machine, the opportunity of results of first-rate importance, all these are greater now. If a more economical and, in our opinion, more effective organisation is to be achieved, the present is now the time for it, for, if we delay, it may become for ever impracticable."

The Committee's proposals for the realignment of the Colonial

Services involved, in the first place, the recognition of a single Colonial Service, and, in the second place, "within this larger whole", the unification of special Services such as Agriculture, Medicine, Education, etc. They did not indicate in detail how these special Services should be organised; it was implied, if not specifically stated, that this would be a task for the new Personnel Division of the Colonial Office, if the Committee's recommendations were accepted. It was clear, in any case, that the initiative would have to rest with the Colonial Office, since much of the information on which the Committee's views were based could not in the nature of things be present to the minds of Governors and their advisers overseas. At the same time, it was recognised that the support of the Colonial Governments would be essential if the project were to be launched under conditions favourable to its success; the Committee therefore recommended that their considered proposal should be brought to the notice of the Governors and other representatives who were about to assemble for the second Colonial Office Conference, and that if the Conference approved in principle, a further Committee should be appointed to draw up a complete and detailed scheme for each branch of the Service, together with the general and special regulations which would be required to bring the new policy into effect. Such schemes, it was hinted, would have to provide for some assimilation of salaries and other conditions of service such as leave and passages; and the creation of a unified Service would imply that officers appointed in future should accept a liability to serve anywhere in the Colonial Empire.

CHAPTER VI

THE UNIFICATION OF THE SERVICE

THE stage was now set for the second Colonial Office Conference, which was to prove a turning-point in the history of the Service. The Conference had many important matters to discuss, but none perhaps of greater significance for the future of the Colonial Empire than the questions of staff organisation arising out of the reports of the two Lovat Committees and the Warren Fisher Committee.

It is safe to say that at the beginning of 1930 most people connected with the Colonial Services would have regarded their unification, however desirable in theory—and as to its desirability there would have been strong difference of opinion—as an impracticable dream. The publication of the reports referred to, with their weight of authority, had, however, in a very short time created a new atmosphere. Particularly impressive was the solemn warning of the Warren Fisher Committee that, if the present opportunity were not seized, the chance of establishing a sound organisation might be irretrievably lost.

In this new atmosphere the Conference was opened by Lord Passfield, the Secretary of State, on 23 June 1930. There were present the Governors of Jamaica, Ceylon, Barbados, Bermuda, Bahamas, the Gold Coast, Uganda, Sierra Leone, Cyprus, Northern Rhodesia, British Honduras and the Leeward Islands; the recently retired Governor of Mauritius; the Resident at Aden; the Colonial or Chief Secretaries of Nigeria, Nyasaland, Palestine, Gibraltar, the Tanganyika Territory and Fiji; and other senior officers representing the Governments of Hong Kong, Malaya, Zanzibar, British Guiana and Kenya, in addition to senior members of the Colonial Office staff. The Conference was thus fully equipped to arrive at authoritative decisions upon questions of policy affecting the Colonial Empire as a whole.

In his opening address, Lord Passfield announced that he had accepted the recommendations of the Warren Fisher Committee with regard to the establishment of a Personnel Division at the Colonial Office, and that an Assistant Under-Secretary of State would be appointed who would devote his attention to questions relating to the personnel and organisation of the Colonial Services. The Committee's very important suggestions for the unification of the Services would be submitted for the consideration of the Conference.

Two Subcommittees were then set up, one to deal with the matters arising out of the Lovat reports, and the other to consider the Warren Fisher Committee's recommendations. The first, under the Chairmanship of Sir Herbert Stanley, then Governor of Ceylon, reported definitely in favour of the establishment of a unified Agricultural Service, though in some particulars they felt it desirable to modify the proposals of the Lovat Committee, in the light of the views which Colonial Governments had expressed to the Secretary of State on the Committee's report. They did not, for example, endorse the suggestion that the Service should include only the senior grades. They considered that all officers with the requisite professional qualifications should be accorded the status of membership from their first appointment. Again, they came to the conclusion that the proposal to finance the Service by means of a cess on revenues was impracticable. They thought, however, that the central fund, to which a number of Colonies had already agreed to contribute so as to meet the cost of an Advisory Council, might also be used to supplement the resources of Colonies which were unable to pay the standard salaries proposed for the unified Service. Otherwise, the normal arrangement by which each Colony was responsible directly for the payment of the staff which it employed, should be maintained.

As regards salary rates, the Subcommittee did not think that the Colonies could afford the full scales proposed by the Lovat Committee, and they recommended the adoption of a standard time-scale running from £480 to £920, with a number of "super-scale" grades carrying salaries of from £1,000 to as much as £1,750. They remarked that, although there should not be any

continuous and indiscriminate transfer of personnel, the acceptance by members of a liability to compulsory transfer was an
essential condition of a unified Service. It was recommended,
however, that the liability should not be enforced, except for
disciplinary reasons, if the transfer would involve the officer
concerned in loss of emoluments or pension privileges.

The Subcommittee did not consider in detail the question of
the Veterinary Service, but advised that this matter should stand
over for consideration by the Adviser on Animal Health, who
was shortly to take up duty at the Colonial Office. They recommended, however, that the question of unifying the Forestry
Services, on the same lines as the Agricultural, should be taken
up as soon as possible.

These reports and recommendations were in due course approved by the Conference, which in particular expressed the
hope that all the Colonial Governments would find it possible
to take part in the Agricultural Service scheme.

Meanwhile, the wider question of general unification was
being discussed by the other Subcommittee, under the Chairmanship of Sir William Gowers, Governor of Uganda. It had
been clear, from the preliminary speeches at the plenary meeting
of the Conference, that some representatives were still disposed
to take the view that until certain fundamental difficulties had
been surmounted the question of unification would have to
remain in abeyance. For their part, the Subcommittee were
inclined to accept the less pessimistic conclusions of the Warren
Fisher Committee. They were especially impressed by that
Committee's argument that, as time went on, the difficulties of
unification would increase, and they felt strongly that if some
definite move were not taken in the immediate future, the
opportunity might not recur.

They set themselves, therefore, to examine the alleged difficulties, and to try to indicate means of disposing of them. In
the first place, they pointed out that in many ways the conditions
precedent to the recognition of a single Colonial Service already
obtained: officers served under the same code of regulations;
their appointments, salaries, pensions, discipline and conditions

of employment were, to a greater or less degree, subject to the control of the Secretary of State, to whom, also, all had a right of appeal; their opportunities of promotion were not restricted to one Colony, but extended over the whole field of the Colonial Empire; in short, it was the nominal isolation of the separate Services, rather than their association, which was not in accordance with existing facts. The Subcommittee saw no reason why a pronouncement that henceforth the Services would officially be known as the Colonial Service should not be made; and they agreed with the Warren Fisher Committee that such a pronouncement would have appreciable advantages, especially from the point of view of recruitment. They felt, however, that unless something further could be done to translate the principle into action, the chief benefits which were to be anticipated from unification would not be realised. They considered it essential, therefore, that, the first step having been taken, an attempt should at once be made upon the next objective, namely, the removal of obstacles in the way of a real and practical unification of the Service.

These obstacles they summarised as follows:

(i) The diversity of salaries, terms of service, climatic and other conditions.

(ii) The existence of different methods of entry for appointments of the same order in different Dependencies.

(iii) The absence of any power of compulsory transfer by the Secretary of State.

As regards the first of these obstacles, which they described as perhaps the most serious, the Subcommittee observed that there was already fairly general agreement that the unification of at any rate the scientific Services was desirable. This, if it proceeded, would automatically make for a simplification and co-ordination of the terms of service generally, since Colonial Governments would presumably not wish to undergo the inconvenience of having two different sets of conditions in force concurrently, for the unified and non-unified branches of their staffs respectively. "We envisage", said the Subcommittee, "an ultimate state of affairs in which the non-technical as well as the technical branches of the Colonial Service will be graded in some sort of way so that the 'real wages' (taking into account climate, pension and leave privileges, amenities and cost of living) in corresponding grades in different Colonies will have some approximation to each other; but we visualise this as coming gradually, and as a natural result of the forces now being put in motion, rather than as being imposed upon Colonial Governments against their wills."

The second obstacle applied only to a limited class of appointments, but the Subcommittee regarded it as one of special importance. They referred in particular to the fact that, whereas the administrative appointments in Africa were filled by the selection system, those in the Eastern group were filled by competitive examination. Although the Warren Fisher Committee had not seen fit to recommend any change in this practice, the Subcommittee held the view that it must, so long as it persisted, retard the realisation of the full benefits of unification. They tentatively suggested that the two methods might be reconciled by adopting for all administrative posts a system of provisional selection, followed by a University course with a serious and stringent qualifying examination at the end, the results of which would determine seniority in the unified Service. In any case, the Subcommittee deprecated any extension of the system of entrance by examination without selection.

As regards the third obstacle, the Subcommittee, after careful consideration, decided that, while the power of compulsory transfer was not likely in practice to be much employed, its existence was inherent in the scheme of unification. They observed, however, that it was more important to take into account the privilege of promotion by transfer, which, from the point of view of recruiting, was a much more significant effect of unification.

The Subcommittee added some observations to forestall possible objections from the political angle. They pointed out that unification would necessarily apply mainly to personnel of the classes normally recruited from outside the Colonies themselves. Those locally recruited need not be put under an obligation or be considered to have a claim to serve outside their own countries; but there was no reason why the adoption of the policy of unification should be allowed to interfere with their being given the fullest scope to serve the State in their own Colonies, or to prevent their being admitted to the unified Service if they so desired and if they possessed the necessary qualifications. Again, in case there should be any apprehension that, by agreeing to participate, Colonies might be "letting themselves in" for unsuitable officers on transfer from elsewhere, the Subcommittee observed that it must clearly be assumed that any scheme of unification would be administered with common sense, and they saw no possible ground for supposing that the Secretary of State was likely to foist upon a Colony persons who were manifestly unsuited to its particular circumstances.

The report of the Subcommittee concluded on a note of warning. If, as they unhesitatingly recommended, the policy of unification were accepted in the interests of the Colonial Empire as a whole, there was bound to be a movement towards standardisation of salaries and conditions of employment. It would no doubt be found that any Colony which failed to come into line would suffer in recruiting, both by original appointment and by transfer. Where it was a question of lack of means, the Subcommittee were confident that some plan would be devised which would protect such Dependencies from being cut off. But where a Government should stand out not from genuine lack of ability but from the refusal of the local legislature to face the facts of the situation, the Subcommittee could only say that it was far better that such a Government should be left to the consequences of its self-imposed isolation than that its non-co-operation should be allowed to hamper the development of the rest.

This report was debated at two plenary meetings of the Conference. The official record reveals that there was a good deal of difference of opinion, and that in particular the question of compulsory transfer gave rise to much discussion. It was generally agreed that a liability to transfer was an essential feature of any scheme of unification, but some representatives doubted whether the imposition of the liability was practicable or desirable. It was also generally agreed that any scheme must be so designed as to leave unimpaired the executive authority of the local Government over its officers. On the whole, the sense of the Conference was in favour of the principle of unification, but it was felt that the practical difficulties were real and would have to be met before the Governments could be expected to commit themselves to the acceptance of any concrete scheme. A momentous discussion concluded with the unanimous passage of the following resolution:

"This Conference considers unification of the Colonial Services desirable if a generally acceptable scheme can be devised, and requests the Secretary of State to appoint a Committee to prepare a detailed scheme for submission to the several Colonial Governments." [1]

Lord Passfield considered that this resolution was at any rate sufficiently encouraging to justify him in taking the initial step recommended by the Warren Fisher Committee, and giving formal recognition to the principle of a single Service. He chose the occasion of the Corona Club dinner on 16 July to announce his decision. (It will be recollected that in Chapter 1 reference was made to this Club as the organisation which arranges the annual Colonial Service Dinner.) The occasion, at which the Conference representatives and large numbers of Colonial officers, past and present, were gathered together, was clearly very appropriate for a pronouncement of this kind.

In his speech at the dinner, the Secretary of State referred with pride to the fact that he was the first Minister of the Crown to be responsible for the Colonial Empire alone. The recent appointment of a separate Secretary of State for Dominion Affairs (the two Secretaryships having been previously held by the same Minister) had been hailed as an important epoch in the history of the relations of the Mother Country with the self-governing Dominions; but he thought that it was no less significant as a landmark in the history of the Colonial Empire. He

[1] Cmd. 3268, pp. 85–90.

recalled Joseph Chamberlain's dream of a great Colonial Service which, in the fulness of time, would take its stand alongside the other great public services of the Empire. It had taken a long time for events to move towards the realisation of that dream. "Even now", said Lord Passfield, "you will find the Press full of tributes, well deserved tributes, to the unselfish devotion and the untiring labours of our colleagues in the Indian Civil Service, but it is not often that you find the newspapers have a paragraph to spare for the equally devoted and equally untiring labours of those who run the ship of the Colonial Empire. The Indian Civil Service presents to the public a simple, easily understandable idea. The complexities and the diversities of our Colonial administration prevent the true realisation of what is actually being done."

Referring, then, to the question of creating a single Service, he said: "Some people may say that it is only a name, but there is a great deal in a name. Yet we need more than a name. The idea of a great single Service spread over those two million square miles, serving alike the bleak fastnesses of the Antarctic Ocean, the scented islands of the Tropic Seas, and the stifling heat of the African bush, ought to fire the imagination. We want to fire the imagination of the young men of Britain in this matter. But it is not much use holding out to them the idea of this great Service if we do not do something to turn it into a reality. We cannot help the diversities of climate and local conditions, though I do not think these are as far apart as they were. We can, however, help to a large extent the diversities of terms of service, which are at present an obstacle to free movement of personnel and to the most profitable utilisation of the great wealth of experience which stands ready at the command of the Colonial Service. We can do it, I think; not at once by a stroke of the pen, not by an arbitrary imposition of authority, but by means of goodwill and co-operation."

Lord Passfield thereupon proceeded to announce, to the evident satisfaction of his audience, that he gladly accepted the recommendation of the Conference, and that he had taken immediate steps to set up, under his own presidency, the

Committee which the Conference had suggested for the purpose of preparing a detailed scheme of unification.

Before we turn to the subsequent proceedings, mention should be made of one practical step which followed immediately on the Secretary of State's decision. This concerned the form of offers of appointment emanating from the Colonial Office. The traditional form of letter was to the effect that the Secretary of State proposed to select the recipient for appointment "as an administrative officer in Kenya", or whatever the post in question might be. The new form decreed by Lord Passfield informed the candidate that it was proposed to select him for appointment "*to the Colonial Service* as an administrative officer", etc.; and continued: "As a member of the Colonial Service, you would be...eligible to be considered, with other members of that Service, at the discretion of the Secretary of State, for appointments in other Dependencies."

This may seem a small thing in itself, and those who have followed this narrative will not fail to recognise that it did little more than register what was already the established practice. But it was of immense significance as marking an entirely new approach to the question of staff organisation in the Colonies. Whereas in the past the emphasis had been strictly on the individuality of the respective public services of the Colonies, and the possibility that an officer might be transferred was deliberately kept in the background as an uncovenanted benefit which should on no account be taken into consideration by the candidate, this possibility was now placed in the foreground as an essential feature of the organisation. By his decision the Secretary of State pledged himself and his successors to action which would ensure that the prospect held out to the candidate was not an empty one, and that in future promotions would be so conducted as to secure, as far as should be possible, to all officers in the Service, wherever stationed, equal consideration and equal opportunity for legitimate advancement.

Having taken and announced his decision, Lord Passfield lost no time in constituting the Committee which was to produce a concrete scheme of unification. As already stated, he had decided to preside over it himself; the members were Sir Warren Fisher, Sir Samuel Wilson and Mr (afterwards Sir George) Tomlinson, who had accepted the new office of Assistant Under-Secretary of State in charge of the Personnel Division of the Colonial Office. The Committee was to co-opt, as might be required, other members of the Colonial Office and Governors and senior officers of the Colonial Service who should happen to be available in this country. It was contemplated that this central or "parent" Committee should appoint, as required, Subcommittees, which would be entrusted with the task of drawing up detailed schemes for the various branches of the Service, in accordance with the general principles which the central Committee should lay down.

The Committee actually began work on 31 July, and the course which they adopted was to instruct a Subcommittee, to be presided over by Mr Tomlinson, to prepare a scheme of unification for the Administrative Service. They selected this branch because it seemed to be in many ways the most difficult to deal with, and also because it was the most numerous branch. If, then, a suitable plan could be devised for the Administrative branch, not only would a large proportion of the whole Service be settled, but the chief difficulties would have been faced and successfully surmounted.

The new Personnel Division of the Colonial Office came into existence on 1 October 1930, and the Subcommittee got to work without delay. Their task was a long one, for it was not merely a matter of reconciling the prevailing diversities in conditions of employment; in the absence of any previous comprehensive attempt to arrive at basic principles by which those conditions of employment should be regulated, it was necessary to survey the whole field, and to consider how far such principles could usefully be laid down, and in what form. In other words, the Subcommittee had practically to begin at the beginning and produce a new set of conditions; they could not be content to take the East African, the West African or the Malayan conditions as a basis and propose that the other places should come into line with them.

While the Subcommittee's deliberations were proceeding, the Colonies, like the rest of the world, were experiencing a serious deterioration of their financial and economic prosperity. To meet the emergency, retrenchments of staff and temporary levies on salaries became unfortunately necessary in many of the Dependencies. Recruitment for the Colonial Service was severely restricted, and for a time a general atmosphere of instability prevailed. By the early part of 1932, the Subcommittee had produced their scheme for the unification of the Administrative Service, but it was obvious that the moment was quite inopportune for proposing to the Colonial Governments that they should consider the adoption of changes of a permanent character in the salaries and other conditions of a large class of officers in the higher ranks of the Service. Such a question called for calm and deliberate consideration in less disturbed circumstances. At that time, no one could venture to predict what modifications in the structure and standards of remuneration of the Service the economic depression might bring in its train.

Sir Philip Cunliffe-Lister (afterwards Lord Swinton), who was the National Government's Secretary of State for the Colonies from 1931 to 1935, was anxious to promote the policy of unification so far as circumstances permitted. Although the adoption of the full scheme was out of the question, he decided that it was both practicable and desirable to create a Colonial Administrative Service, even if the assimilation of the conditions of employment to a common standard should have to be postponed. There were many respects in which the conditions could be assimilated without financial repercussions; one of these to which the Secretary of State attached particular importance concerned the method of entry.

As we have seen, the Colonial Office Conference Subcommittee had expressed the view that a unified Service pre-supposed a single method of entry, and that circumstances made it necessary that this method should be the selection rather than the examination system. On the other hand, it was clear that, in the Dependencies where the traditional entry to the administrative Services was through the Home and Indian Civil

Service examination, there was a natural reluctance, at any rate in some quarters, to make a change which did not appear to be dictated by any local considerations, and which, it was feared, might actually be to the disadvantage of the Governments concerned.

The Secretary of State's views, and his decision, were explained in a despatch published in the *Federated Malay States Gazette* of 24 March 1932. While giving full weight to the possible objections, and frankly admitting the excellent service which the examination system had rendered to the Eastern Dependencies in the past, he gave it as his considered conclusion that the interests of the Eastern Services were so closely bound up with those of the Colonial Service as a whole, and those of the Colonial Service as a whole so closely bound up with the maintenance and development of the selection system, that the balance of advantage was strongly in favour of applying that system to the whole Colonial Administrative Service, and abandoning the system of recruitment by examination.

Sir Philip Cunliffe-Lister decided, then, to create a Colonial Administrative Service, with effect from 1 July 1932, based on the following plan. First of all, it would have a single method of entry: selection by the Secretary of State, on the advice of the Colonial Service Appointments Board. The appointment, confirmation, promotion, transfer and retirement of members of the Service would be governed by the directions of the Secretary of State. A list of posts would be drawn up, which would normally be filled by members of the Service. All officers holding listed posts on 1 July 1932, would automatically become members of the new Service; but thereafter membership of the Service would not depend on the holding of a particular post, but on the nomination of the Secretary of State. All persons appointed as members after the commencing date would be liable to be transferred by the Secretary of State to any of the listed posts, with or without promotion, subject to two important qualifications: first, that no officer who was at the time of his appointment ordinarily resident in the Colony in which he was to be employed would be liable to transfer out of that Colony without his own consent; second, that no officer would be obliged to accept transfer to a post which, in the opinion of the Secretary of State, was of less value than that which he already held, due regard being had to climate and other relevant considerations. Apart from these special regulations, officers of the Service would be subject to the ordinary rules of the Dependency in which they were employed.

A detailed description of the Colonial Administrative Service is reserved for a later chapter; here we must proceed with the subsequent history of the development of unification. With the decision to create a unified Administrative Service, two lines of advancement opened out. On the one hand, there was the question of forming other unified branches on the same plan as had been adopted for the Administrative branch. On the other hand, it was necessary to pursue, as opportunity should permit, the search for a reasonable standard of conditions of employment, and the endeavour to assimilate existing conditions to that standard when found. It will be convenient to follow up these two lines separately, in a fresh chapter.

CHAPTER VII

PROGRESS OF THE POLICY OF UNIFICATION

As soon as the unification of the Colonial Administrative Service had been accomplished, consideration was given by the Secretary of State to the question of proceeding, upon similar lines, with the unification of other branches. The first to be dealt with was the Legal branch, and this was constituted as the Colonial Legal Service with effect from 1 July 1933. Like the Colonial Administrative Service, this was based on a list, or "schedule" of posts, the holders of which on the appointed date automatically became members of the new Service. The schedule comprised those posts in the Colonial Empire the duties of which call for the employment of qualified barristers or solicitors, and which are normally filled by persons recruited from outside the Colonies themselves. Some legal and judicial posts in certain Colonies were customarily filled by locally appointed lawyers, and were therefore unscheduled; but, broadly speaking, the schedule comprised all the higher legal and judicial posts in the Colonies, that is to say, on the legal side the Attorneys-General, Solicitors-General and Crown Counsel, and on the judicial side the Chief Justices, Judges and professional Magistrates.

After a short interval there followed the creation of the Colonial Medical Service, which came into existence on 1 January 1934. The scheme for this Service was similar in principle to those already described, but one or two special points had to be considered. First there was the question of defining the professional qualification for membership. In a large number of Colonies, but not all, the possession of a medical qualification rendering the holder eligible to be registered as a practitioner in the United Kingdom is a necessary condition of admission to the local medical register. In any event, there are few of the higher medical posts in the Colonial Service for which the possession of such a qualification would not be regarded as essential, irrespective of the provisions of the local registration law. Accordingly, while no restriction was placed on the automatic admission to the⁻ Service of officers already holding scheduled posts, whose qualifications did not happen to entitle them to registration in the United Kingdom (though registrable in the Colony concerned), it was decided to provide that, after the commencing date, only officers with qualifications registrable in the United Kingdom would be eligible for appointment as members of the Service.

A further question which had to be considered was that of private practice. The rules and customs in this matter varied considerably in different Colonies, according to local circumstances, and while there was no question of introducing uniformity, it was considered desirable to incorporate in the regulations of the new Service some general expression of policy. It was accordingly decided to lay down that, subject to the preservation of rights acquired prior to 1 January 1934, no officer of the Colonial Medical Service should be entitled as of right to practise on his own account. The conditions, if any, under which officers might be allowed to engage in private practice were to be determined by local regulations framed in accordance with the circumstances of the various Dependencies and approved by the Secretary of State. In other words, the Colonial Medical Service was envisaged as primarily one consisting of whole-time officials, and it was not expected or desired that officers should enter it in the hope of adding substantially to their emoluments by private practice. At the same time, provision was retained for permitting private practice to officers the nature of whose duties did not preclude it, and who might be serving in places where the needs of the population could not be met by private practitioners.

The creation of the Colonial Medical Service involved the absorption into the new organisation of the important regional medical services in West Africa, East Africa and Malaya, which now ceased to exist as separate units.

The following year (1935) saw the establishment of the Colonial Forest Service, the Colonial Agricultural Service and the Colonial Veterinary Service. In the case of all three, specific professional qualifications were laid down for new entrants. For the Forest Service, the prescribed qualification was the possession of a degree in Forestry of a British University, and the candidate must also have attended an approved course of study at the Imperial Forestry Institute at Oxford. The entrant to the Agricultural Service must possess a University degree in Agriculture or Natural Science, or a diploma of an Agricultural College of University status, the acquisition of which involved at least a three-year course of study in agriculture or horticulture; he must also have had not less than two years' post-graduate training in agricultural sciences or two years' approved post-graduate experience. For the Veterinary Service, the prescribed qualification was the possession of a diploma of membership of the Royal College of Veterinary Surgeons, or of a veterinary qualification obtained in one of the self-governing Dominions.

The Colonial Police Service, covering what may be conveniently described as the "commissioned" ranks of the Colonial police forces, was constituted with effect from 1 January 1937; and the tale of Services so far unified concludes with a batch dating from the beginning of 1938, namely, the Colonial Survey Service, the Colonial Mines Service, the Colonial Geological Survey Service, the Colonial Customs Service and the Colonial Postal Service. It is legitimate to assume that the extension of the principle to other branches is only a matter of time and opportunity, and that in due course other unified Services will be set up on similar lines, until the whole field of appointments mainly or substantially recruited from outside the Colonies themselves shall have been covered. Educational, engineering and nursing posts, amongst others, suggest themselves as being potentially suitable for the application of the policy of unification.

Meanwhile, parallel consideration was being given to the question of standardising, within practicable limits, the conditions of employment. The reader will have gathered from the earlier pages of this book some idea of the complexity of this question. If full effect were to be given to the principles of unification, and if the benefits of the policy were to be fully realised, it was evident that the actual conditions of employment in all parts of the unified Service must rest upon some basis of broad equality. At the same time, it would be idle to contemplate a scheme which did not make due allowance for the many and real differences which exist in the Colonial Empire, in climate, amenities, cost of living, and the financial circumstances of Colonial Governments. Moreover, the matter was one over which the Secretary of State could exercise only a limited control. In making any changes he must carry with him not merely the official heads of the numerous separate administrations which might be affected, but in a large number of cases the unofficial representatives, in the local Legislatures, of the Colonial taxpayers, who, after all, would have to find the money and were entitled to their views as to how it could be spent to the best advantage.

In these circumstances there was no question of reaching the objective by any short cut. The first necessity was to determine, as far as might be possible and as opportunity should serve, what, on the basis of general principles, could properly be regarded as reasonable terms of employment for officers possessing the personal and professional qualifications required for the Service, and employed under average Colonial conditions. If a standard of this kind could be defined, the problem would at any rate be reduced to one of adaptation of the basic terms to the financial and other circumstances of each Dependency.

As has already been noted, the Subcommittee which produced the scheme for the unification of the Administrative Service did in fact attempt to draw up such a set of standard terms, but the scheme appeared at an inopportune moment for securing general acceptance, and the extension of the unification policy to other branches of the Service made it necessary for the various aspects of the matter to be considered more exhaustively and on a wider basis. In the result, as will be seen, it became advisable to deal separately and by different methods with different heads of the question.

The most fundamental and at the same time the most difficult question was that of salaries. The absence of a recognised standard had led to an almost unlimited number of variations amongst corresponding posts in what were to be the unified branches of the Service, although, as has been recorded, there was some co-ordination within certain geographical groups. However, the Administrative Service scheme provided a starting-point. It had contained proposals for a standard basic "time-scale" running from £400 a year by twenty annual increments to £1,000 a year. These figures were based on the assumption that free quarters would be provided; if not, certain additions were to be made. It was also contemplated that the scale should be supplemented by non-pensionable local allowances as the individual circumstances of Colonies might dictate.

It happened that other considerations rendered it desirable at this time to revise the salaries of Administrative officers in East Africa, and the Secretary of State decided to introduce in that area a modified form of the unification salary scheme. The main modification was that the initial salary was fixed at £350 instead of £400, this being compensated to some extent by higher subsequent increments. A definite decision having thus been reached with regard to Administrative salaries in East Africa, it was possible to work outwards from this central point, and to consider what would be the appropriate related salaries for other branches of the Service in East Africa, and for the corresponding branches in West Africa and elsewhere. There ensued a long series of discussions and correspondence between the Secretary of State, his advisers at home, and the Governors of the African Dependencies, with the ultimate result that by the end of 1936 a complete scheme of interrelated salary scales had been worked out for new entrants to all the main branches of the Service in East and West Africa; and these were available as a standard to which it would be possible to relate the salary schemes of other Colonies if occasion should arise to make changes.

Hardly less important than the question of salaries was that of pensions. Ideally, a unified Service should have a simple and uniform scale of pensions, applicable irrespective of the accidents of transfer from Colony to Colony. We have already seen that such an ideal is far from being easily attainable in relation to the Colonial Service, where pensions are the subject of separate legislation in each Dependency. Pension legislation is at best a complicated affair; there are so many possible contingencies to be provided for; and even the Imperial Superannuation Acts, if one may say so without irreverence, are hardly a simple set of documents. But at least they are enacted by one Parliament, and concern a homogeneous Service. The complexities of the question in relation to the Colonial Service are obviously and inevitably much greater. Here again, the first requirement was a standard. Actually, in 1930, there was no model Pensions Ordinance to which Colonial Governments could look for guidance in framing their legislation; and one of the most important tasks carried out by the Personnel Division of the Colonial Office during the early years of the unification movement was the preparation of such a model, based on the various rulings which had been given from time to time on questions which arose in the course of dealing with pension matters in different Colonies and in the Home Service, and on the forms of legislation which had been found in practice to work most satisfactorily.

A cognate subject is that of pensions for the widows and orphans of deceased officers. To review this question the Secretary of State set up, in May 1934, an expert Committee under the Chairmanship of the Government Actuary, the late Sir Alfred Watson. This Committee took steps to obtain the views not only of the Colonial Governments but also of the staff associations in the Colonies, where these existed, and of representative serving officers. In their report,[1] which was completed just before the Chairman's death and published in May 1936, the Committee (with one exception) recommended the establishment of a Central Fund to cover the dependents of all officers of the unified Services and others of corresponding status. This

[1] Cmd. 5219.

Fund would be financed by contributions from the officers themselves and from the employing Governments, and would provide pensions for widows and orphans in accordance with a single set of actuarial tables. These recommendations have been accepted in principle by the Secretary of State, subject to their receiving support from a sufficient number of the Colonial Governments to justify the institution of the proposed Central Fund. At the time of writing the matter is still under consideration, and it is not possible to do more than hazard a prediction that, in view of the disadvantages of the existing system and the added convenience which a Central Fund would secure, means will be found to overcome the difficulties inherent in the scheme.

Questions relating to leave and passages were referred by the Secretary of State in October 1932 to another important Committee, presided over by the then Parliamentary Under-Secretary of State, the Earl of Plymouth. Their report was published in November 1934.[1] Once again it was necessary to face and surmount the difficulty of the absence of any standard. The first paragraph of the Committee's report puts the position succinctly:

"At the outset we would remark that, so far as we are aware, no comprehensive investigation of the kind which we have now completed has been undertaken on any previous occasion. The regulations hitherto in force appear to have been drafted *ad hoc*, as occasion demanded, to meet the requirements of particular Colonies and without reference to any authorised standard. Indeed this was necessarily the case since no general standard of conditions of service existed to which the regulations of individual Colonies might have been made to conform."

The Committee accordingly set themselves to determine what should be the general considerations which should govern the leave and passage conditions of officers of the unified Services and others of corresponding status. The principles which they laid down were, briefly, that such officers should be entitled to home leave at fixed intervals, which should vary according to climate and other circumstances, but should in no case exceed

[1] Cmd. 4730.

four years; that free passages should be granted to officers and their wives; and that the ratio of leave to resident service should ordinarily be so adjusted as to allow the officer from four to six months' full pay leave in his home country on each occasion, more being allowed if he should be in ill health. They also considered that in general leave should be granted rather more frequently after ten years' service than during the first ten years.

It will perhaps strike the reader with some surprise that such principles should require enunciation at all in relation to the Colonial Service; and indeed the regulations of all the African Dependencies, Malaya, Hong Kong, Ceylon and certain others did already conform to them in substance, although differing considerably in detail. But in many of the older Colonies the regulations were really based upon principles which rested in their turn on the assumption that the officer was either already an inhabitant of the Colony or proceeded to make his home there. The leave allowances were not ungenerous, but there were no fixed arrangements for officers to take home leave at regular intervals; and, while in some cases assistance towards the cost of passages was given, in others none at all was forthcoming. Thus officers might often have to serve for prolonged periods without overseas leave, especially as the salary scales ruling in the Colonies in question were not generally such as to allow much margin for an officer to save money to meet the cost of passages. Whatever justification there might be for the regulations as applied to locally recruited staff, it was clear that their suitability for officers recruited from outside the Colonies concerned was questionable.

The Committee therefore found it necessary to point out in some detail that the interests of the Colonies themselves demanded that officers should be given the opportunity of periodical change of surroundings and contact with the world outside, "if the evils of parochialism and the deadening effects of monotony are to be avoided". They observed that a judicious outlay on leave privileges was economically sound. Further, leave should be granted on sufficiently generous conditions to enable the officer to derive full benefit from it. The basic principles upon which leave was granted should be the same for all Colonies; what was required was a scheme which, while preserving uniform principles and eliminating unnecessary diversity of practice, was sufficiently elastic to meet the needs of the widely varying conditions to be found in the Colonial Empire.

Proceeding, in the light of these general ideas, to study the problem Colony by Colony, the Committee came to the conclusion that many of the existing divergencies did not appear to rest upon any definite principle, and that the construction of such a scheme as they had envisaged was not so difficult as had at first sight appeared. In putting forward their proposals they laid emphasis on this point, deprecating any supposition that in their desire for simplification they had created a bed of Procrustes, to which conditions of service must be adapted irrespective of reason.

It seemed to the Committee that, granted the general principles which they had enunciated, any necessary variations of detail could be effected by dividing the Colonies into a series of groups, on a basis partly geographical and partly climatic. While they thought that it would be unwise to divide the Colonies into less than four such groups, they saw no necessity for having more than four. The grouping which they proposed was as follows:

A. In the first class they placed the Mediterranean Dependencies (Palestine, Cyprus, Malta and Gibraltar), where, in view of their comparative proximity to England, the Committee thought that a biennial holiday of 2 to 3 months would be the most satisfactory arrangement.

B. In the second class the Committee placed the four West African Dependencies and Somaliland. Here they recommended no very substantial change in the existing arrangements, under which officers were allowed a week's leave at home in respect of each month of resident service, the normal tour of service being 18 months (with a minimum of 12 and a maximum of 24) in West Africa, and 12 to 15 months in Somaliland.

C and D. The remaining Dependencies were divided between these classes, some being included in both for different sections of the staff. In class C, the tour of service was to be 2 to 3 years, and the allowance of leave at home 5 days for each month of resident service. The Dependencies assigned wholly to this class were British Honduras, Northern Rhodesia, Nyasaland, Tanganyika Territory, Uganda and Zanzibar. In Class D, the tour of service was to be 3 to 4 years, and the leave allowance 4 days per month; the Dependencies wholly assigned to this class being Bahamas, Bermuda, Falkland Islands, St Helena and Seychelles. In the Dependencies not already mentioned, it was proposed that senior officers should be treated as if the Dependency were in Class C, and junior officers as if it were in Class D. "Senior" and "junior" officers the Committee defined as those with respectively more and less than 10 years' public service.

The Committee also made detailed recommendations with regard to passages, sick leave, and other matters within the scope of their inquiry. They were particularly impressed with the existing lack of any accepted principle in connection with even so fundamental a question as that of the provision of free passages, and they expressed their opinion on this subject with especial vigour. "We regard this question", they said, "as one of paramount importance to the proper organisation of the Service. We do not think it too much to say that those Colonial Governments which at present refuse free passages to officers of the grades to which our recommendations apply are failing to carry out their reasonable obligations towards their employees.... We would strongly urge that the provision of passages should be recognised as a necessary, not an optional, item in the public expenditure of a Colony." The Committee accordingly recommended that, in all cases where this was not already done, officers should receive free passages of an appropriate grade on all normal occasions of travel between a Colony and the United Kingdom, or on transfer from one Colony to another. They recommended also that on the like occasions every officer should receive a free passage for his wife. In view of the differences in local conditions they did not feel that it was possible to advise that free passages should be allowed as a matter of course for children, and preferred to leave the question of children's passages to be decided at the discretion of the individual Governments.

The Committee's report was accepted by the Secretary of State as a basis of future policy, and since its publication much progress has been made in securing the adoption of its principles in the Colonial Empire, in so far as they were not already in operation. Model Leave and Passage Regulations have been drafted and put into force in many places, and the rules relating to the provision of passages on transfer have been clarified and improved. The resulting position will be outlined in the second part of this book.

Apart from these main heads of the conditions of service, a great deal has been done, through the operation of the Personnel Division of the Colonial Office as a clearing house, to secure a broader equality of treatment and of opportunity throughout the Service than was possible before, and thus to make the unified Service a living reality. For instance, in 1933 a new edition of the Colonial Regulations (more properly called "Regulations for His Majesty's Colonial Service")[1] was issued, and in this edition the Regulations were divided into two parts: one dealing with Public Officers, and the other with Public Business. The first part contained several new rulings on conditions of service, designed to clarify procedure and to promote uniformity in the broad principles governing practice in respect of officers serving in different Colonies. Again, there has been considerable development of the practice of communicating to the Colonial Governments generally, by means of circular despatches, the Secretary of State's views and decisions on questions of general interest which arise in connection with particular Colonies or individual cases, so that experience gained in one quarter may be made available in the others.

It is an accident, not perhaps in the long run altogether un-

---

[1] The word "Service" appeared in the singular in this title from the first issue of the Regulations until the edition of 1928, when it was altered to the plural with the express intention of correcting the erroneous impression that there was a single Colonial Service. The altered form was short-lived, for naturally, after the Secretary of State's decision of 1930, the first opportunity was taken to revert to the singular.

fortunate, that the inception of the policy of unification had to be undertaken at a time of financial stringency. I do not, of course, mean that the stringent economies were not unfortunate for those who suffered as a result of them, but that it may have been to the advantage of the future Service that it should have taken shape under conditions which ensured avoidance of redundancy and due care for the necessity of making the wisest possible use of available resources. This necessity led to an examination of first principles, such as had never before been attempted, and as a result it was found possible to define standard minimum terms of employment. The pressure of economy also led to a revision in many cases of current ideas as to the extent to which it was really necessary to employ officers from overseas in preference to locally recruited staff. It is clearly not in the true interests of the former that they should occupy posts to which the latter may properly aspire, and in which their services are in danger of becoming superfluous.

The years of general economic depression were difficult ones for the Colonial Service no less than for other people in public or private employment. Many of the Colonial Governments were forced to adjust their expenditure to new levels by retrenching staff and applying temporary levies on salaries. Retrenchments affected nearly all branches of the Service in nearly all parts of the Colonial Empire, but the branches to suffer most were, naturally, those concerned with activities such as public works, surveys and railways, which were automatically curtailed by shortage of funds. Everything possible was done to minimise the hardship to individuals. As far as was practicable, officers willing to take their pensions were selected for retrenchment. A considerable proportion of those who did not wish to retire were found alternative employment in other Colonies, either at once or after a short interval. Particular care was taken to ensure that those who had to be retired were given ample notice, and in many cases special gratuities were awarded to any who were not in the ordinary course qualified for pension or gratuity. It would be misleading not to admit that the retrenchments of 1931 and the following years were an unhappy episode in the history of the Colonial Service, but the Colonies, like the rest of the world, were rudely attacked by the sudden tempest, and it may fairly be claimed that the lesson has been learnt, and that the new Service is built upon surer foundations than the old. In particular, it may confidently be assumed that a unified Service can more readily be adjusted to meet whatever changes and chances the future may have in store than could the Services as they existed prior to unification.

The salary levies which many Colonies had to impose, in much the same way as the Home Government found it necessary to impose certain cuts in civil service salaries here, are happily now a thing of the past, and it is to be hoped that circumstances will not on any future occasion demand recourse to so unusual and repugnant a measure. The best guarantee against it is the sound and efficient organisation of the Service on whose efforts rest to a large degree the maintenance and development of the prosperity of the countries which it exists to serve.

It remains to chronicle an interesting development in Kenya which illustrates a tendency in harmony with and complementary to the policy of unifying the Service in the grades normally recruited from outside the Colonies themselves. In Kenya, as in the other African territories, it has been customary in the past to have a single set of conditions of employment for all European officers irrespective of rank. The experiment which has been begun in the last few years is to divide the European public service of the Colony into an "overseas service" and a "local civil service". The former coincides approximately with the schedules of posts already included in unified Services or likely to be so included, and the salaries and other conditions attached to this division are related to those applicable to similar grades in other parts of Africa and elsewhere. The "local civil service", on the other hand, comprises posts for which as a rule special professional training is not required, and which it is considered can be filled satisfactorily by candidates already resident in Kenya, or failing them by persons who will be prepared to make the Colony their home. The conditions of employment are based on this consideration, and differ from those applicable to the "overseas service" in regard to leave, passages, the non-provision of quarters and the substitution of a provident fund for the orthodox pension system. The progress of this novel experiment will certainly be watched with interest; in any event it seems clear that in other places as well as in Kenya the definition of the unified Services, and of the conditions under which the members of those Services may properly expect to be employed, will help to stimulate consideration of the best means of organising local resources to carry out those functions for which it is unnecessary and uneconomical to recruit from outside.

We have now completed the historical review of the developments which have created the Colonial Service of to-day, and in the following chapters an endeavour will be made to describe that Service as it is now constituted. The picture is very different from that of the Services as they existed before and for some years after the War. The unification of the Service has enabled recruitment to be organised on a scientific basis, with the selection system universally established. Post-selection training has been developed, so that in nearly all the main branches of the Service the selected candidates receive intensive and specialised instruction, from the best authorities available, to fit them for their duties and to increase their efficiency. Conditions of employment have been improved, where necessary, and to a large extent assimilated to carefully thought-out standards. The flow of promotion has been regulated, and the interchange of officers facilitated.

PART II
THE COLONIAL SERVICE TO-DAY

*

CHAPTER VIII

GENERAL STRUCTURE OF THE SERVICE

UNIFICATION of the Service has not affected the primary fact that each Dependency has its own public service, paid for from its own funds. Since the Colonial Service, whether unified or not, consists of the aggregate of these local public services, it is natural and right that the accepted policy should be to allow the inhabitants of any Dependency the first claim to staff the public service of their own country up to the limit of their capacity to do so efficiently. This limit naturally varies at different times and in different places.

All appointments to posts in the public service of a Colony are made by the Governor. Under the Colonial Regulations, the Governor has certain powers of appointing persons resident in the Colony to public offices. Where the office carries initial emoluments of up to £200 a year, he may appoint on his entire responsibility. Where the initial emoluments are from £200 to £400, he may make a provisional appointment, which must be reported to the Secretary of State for confirmation; this is seldom withheld. For posts carrying over £400 he may recommend a local candidate, but on the understanding that the Secretary of State will make the final selection at his complete discretion. These salary limits have been varied to suit the circumstances of different Dependencies, but the principle remains the same. For practical purposes, then, the unified Service affects only the posts in the third category, and even in regard to these there is full scope for the employment of locally recruited personnel if candidates exist who possess the requisite qualifications for the post in question.[1]

---

[1] Discussions are at present proceeding with regard to a proposal for revising the regulations so as to enlarge the Governors' powers of making local appointments without reference to the Secretary of State, and to confine the latter's control to posts included in the unified Services and only to such other posts as carry salaries of not less than £600 a year.

It should be understood, however, that in any case it is the *Governor* who appoints any person to hold office in the Colony, whether that person is a member of the unified Service or not, and whether or not he is selected by, or appointed subject to the approval of, the Secretary of State. The latter only selects or approves; he does not appoint to a post. He does, however, appoint at his discretion to membership of a unified Service; this is a matter of status only, and such membership does not in itself confer upon an officer the right to draw pay from the Colony's funds, or to exercise official functions. These rights are derived from the officer's appointment by the Governor to his particular post in the Colony's public service, such appointment being usually conveyed to the officer by a formal letter sent at the Governor's direction, and to the public at large by a notification in the official Gazette. Constitutionally, the Secretary of State's power of securing posts for persons whom he appoints to membership of a unified Service, or whom he selects for any Colonial appointment, rests upon the fact that the Governor, as the representative of the Crown in the Colony, is bound by the instruments of his own appointment to carry out the instructions of the Crown as conveyed by the Secretary of State.

The expenses of the public service of a Colony are met from the funds of the Colony, derived mainly—in most cases entirely— from local taxation. They are provided for in the annual Estimates of the Colony, and have to be voted by the Legislature where one exists. It is an obvious practical necessity that the Secretary of State and the Governor should possess some effective means of control, so as, when occasion may demand it, to secure to an officer the salary or other conditions which he has been offered in the name of the Colonial Government, or to protect him from the consequences of an adverse vote of Council. Such occasions are naturally rare, but an officer may legitimately ask for assurance as to his position in this respect. In Dependencies where there is an official majority on the Legislative Council, the requisite safeguard is provided by the power of the Executive to carry a vote by the use of that majority, the official members being bound to vote for the Government's policy if so instructed.

Where, however, a Dependency has reached the stage of having an unofficial majority, other means have to be found, but, without entering into details, it may be assumed as a general principle that, in the last resort, the administration of a Colony is usually empowered to act without the support of the legislature in any matter of paramount importance to the public interest. Such a ground would naturally be relied upon only in most exceptional circumstances, such as a case in which a question of public faith was involved. Circumstances of this kind are not likely to arise in practice, but the point is mentioned in order to show on what basis the security of tenure of an officer in the Colonial Service rests.

In more recent changes of constitution, moreover, it has been the practice to pay special attention to this question of the position of the public servant. Thus, in the Order in Council embodying the new constitution granted to Ceylon in 1931, following the report of the Donoughmore Commission, it is specifically provided that the appointment, promotion, transfer, dismissal, and disciplinary control of public officers is vested in the Governor. It is further provided that no vote of any kind affecting any officer serving at the date of the change of constitution and involving any alteration in his pay, pension, or conditions of service may be introduced into the State Council without the sanction of the Governor, and that no vote involving any such alteration which, in the opinion of the Governor, is prejudicial to the officer shall take effect without the sanction of the Secretary of State. A similar protection is provided for officers appointed after the change of constitution whose appointments are subject to the approval of the Secretary of State. The Governor is, moreover, given special powers to put into effect any measure the passage of which may be necessary in order to preserve any rights or privileges which are intended to be safeguarded by the Order; for instance, to secure the payment of an officer's salary.

Another recent example is furnished by Mauritius, where the Council of Government was reconstituted in 1933 with an unofficial majority. Here no such elaborate provisions were made as in the case of Ceylon; but in the new "Letters Patent" it was laid down that, if the Governor should consider it "necessary in the interests of public order, public faith or other essentials of good government" that any Bill, vote, etc., should have effect, and if the Council should fail to pass it within such time as he thought reasonable or expedient, he might declare at his discretion that it should have effect, and it would then have the full force of law. The Governor is required to inform the Council of his reasons for any such declaration, and to report the matter forthwith to the Secretary of State.

It is legitimate to presume that safeguards of a similar kind will be associated with any future developments in the direction of the grant of self-governing institutions to Colonies. We may therefore assert that the Colonial Service enjoys, equally with the other great British public services, that reasonable security of tenure which is rightly regarded as an essential condition of efficiency and of incorruptibility.

If an attempt were to be made to represent the Colonial Service diagrammatically, one might picture it as a graph divided vertically into separate columns, and horizontally by an irregular line. The vertical columns, of very varying width, would stand for the individual public services of the different Dependencies, the aggregate of which composes the Service. The irregular horizontal line would mark off the grades comprising the unified branches, and other grades of corresponding status, the members of which depend for their appointments upon the approval of the Secretary of State. Staffs above the line would normally be recruited from outside the Dependency, and would be interchangeable amongst the Colonies generally. The line would be irregular, because the point of demarcation would vary from Colony to Colony, and even from department to department within the same Colony, and from time to time within the same branch of the Service. Moreover, the imaginary line would not represent a barrier between the two classes. Officers serving below the line would be fully eligible to cross the line if they were qualified to occupy posts above it. Nor would it necessarily imply any differentiation in terms of service. In some Colonies all officers are employed under the same general conditions, whatever their status; in others, there are separate regulations for European officers as such and for non-Europeans; in others, again, there may be differences related to the salaries drawn. All that can be said is that, in the case of those above the line, there is a definite tendency for certain minimum standard conditions to be accepted, based on the assumption that the officers concerned will for the most part be recruited from outside the Colonies, irrespective of whether the same or different conditions are regarded as suitable for those members of the staff whose homes are in the Colony in which they are employed.

In the case of the latter, the conditions of employment are primarily the concern of the local Government, which is in the best position to judge what is suitable, having regard to the particular circumstances of the Dependency. The conditions will clearly be determined by such considerations as the local cost of living, the customary standards of living, the prevailing rates of wages in non-Government employment. Considerations external to the Colony itself do not enter into the matter very much if at all. The Secretary of State is not likely, therefore, to intervene to any great extent in these arrangements, unless he feels it necessary to do so in the exercise of his financial control, or in the interests of equity. But all officials of the Colonial Service, of whatever grade or status, have the right to appeal to the Secretary of State, either individually or collectively, if they feel aggrieved, provided that they do so through the Governor; and any such appeals receive the most careful and impartial consideration.

It would be tedious, and of doubtful value, to attempt a detailed analysis of the conditions of service of the locally recruited staffs, which, as has been shown, must inevitably vary from one Colony to the next. We shall confine our study to the conditions obtaining in regard to the unified branches and the grades of corresponding status; but first it will be well to examine the general structure of the public service of a Colony, and see for what purposes the different grades are employed.

It is hardly possible to pick on a typical Colony, for they all have strong individual characteristics; but there is a fair similarity in the structure which years of experience, passed on from one to another by transfers of staff and through the co-ordinating medium of the Colonial Office, have evolved. The head of the administration is, of course, the Governor. He is usually assisted by a kind of Cabinet, called the Executive Council, which may include unofficial members, but will certainly include the leading officials, that is to say, the heads of the more important departments of the Governments. There is also usually a Legislative Council, which is in effect a Parliament, but unlike our own Parliament in consisting largely of permanent officials, who may even be in a majority. (As will have been gathered from the Introduction, this general description is subject to all manner of local variations.[1])

The departments of a Colonial Government will generally include, according to the requirements of the particular Colony, the following:

THE SECRETARIAT: the head office of Government, through which pass all matters requiring the Governor's decision. This office is directed by the Colonial Secretary (called Chief Secretary in Dependencies which are not Colonies), who is the principal executive officer under the Governor. In many of the larger Colonies the Secretariat includes an important officer designated "Financial Secretary", who, as his name implies, is the chief adviser of Government on economic and financial questions. (See Appendix I.)

THE TREASURY, or ACCOUNTANT-GENERAL'S DEPARTMENT: dealing with all matters relating to the receipt and expenditure of Government funds.

THE LEGAL DEPARTMENT: consisting of the Attorney-General and the officers (Solicitor-General and Crown Counsel) who assist him in his work as legal adviser to the Government.

---

[1] For a full account of the organisation of the Colonial Governments, and the functions of the various departments, the reader may be referred to *The Colonial Service*, by Sir Anton Bertram (Cambridge University Press, 1930). A detailed and up-to-date description of the administrative machine in one of the larger Colonies is contained in Sir Alan Pim's report on the financial position of Kenya (H.M. Stationery Office, 1936).

THE CUSTOMS DEPARTMENT: responsible for the collection of what in most Colonies is the principal source of revenue.

THE MEDICAL DEPARTMENT: dealing with all matters concerning the public health.

THE EDUCATION DEPARTMENT.

THE AGRICULTURAL DEPARTMENT.

THE VETERINARY DEPARTMENT.

THE FOREST DEPARTMENT.

THE PUBLIC WORKS DEPARTMENT: responsible for all Government buildings, roads, waterworks, drainage schemes and so on.

THE LAND, or SURVEY DEPARTMENT.

THE POSTS AND TELEGRAPH DEPARTMENT.

THE RAILWAY DEPARTMENT. (Practically all Colonial railways are run as Government concerns.)

In addition to these departments, there are the Judiciary, the Police, and the Provincial or District Administration, together with such special organisations as the individual circumstances of the Colony may call for.

This departmental structure differs in kind as well as in scale from that with which we are familiar in this country. The first and most obvious difference is that the heads of departments are not, as here, Ministers responsible to the electorate; they are permanent officials removable only by the Crown, and safe-guarded in their positions by an elaborate code of procedure. (I should perhaps say here that in attempting to give a general picture I am deliberately omitting reference to exceptional cases such as Ceylon.) This is not, of course, to say that they are irresponsible; they are responsible ultimately to the Imperial Parliament, and there are many ways in which public opinion in the Colonies themselves can and does make itself felt, and influences, if it does not control, the actions of the Government. Discussion of this point would, however, be outside the scope of the present study.

Apart from the fact that the Executive is composed of permanent officials, there is another important difference from the practice of this country. Here, the permanent heads of departments are administrative officers, drawn from the administrative class of the Home Civil Service. But in the Colonies, the heads of the professional and technical departments are usually themselves professional or technical officers. The head of the Medical Department is a doctor; the Director of Public Works an engineer, and so on. In some Dependencies administrative officers may be attached to technical departments in a secretarial capacity; while, in others, examples may be found of such officers acting as heads of semi-technical departments, such as the Customs Department, or the Post Office. Broadly speaking, however, the Colonial practice is that the heads and superior staffs of the various departments are specialist officers trained in the particular work of the department, and only in very exceptional circumstances transferring from one department to another within the Colony, though they may frequently transfer to a corresponding department in another Colony.

It is to fit in with, and to enrich this system of organisation that the unified branches of the Service, the formation of which has been chronicled in the first part of this book, have been established. A Colony may have, for example, a small Medical Department, but it will need for this department a staff of medical men of high professional attainments, and at the head one who is not only a good doctor but an officer of administrative and executive ability, qualified both to manage his department and to take his part in the general counsels of the Government. The Colony might or might not be able to provide continuously for these requirements by its own efforts; but once the Medical Department, without losing its individuality, is included in a unified Colonial Medical Service, the field of selection is greatly increased, and the department gains a status far higher than it could hope to secure by itself.

The unified Services, then, are a part of the general structure of the Colonial Service, created for the benefit of the Colonies and having a special purpose and special characteristics. An officer who is a member of one of these Services is not the less for that reason a member of the public service of the Colony in which he is employed and by which he is paid. There is no question of a divided loyalty. But the membership of the larger community implies a professional status, a readiness and capacity for general service, the prospect of a wider career, a guarantee of supervision by the Secretary of State of the conditions of employment. In the succeeding chapters I shall endeavour to give some account of those conditions in relation to the unified Services and other branches which, if not yet formally unified, are of similar standing, and to describe the functions and organisation of these Services and branches as they exist at the present time.

At this point it is perhaps desirable to recapitulate the progress so far made with unification, and the plan upon which the unified Services have been inaugurated. The list of the Services already constituted is as follows:

The Colonial Administrative Service;
The Colonial Legal Service;
The Colonial Medical Service;
The Colonial Forest Service;
The Colonial Agricultural Service;
The Colonial Veterinary Service;
The Colonial Police Service;
The Colonial Survey Service;
The Colonial Mines Service;
The Colonial Geological Survey Service;
The Colonial Customs Service;
The Colonial Postal Service;

to which must be added the Colonial Audit Department, which has existed as in essence a unified Service since 1910.

It may be assumed to be the intention of the authorities that other Services should be organised on similar lines until all those branches to which the principles of unification can with advantage be applied have been covered. From what has already been accomplished it is possible to draw a clear conclusion as to what those principles are, and on what basis it would be judged whether they should be applied to a given case.

The first principle is that unification is of value only in relation to classes of staff common to a number of Colonies and necessarily recruited to a substantial extent from outside the Colonies themselves. Any attempt to "unify" staffs locally recruited in the various Dependencies would be impracticable even if it were not undesirable. Within this specific limit, unification implies the maximum amount of co-operation amongst the Colonial Governments for securing and retaining personnel of the highest quality obtainable in each branch. This in its turn suggests, as the characteristics of a unified Service: (i) a recognised common standard of qualification; (ii) a broad equality of conditions of employment; (iii) a career as far as possible open to all members on the basis of merit, and unaffected by accidents of geographical posting. At the same time, these principles have to be given effect, not in one homogeneous and centrally controlled organisation, but in a world-wide series of different administrations with greatly varying geographical, political, social and economic circumstances.

The policy adopted, then, has been to select for the application of the principles a number of professional classes, and to constitute them as unified Services on the following plan:

First, in each instance, a schedule has been drawn up of posts actually existing in the Colonies which are not customarily, in present circumstances, filled by local recruitment, and which share a common similarity of function and of professional qualification. This qualification may be definite, as in the case of the Medical or Veterinary Service; or if indefinite, as in the case of the Administrative or Police Service, yet recognisable as the ability to discharge with full efficiency a certain class of work. The schedules have been drafted in the Colonial Office, and submitted to the Governors of the Colonies for their observations before being actually promulgated. A date has then been fixed by the Secretary of State on which the unified Service in question shall come into being. For each new Service the Secretary of State has issued a set of Special Regulations, drawn up on a common basis, with such variations as the different requirements of different Services have demanded. These Special Regulations provide, in the case of each Service:

(i) That the Service shall be constituted with effect from a specified date;

(ii) That a schedule shall be drawn up of posts which shall normally be filled by members of the unified Service;

(iii) That every officer substantively holding a scheduled post on the specified date shall *ipso facto* become a member of the Service;

(iv) That after the specified date, membership of the Service shall be acquired not through holding a particular post, but only by the person concerned being appointed by the Secretary of State to be a member;

(v) That the appointment, confirmation, promotion and retirement of members, and the transfer of members from one Dependency to another, shall be governed by the directions of the Secretary of State;

(vi) That officers appointed after the specified date shall be liable to be transferred by the Secretary of State to any scheduled post, whether or not such transfer represents promotion, provided that: (a) no officer whose appointment is to an office in a Dependency in which he was ordinarily resident at the time of appointment shall be liable to be transferred outside that Dependency, unless and until he has accepted an office in another Dependency;[1] (b) no officer shall be transferred without his own consent to an office which in the opinion of the Secretary of State is of less value (due regard being had to climate and other circumstances) than that which he already holds;

(vii) That an officer who, with the Secretary of State's approval, transfers to a post which is not at the time of transfer a scheduled post, shall not (unless it is provided otherwise in the conditions attaching to the new appointment) thereby cease to be a member of the unified Service;

(viii) That, in addition to the Special Regulations, members of the Service shall be subject to the Colonial Regulations, the laws and regulations of the Colonies in which they are employed, and any special conditions specified in their individual letters of appointment.

It will be seen that these constitutions provide for both the

---

[1] This proviso (a) was deleted from the regulations of the various unified Services in 1937, the Secretary of State taking the view that it was not appropriate to make any distinction in the matter of liability to transfer between officers who were recruited from outside the Colonies and those recruited from within.

central control essential to unification, and the elasticity necessitated by the circumstance that each member of the Service
will be in the employment of a particular Colonial Government.
The officer entering the Service knows what posts will normally
be open to him, and is assured of the supervision and protection,
if necessary, of the Secretary of State. He is not bound to accept
any but a scheduled post; but, on the other hand, he may accept
opportunities, if they occur, of going to unscheduled posts
without forfeiting his status as a member of the Service. On the
other side, the Secretary of State is not absolutely restricted to
members of the Service in making appointments to scheduled
posts, and reserves his liberty to select others if in a particular
case he judges that it is in the public interest to do so. Again,
it is open to him to adjust the schedule to changing conditions
by the addition or removal of posts.

In the Colony itself it makes little practical difference to the
Government whether a post is included in the schedule of a
unified Service or not, or whether an individual officer is or is
not a member of the Service. The inclusion of a *post* merely
registers what is in any case the fact, namely that the Secretary
of State has the right of selection and claims to supervise the
conditions of employment. The inclusion of the *individual*
confers upon him no status in the Colony; his status there
depends upon the office which he occupies, and he is in all
respects subject to the local regulations like any other officer in
the public service of the Colony. The status conferred is one
relating to the Service at large. Its outward and visible sign is
the inclusion of the officer's name in the "List" which it is the
practice of the Colonial Office to publish periodically, in respect
of each of the unified Services, containing the schedules of posts,
the Special Regulations, and biographical notices of all the
current members. By this and other means it is sought to create
an *esprit de corps* for the unified Service as a whole, complementary to and not in any way conflicting with that *esprit de
corps* which is the natural and proud possession of the public
service of each Colony, whether it be small or large.

CHAPTER IX

CONDITIONS OF EMPLOYMENT

IN this chapter I shall endeavour to give a general account of the conditions of service upon which the members of the unified branches, and other officers of similar status, are employed. Practically every generalisation about the Colonial Service is, however, subject to more or less important exceptions, and while I shall attempt to indicate the more notable of these, I must ask the indulgence of the reader if I do not undertake to deal completely with every variation. Perhaps his indulgence would be even more necessary were I to do so. At the same time, the movement towards assimilation of conditions to a common standard has gone far enough to make the task of description a much easier one than it would have been even a few years ago; and under most heads it will be possible to state without undue confusion what practice is applicable to most of the classes of officers to which our survey is limited.

Strictly speaking, it is not even possible to begin by stating that the officers of the Colonial Service are in the employment of the Crown; for, while broadly this statement would be correct, it would not be properly applicable to officers employed in certain native States, such as those of the Malay Peninsula. In practice, however, the distinction is unimportant, since local regulations are in force which have the effect of placing the officers concerned in the same position as those directly in the Crown service; while, in the case of those who are members of one or another of the unified branches, the officer has a special relation to the Minister of the Crown, that is to say, the Secretary of State, as well as to the local administration, however constituted. For practical purposes, then, we may assume that all members of the Colonial Service are in the service of the Crown. This means that their appointments are made by His Majesty's authority, and are held during His Majesty's pleasure.

The pleasure of the Crown that a person in the public service should no longer hold his office may be signified through the Secretary of State at any time, and without special formalities. While the use of this power is not unknown, it is naturally reserved for very exceptional circumstances.

As has already been stated, a candidate for appointment who is resident in a Colony may be selected or recommended by the Governor, but the selection of candidates from outside the Colony rests with the Secretary of State. Most of the officers with whom we are here concerned enter the Service by the Secretary of State's selection. The candidate, having decided for which branch of the Service he proposes to present himself, submits an application to the Director of Recruitment (Colonial Service) at the Colonial Office. After such enquiries and interviews as may be deemed necessary, and after the selection has been approved by the Secretary of State on the recommendation of the Colonial Service Appointments Board, the successful candidate receives an offer of appointment from the Colonial Office. This is a letter giving full particulars of the post for which the Secretary of State proposes to select the candidate, subject to his being passed as physically fit. The candidate is asked, if he wishes to accept the offer, to take an early opportunity of presenting himself to one of the Consulting Physicians to the Colonial Office for medical examination. The physical requirements may, of course, vary within certain limits, according to the nature of the appointment in question, but in general a candidate should be a "first class life" for insurance purposes. In the case of most appointments, selection will be conditional on satisfactory attendance at some course of instruction. Assuming that he satisfies the medical and other requirements specified in the "offer", and that he has duly accepted, the candidate receives a further letter from the Colonial Office, confirming his selection and conveying any necessary instructions with regard to his passage. He is also informed that he will receive a formal letter of appointment from the Governor on his arrival in the Colony.

It will have been noted that, while the candidate may be

offered membership of one of the unified Services, the offer is always attached to a specified post in some Colony. In allocating candidates to posts, the preferences of individuals as to the Colonies in which they are to serve are met as far as may be practicable. An officer may sometimes be offered in the first instance appointment to the Service in general, his allocation to a Colony to be settled later. But, inasmuch as pay and pension are attached only to actual posts in the service of some Colony, an officer must, before his appointment can become a reality, have been offered and have accepted a specific post.

There is a further method of appointment, which should be mentioned here for the sake of completeness. Engineering and certain other technical posts not as yet included in unified branches, but recruited from the United Kingdom, are filled by the Crown Agents for the Colonies. Candidates selected by the Crown Agents are engaged on agreement in the first instance, for a specified period of service. At the end of the engagement the agreement may or may not be renewed, or the officer may be taken on permanently.

Except in the case of those engaged on agreement, officers are normally appointed on probation for a period of two or three years. The purpose of the probationary period is, of course, to enable the Government to satisfy itself by practical test that the candidate is likely to prove a satisfactory officer for permanent retention. In most cases, as well as having to satisfy the authorities as to his character and ability, the officer has to pass certain specified tests in local languages, laws, etc., according to the nature of his appointment. During the probationary period, the Governor has power to terminate the appointment at any time, without assigning any reason. An officer whose probationary appointment is terminated on account of misconduct forfeits all privileges, and may have to repay the cost of his outward passage and any money spent by the Government on his training; but if the reasons for termination are not discreditable the officer is usually given a passage home and some leave with salary, and treated liberally as regards his liability to repay the Government's outgoings on his behalf.

While every effort is made to see that probation is a real thing, so as to avoid as far as possible the retention of "misfits", which would be in the interests neither of the Government nor of the persons concerned, the termination of a probationary appointment is in practice very exceptional. In the normal case the officer successfully completes his probation, and he is then confirmed in his appointment and becomes a permanent and pensionable member of the Colony's establishment. The approval of the Secretary of State is required for the confirmation, or the extension or termination of the probationary appointment, of an officer who is a member of a unified Service, or who was selected for appointment by the Secretary of State.

Some reference has already been made to the security of tenure enjoyed by duly confirmed officers of the Colonial Service. Subject always to the overriding powers of the Crown, which have been mentioned, such an officer is in practice assured of continued employment so long as he avoids serious misconduct, and remains efficient and of good health, until he reaches the retiring age laid down for the Colony in which he is employed. He is also assured of a pension or gratuity, according to his length of service, if retired on account of age, ill-health or abolition of office, or even on account of general inefficiency. Dismissal for misconduct naturally implies loss of pension. If at any time he is charged with misconduct or inefficiency, the Colonial Regulations contain carefully framed rules of procedure to secure him a fair hearing, and the final decision rests not with his local superiors but with the Secretary of State, to whom, as has been previously observed, every officer has a right of appeal at any stage of his career if he feels dissatisfied with any matter connected with the conditions of his employment.

The Colonial Regulations just referred to are not only the officer's charter of security, but a compendium of the rules of conduct to which he is expected to conform. They prescribe, for example, that he must not be absent from his Colony without leave; that he must not engage in trade or commerce; that he must not directly or indirectly acquire, without permission, investments or interests in local businesses; that he must not, without permission, publish any matter which may reasonably be regarded as of a political or administrative nature; that he must not accept presents.

These, then, are the general rules and traditions of the Service. We now turn to a consideration of the more detailed terms and conditions upon which officers are employed.

The first and basic question is that of pay. While it will be more convenient to deal with actual salary scales in connection with the respective branches of the Service, some general observations may be made at this stage. Broadly speaking, the scales of salary for the University graduate class, of which the bulk of the unified branches is composed, start at not less than £400 a year and run up to at least £1,000 a year. The run may be uninterrupted, subject to efficiency, or it may be conditional on promotion; but, in general an officer who remains in the Service for as much as 20 years and maintains a reasonable standard of efficiency can count on reaching the higher figure mentioned. There are, as will be seen, in the various branches, numerous posts above the £1,000 mark to which a proportion of officers may be promoted on the basis (to quote the Colonial Regulations) of "official qualifications, experience, and merit".

Salaries of this order, while not large by some standards, are intended to be adequate, so far as it has been possible to judge from experience, to enable officers to live comfortably at the various stages of their careers in the actual conditions of Colonial life, due allowance being made for the fact that in the normal case an officer will wish to marry and have children who will usually have to be educated at home. In comparing salaries in the Colonial Service with the remuneration obtainable in other walks of life, care should be taken to allow for other important factors as well as the actual cash salary. Not only is it necessary to take into account the conditions relating to pensions, passages, housing, medical attention, widows' and orphans' pensions, etc., attached to the particular post or to employment in the particular Colony under consideration, but in general it should be borne in mind that taxation in the Colonies, apart from import duties, is low. It will be found on examination that in almost every case the "real wages" of an appointment are very substantially more than the salary alone would suggest.

It will have been gathered from earlier chapters that, until the advent of unification, little had been possible in the direction of the co-ordinated planning of salary scales for the Service as a whole. The effect of the reforms of the last few years has been to place the salary schemes applicable to large sections of the Service on a common basis, and, while many Colonies still retain their own arrangements, those in which most of the members of the unified branches are employed are now associated in a general plan. As stated above, the underlying principle of this plan is that the average administrative or professional officer who is reasonably efficient should have the prospect of rising to a salary of at least £1,000 a year, with the chance of promotion to posts carrying higher salaries. In Tropical Africa, all administrative officers are on a "long scale" with a maximum of £1,000 plus free quarters. Medical and legal officers are on a scale with the same maximum, but with a higher minimum. Other professional officers are on a common scale which commences at different points (corresponding roughly to differences in the length and expense of professional training) but rises to a common maximum of £840. Here there is a "promotion bar", leading to a higher grade on the scale £880 to £1,000. One object of this arrangement is to provide as it were a point of focus at which the interchange of officers on promotion from one Colony to another can be considered. It has been found that the existence of unbroken "long scales" causes, amongst other things, some difficulties in the way of free interchange, and makes for inequality of opportunity. This disadvantage is less marked in relation to the administrative than to the professional branches. It is the intention that, when the unification schemes have been fully worked out, the establishments of each branch, taking the Service as a whole, should be so adjusted that there is a reasonable flow of promotion from the lower to the higher incremental grade, and that no efficient officer should be "blocked" at the £840 bar.

Outside Tropical Africa, the Dependencies employing the largest numbers of members of the unified branches are the

Malayan group. Here the salary schemes differ considerably in detail from those in force in Africa but will be found, on examination, to be based on very similar principles. The cash salaries are generally higher, but the difference is to some extent offset by the non-provision of free quarters. Thus, the Malayan administrative "long scale" rises to a maximum of £1,400 a year. The "professional" scale rises to a maximum of £1,120, but the posts above this "promotion bar" are as a rule on fixed salaries and not, as in Africa, on a further incremental scale.

The Malayan and African Services therefore form a reasonably homogeneous "block", covering most of the officers included in the unified branches. Hong Kong has recently adopted a set of salary scales based on the West African scheme, with supplementary provisions to suit local requirements. Similarly, in other Dependencies there is visible a tendency to adapt for local use the general principles of the main salary schemes, wherever substantial numbers of officers of the unified branches are employed.

In the good old days, when there was little fluctuation in the relative exchange values of different currencies, it was customary for salaries to be expressed in sterling, even though some currency other than sterling was, for reasons of convenience, actually in use in the Colony concerned. We have seen something of the difficulties which resulted from this in the East African Dependencies after the War. Difficulties of the same sort have occurred elsewhere, and even now the possibility of their occurrence cannot be dismissed from consideration. For this reason, it is now the general (though not universal) practice for salaries to be expressed and paid in the currency of the Colony, unless that currency is sterling or statutorily linked with sterling, as is the case, for instance, in the East and West African Dependencies and many others. Thus, in Malaya, salaries are expressed in the Straits dollar, which is normally stable at 2s. 4d. sterling. In Ceylon, some salaries are expressed in rupees and some in sterling; in the latter case they are at present converted into rupees for the purpose of local payments at Rs. 15 to the pound. In Mauritius, on the other hand, all salaries are expressed and paid in rupees. In Fiji, salaries are expressed in the local pound, which is worth somewhat less than the pound sterling. It is perhaps unnecessary to attempt a complete catalogue.

As has been pointed out, salaries in the Colonial Service have in many cases been subject to severe vicissitudes since the War, and it is only comparatively recently that any general degree of stability has been achieved. For the sake of simplicity and clarity I shall, when describing in the following chapters the ruling salaries in the different branches, confine myself to stating the salaries now in force for officers newly appointed to the posts or grades mentioned, leaving out of account the fact that, in many cases, officers appointed up to even quite recent dates may be serving on salary scales which are obsolescent. To attempt to trace in detail the history of the salary schemes of every branch of the Service in every Colony would involve a mass of detail, and it seems more satisfactory and more profitable to limit description to the conditions which, so far as can be anticipated, will substantially hold the field for an indefinite time to come.

Similarly, in regard to other conditions of employment, I shall in the main deal with them as they are presented to the officer who enters the Service to-day. Inasmuch as these conditions, unlike salaries, which necessarily vary not only from Colony to Colony but from one branch to another within the same Colony, are generally speaking applicable without distinction to all officers, in the classes which we have under consideration, who are employed in any one Colony, it will be convenient to take note of them in this chapter.

Pensions. Reference has been made more than once to the difficulties which have been encountered in the attempt to devise a simple system of pensions applicable equally to the officer who serves in one Colony only and to the officer who has been transferred from one to another in the course of his service. The aim of recent years has been to establish a general arrangement by which pensions are calculated at the rate of 1/600th of the officer's final pensionable emoluments for each month of his service, and this rule is now very widely in operation. The expression "final pensionable emoluments" means salary plus any other allowances, such as the value of free quarters, where these are provided (see below), which according to the law of the Colony concerned are pensionable. (In some cases an average of the emoluments drawn during the last three years of service is taken.) Thus, an officer who retires after 25 years' service, and on retirement is receiving a salary of £1,200 a year, with free quarters valued at £150 a year, will be granted a pension of £675 a year. There is a maximum limit of two-thirds of the final pensionable emoluments, which limit is reached after 33 years, 4 months' service; so that an officer who serves from 22 years of age to 55 practically qualifies for the maximum pension.

It is also the general practice to make provision for the pension to be converted, in some cases at the officer's option, but in others compulsorily, into a reduced pension and a lump sum gratuity. The standard arrangement in force is that the pension is reduced by a quarter, and the lump sum represents ten times the amount by which the pension is so reduced.

Officers who retire before completing ten years' service do not receive a pension in the ordinary course, but if their retirement is on account of ill-health and not on account of voluntary resignation or misconduct they receive a gratuity usually equivalent to five times the pension which they might have been granted if there had been no qualifying period. After completing ten years' continuous public service, whether in the Colony from which he retires or elsewhere, an officer becomes eligible for pension on retirement at the prescribed retiring age or prematurely, if the premature retirement is occasioned by ill-health.

Except in Bermuda, all pensions are *non-contributory*.

The above is a brief summary of the pension conditions which apply to officers now entering the Service in the African Dependencies, Malaya and Hong-Kong; in other words to something like nine-tenths of that part of the Colonial Service with which we are mainly concerned. The extension of the system described to other Dependencies is being pursued as opportunity offers, and it is probable that before these words appear in print several of the remaining Colonies will have come into line. It seems unnecessary, therefore, to enter into details of the many variations at present existing in different Colonies which do not, on the whole, employ many members of the unified branches. It should, however, be added that, by the operation of the arrangement described at the end of Chapter III, officers are now generally able to count, for practical purposes, on receiving a pension as if their whole service had been in one Colony, even though they may have been transferred once or more than once in the course of their careers.

Supplementary Pensions for Ill-Health, etc. The pension rate of 1/600th is designed to be supplemented by an additional pension in the event of forced premature retirement. Most Colonies grant supplementary pensions, as compensation for loss of career, to officers who may have to retire on account of retrenchment or abolition of office. They also award special additional pensions to any who retire as a consequence of injury sustained on duty. In West Africa, a scheme for the grant of supplementary pensions (on a sliding scale, decreasing with length of service) to officers retiring on medical grounds has been adopted, and it is contemplated that in course of time some such scheme may be applied in other parts of the Colonial Empire.

Retiring Age. Here again, many of the diversities which formerly existed have been swept away in recent years, and a normal retiring age of 55 is now fairly generally in force. In the Dependencies where most of the officers included in the unified branches are employed, provision is, however, made for retirement at or after the attainment of the age of 50 in special cases, if either the officer himself or the Government by which he is employed should desire it for reasons which the Secretary of State is prepared to accept as sufficient. The principal exceptions to the general rule that the retiring age is 55 are:

(i) In a few of the West Indian and other temperate Colonies the retiring age is 60;

(ii) It is a rule that Judges should not be called on to retire before the age of 62, though they are at liberty, if they wish, to retire at the ordinary retiring age of the Colonies in which they are employed;

(iii) Some Colonies allow women officers to retire at 45.

Death Gratuity. Most Colonial pension laws now provide for the payment to the estate of an officer who dies in the Service of a gratuity representing one year's pensionable emoluments. This most valuable form of free life insurance is quite distinct from the arrangement for widows' and orphans' pensions, which is described in a later paragraph.

Leave and Passages. It might be regarded as axiomatic that an officer should be given a free passage to his Colony on first appointment, but actually there are a few posts in the West Indies to which this condition is not attached. With these minor exceptions, however, the rule is general, and in addition to the officer himself most Colonies pay for his wife and many also for his children.

As regards leave and passages in general, the principles if not in all cases the details of the Plymouth Committee's recommendations[1] are now widely accepted and applied so far as officers of the unified and similar Services are concerned. There are, however, still some Colonies which have not yet brought their arrangements into harmony with the principles laid down by the Committee.

In West Africa, Somaliland and Aden, the normal "tour" of service is from 18 to 24 months (12 to 15 in Somaliland), but in special cases leave may be granted at any time after 12 months' resident service have been completed. Leave is at the rate of one week in the United Kingdom in respect of every month of resident service. Thus an officer serving in West Africa can count on having from 4 to 6 months at home in the course of every 2 years or so. While West Africa has its disadvantages, in that it is often impossible for an officer to have his wife with him throughout his tour, and that young children cannot usually be taken there at all, the short tours and frequent leave are of great benefit to those who have children at school, since they can keep in touch with them to an extent impossible to those who serve where tours are longer. Free passages are granted to officers and, since 1 January 1937, to their wives on all normal occasions of travel between the United Kingdom and the Colony.

[1] See Chapter VII.

In Uganda, Zanzibar and Nyasaland, regulations following the Plymouth Committee's recommendations have also been introduced from 1 January 1937. The tour of service is from 24 to 36 months, and the leave ratio 5 days in the United Kingdom in respect of each month of resident service. Free passages are provided for officers and their wives. The adoption of similar rules for the Tanganyika Territory and Northern Rhodesia is under consideration; in the meantime the regulations in force in those Dependencies are somewhat different in detail, and wives receive assisted passages only. In Kenya the rules regarding tour and leave are similar to those for Uganda, so far as senior officers are concerned, but in accordance with the Committee's recommendation junior officers serve a tour of 3 to 4 years and have a leave ratio of 4 days per month. Free passages are granted to officers, but at present assisted passages only to officers' wives.

Gibraltar, Malta, Cyprus and Palestine have adopted for officers of the unified Service classes regulations on the lines advocated by the Committee, that is to say with a tour of 18 to 24 months and a leave ratio of 3½ days per month. In Palestine, however, a ratio of 4 days has been allowed, on account of the particularly arduous nature of the work of the officials there. All these Colonies grant free passages to wives as well as to officers themselves; Palestine and Cyprus also provide assistance for children's passages.

Malaya, again, has adopted the Committee's scheme, the leave arrangements being similar to those already noted in connection with Kenya. Malaya grants free passages to an officer's children under the age of ten, as well as to the officer himself and his wife. Ceylon and Hong Kong have arrangements which differ from the Committee's scheme in detail, but are in general accord with its spirit.

Enough has been said to show that over an area covering the greater part of the unified Services and similar classes reasonable and generous leave and passage rules are in force, based on well thought out principles. It is perhaps unnecessary to particularise further. Some of the Colonies which have not been mentioned have adopted the Committee's principles in whole or in part, according to their ability; others have not done so but still have the matter under consideration. In a few it seems unlikely that the Committee's proposals will commend themselves to the local legislatures, but these are Colonies where, as a rule, there is little scope for the employment of officers from outside. For practical purposes we may say that in general the Colonial Service now offers its members, as a basic condition of employment, leave at regular and reasonably frequent intervals, with free passages for officers, free or at least assisted passages for their wives, and in many cases free passages for children.

Housing. In most cases officers of the unified branches may expect to be provided with Government quarters. Throughout the Tropical African Dependencies such quarters are provided free and partly furnished. The quality of the quarters naturally varies according to local circumstances and the status of the officer, but in general it can be confidently stated that officers in Africa are reasonably well housed, without trouble or expense (apart from rates and similar outgoings, and such personal matters as table linen, cutlery, etc.), and that the standard of accommodation is continually improving. "Rest houses" are provided where possible for officers travelling on duty.

Outside Tropical Africa, while there are few cases, except in the West Indies, in which an officer is left to find his own accommodation, it is not unusual for officers to be required to pay rent to the Government for the quarters assigned to them. This is not, however, necessarily an economic rent, but generally takes the form of a fixed percentage of salary, 6 per cent. being an average figure. In any comparison of the salaries of corresponding grades in different Colonies, care should be taken to make any necessary allowance for differences in the arrangements relating to the provision of quarters.

Medical Attendance. In all the Tropical African Dependencies, Malaya, Hong Kong, and several other Colonies, officers are entitled to free treatment by the Government medical staff while in the Colony. If admitted to hospital they usually have to pay certain hospital charges, but these are on a moderate scale. In some cases similar privileges extend to the families of officers. Free dental treatment is also provided in Colonies which maintain a Government Dental Surgeon. Officers are not entitled to free medical treatment when outside the Colony, but any officer on leave whose condition appears to require it is sent to a consultation with one of the Colonial Office Consulting Physicians at the Government expense, and those who need hospital treatment can obtain it on special terms at the Tropical Diseases Hospital or one of the other institutions maintained by the Seamen's Hospital Society, or at the Royal Infirmary, Liverpool. In a Service employed for the most part in the tropics, where the risks to health, though greatly reduced as compared with former times, are still not negligible, it is only right that the attention of the authorities should be continually directed to the question of the health of the individual officer, and it may be stated with confidence that in no public Service is more care given to this important matter than in the Colonial Service. Under the Colonial Regulations every officer has the right to request at any time that he may be medically examined with a view to its being ascertained whether he is fit for duty; and if he is not satisfied with the decision reached in consequence of an examination, he is entitled to protest, in which event the Secretary of State, or the Governor, as the case may be, may at his discretion call for further medical evidence. All officers are, as a matter of course, examined before admission to the Service; an officer is also, usually, examined before being transferred from one Colony to another. In the African Dependencies all officers are examined before proceeding on leave, and the examining doctor advises them as to any special measures or precautions which they ought to take, and reports to the Colonial Office whether they should be seen by a Consulting Physician on arrival at home. This practice has lately been extended to some non-African Colonies. It may be claimed, therefore, that a continuous effort is made to keep the health of each individual officer under constant review, and to ensure, as far as is practically possible, that no officer is exposed to undue risks.

It is perhaps relevant to mention here that standing arrangements exist by which any case of dangerous illness of an officer in a Colony is reported by telegram to the Colonial Office, which sees that the officer's relatives at home are kept in close and constant touch with his progress.

Widows' and Orphans' Pensions. Contributory schemes for the provision of pensions to the widows and orphans of officers have been maintained in all the Tropical African Dependencies and most of the other larger Colonies for many years past. It is too early to say at present what changes may be made as a result of the report of the Watson Committee, to which reference was made in Chapter VII, but it may be assumed that any such changes will be in the nature of improvements, at all events in the direction of making the arrangements more nearly all-embracing, so far at least as members of the unified branches and other officers of corresponding status are concerned. At present, while most of such officers serve in Colonies in which a widows' and orphans' pensions scheme is in force, some do not, and must make their own provision for their dependents.

The general principle upon which the existing schemes are constructed is that every officer is obliged to contribute a fixed proportion of his salary (usually about 4 per cent.) to the revenue of the Colonial Government. No actual fund is maintained, but the Government guarantees to pay certain pensions to the officer's widow, or if his wife predeceases him, to his children until they reach a specified age. The pensions are calculated actuarially, according to the respective ages of husband and wife, as if the officer's contributions had been invested in a fund and had earned a fictitiously high rate of interest. The standard rate of assumed interest for some years has been 8 per cent., but it is now usual to calculate the actuarial tables on a 6 per cent. basis, since this is considered to afford a reasonable extent of Government subsidy in comparison with the current yield of trustee securities.

Although the Watson Committee considered that in some respects the existing arrangements were capable of improvement, they pointed out that there was no doubt that those arrangements had been an inestimable boon to those sections of the

Service to which they had been applied. The pensions available for the widows of officers who die in the Service or after retirement are usually substantial enough to liberate the Colonial officer to a large extent from the fear, so real to many in other walks of life, of leaving his wife and family inadequately provided for in the event of his premature death.

Allowances. While there is considerable variety as regards details, it is the general practice of the Colonial Service to pay officers a consolidated salary on the basis of full-time employment, and to give allowances only in reimbursement of expenses of an unusual nature. Some posts have a "duty allowance" attached to them, but the number tends to diminish; and a few officers draw special allowances for performing work outside the normal scope of their appointments. But in general allowances are given only in connection with travelling, upkeep of motor cars, etc. The fact that the Government as a rule does grant reimbursement or extra remuneration in the circumstances mentioned is a factor to be taken into account in estimating the adequacy of the salaries offered. As regards initial expenses on entering the Service, outfit allowances are not generally granted nowadays, but officers are readily allowed an advance of a month's pay, which at any rate goes some way towards enabling them to equip themselves for the first tour.

Acting Allowances are generally paid to officers acting in higher appointments.

Children's Allowances are granted in Malaya to European officers with children. This is an arrangement of recent introduction, and does not at present apply elsewhere.

Expatriation Allowances. The only Dependency in which a definite system of "expatriation allowances" exists is Palestine, where officers who are neither Palestinians nor natives of neighbouring territories receive pensionable expatriation allowances varying from £50 to £200 a year according to the rate of substantive salary drawn. The Committee on the unification of the Colonial Administrative Service proposed that 10 per cent. of the salaries which they recommended should be regarded as expatriation pay; that is, the rates of salary would be reduced by that percentage in the case of locally recruited officers. There has, however, been little movement as yet in the direction of adopting any such formal arrangement. In general, salaries are attached to posts, and an officer receives the salary of his post, whether he is recruited locally or from outside; any differentiation made is usually attached to leave and passage privileges, or the provision of quarters, rather than to salary. It remains to be seen whether development will continue along existing lines or whether there will be an extension of the expatriation allowance system, which, in the circumstances presented by the Colonial Service, evidently has much to recommend it from the point of view of practical convenience and economy.

Promotions and Transfers. The unification of the Colonial Service made *de jure* the arrangement which already existed *de facto* under which every member of the Service is potentially eligible to be considered for any appointment in the Service for which he may be qualified, whether such an appointment becomes vacant in the Colony in which he is serving or in any other. The Secretary of State now appears, not as the dispenser of "patronage", but as the central authority controlling appointments and promotions throughout the unified Service. I referred at the beginning of the previous chapter to the regulations which limit the powers of the Governors to make appointments without the approval of the Secretary of State. The effect of these regulations is to place in the hands of the Secretary of State the control of all posts included in the unified Services and others of commensurate status. When a vacancy occurs in any such post, the Governor is required to report it to the Secretary of State; he may, and often does, recommend the promotion of one of his own officers, and any such recommendation is assured of the most careful consideration; but the Secretary of State is entirely free to fill the vacant appointment in the manner which he thinks in all the circumstances of the particular case is most in the public interest.

The Colonial Regulations lay down two principles which govern promotions in the Service. The first is that, other things being equal, the claims of meritorious officers in the Colonial

Service are considered before any post is filled by recruitment from outside. The second is that officers are considered for promotion on the basis of "official qualifications, experience and merit". It is to be noted that seniority as such is not mentioned in this connection. Earlier editions of the Regulations prescribed that officers should be considered for promotion in the order of their seniority, but this provision has been deliberately excluded from the modern version. This is not to say that seniority is of no account; it has to be taken into account in practice, especially when promotion from a lower to a higher grade is virtually a matter of course; but no officer can claim promotion on the ground of seniority alone, and the regulations rightly emphasise the fact that it is the experience gained in the course of service, rather than the length of service in itself, which constitutes a qualification for promotion.

The principal source of the information on which the Secretary of State bases his selection of candidates for promotion is the annual confidential report. Under the Colonial Regulations, each Governor is required to render annually to the Secretary of State a confidential report on all the officers serving under him who fall into the following categories:

(a) All members of unified Services who have been confirmed in their appointments;

(b) Other officers drawing £700 a year and over;

(c) Officers not included in the above descriptions who are heads of departments or who are regarded as specially fitted for promotion or transfer.

The prescribed form of confidential report is divided into three sections. The first is filled up by the officer himself: here he gives particulars of his age, appointment and salary, and spaces are provided for him to note any special qualifications or experience which he may have gained during the year, and any special wishes which he may desire to express as to the nature of the work which he prefers. He is also asked to state whether, if the opportunity offers, he wishes to be considered as a candidate for transfer, and, if so, whether there are any Colonies to which he does not desire to go.

The second section is filled up by the head of the officer's department, who is required to report on his conduct and personality, his general or special ability, and his suitability for promotion. A space is added for any remarks by the Colonial Secretary in the case of administrative officers, and the final section is reserved for such observations as the Governor may feel able to offer.

(The question whether an officer should be shown his confidential report, as is the rule in the Army, has been the subject of some discussion from time to time. The Colonial Service rule follows the recommendation of a Committee of the Colonial Office Conference of 1930, which was in these terms: "We have considered the question whether adverse confidential reports should be imparted to the officer concerned. We consider that such reports should not be shown to the officer, except on the orders of the Governor, but that the substance of such reports should be communicated by the head of the department to the officer where they relate to such faults or shortcomings as it may be in the officer's power to amend."[1] In pursuance of this policy, the second section of the report form includes a statement to be signed by the reporting officer as to whether or not the substance of the report has been communicated to the person on whom the report is made.)

These reports, as has been said, form the basis of the Secretary of State's consideration of candidates for promotion, but they are supplemented by information obtained through personal interviews with the officers themselves and through discussions with Governors and heads of departments when on leave. In the light of all this information, when a vacancy of any kind is reported it is possible to compile a list of suitable candidates, from which the Secretary of State selects the officer whom in all the circumstances he considers to be most fitted for the appointment in question. Further particulars of the machinery employed will be given in Chapter XVII.

[1] Cmd. 3628, p. 91.

Transfers in the Colonial Service are naturally irregular in their incidence, and it is only possible to say that in general they occur with greater frequency, relatively to the numbers of the staff, in the professional and technical than in the administrative branches, and in the senior than in the junior ranks. The prospects of an individual can rarely be estimated, owing to the immense variety of the circumstances which may affect them; but the days are gone when it was deemed necessary to warn entrants to the Service that they should not expect to be transferred. Those who enter the unified branches now accept a liability to transfer, and all are eligible for consideration. The Colonial Service is kept as far as possible as a career open to the talents, and restrictive rules are sedulously avoided.

Conditions of Living. Obviously nothing more than the briefest sketch can be attempted here of the sort of life led by an officer in the Colonial Service. There are the widest conceivable varieties of conditions in practically every department of life; varieties arising from climatic and geographical considerations, from the requirements of different jobs, from the differences in the amenities available in different Colonies at different stages of development. Yet there are some generalisations which it is possible to make. Thus, it is almost true as a general proposition that officers of the Service are employed in countries where a European cannot settle down and make a home. There are, of course, exceptions, but the number of posts in "white men's countries" which are not filled locally is not large in proportion to the Service as a whole. Even in Dependencies like Kenya and Northern Rhodesia, where considerable numbers of the unified Services are employed, it must be remembered that only certain parts of the territories are suitable for white settlement, and that officers from overseas are to a great extent employed in the less-favoured areas.

Generally speaking, then, an officer of the Colonial Service must make up his mind to a life of separation from the surroundings which are natural to him. It is not necessarily, nor, it is to be hoped, usually an unpleasant form of separation; but anyone who attaches importance to the amenities of what we are accustomed to call civilisation should not take up the Colonial Service as a career. Again, anyone whose interests lie in the direction of art, music or literature, may expect to find his opportunities for such pursuits restricted, unless he is exceptionally fortunate. Except in the few large cities of which the Colonial Empire boasts, it is difficult for an officer to get away from the atmosphere of "shop". He cannot leave his work behind him when he quits his office in the evening.

Family life, again, is subject to some inevitable restriction. There are, however, now very few Colonies or stations where a married officer cannot be accompanied by his wife; and it is the policy of the Governments to try to make conditions as comfortable as possible for the married officer. In West Africa most officers manage to have their wives with them for at least twelve out of the 18 months of the normal tour; elsewhere, wives can generally stay out the whole time if they wish to do so. In practically all Colonies except those in West Africa children thrive up to 6 or 8 years of age. After that time it is usually advisable for them to be sent home. Educational facilities for European children in the Colonies are as a rule very restricted.

These considerations must be set on the debit side of the account; but there are corresponding advantages to be noted on the credit side. It may safely be said that an officer of the Colonial Service can enjoy in many ways a higher standard of living than would be possible on a similar salary in this country. He can command much more in the way of personal service though the service may not be of the most efficient. He has a definite rank and social position, and does not, outside his office, become merely one of the crowd. He has, usually, opportunities for sport and outdoor recreation to a far greater extent than the ordinary worker at home. Finally, and most important of all, there is the interest of the work itself. That work lies mostly, though not exclusively, amongst peoples in a more or less primitive state of development, and its object is to assist such peoples towards self-realisation and self-sufficiency within the framework of the British Commonwealth of Nations. To those who have faith, not in old-fashioned Imperialism, but in the belief that we British have something of value to pass on to others, this mission cannot fail to appeal. Granted such a faith, and a spirit of sympathy with the aspirations of the smaller communities which share with us the privilege of citizenship, anyone entering the Colonial Service may hope to have opportunities for constructive work, within the sphere of his particular profession or vocation, such as are hard to meet with elsewhere. He will be dealing not so much with paper problems as with men and women; he will be entrusted with responsibility, and will be able, according to his position in the Service, to reach decisions for himself, to take practical action on his decisions, and to see the results of his work.

This general survey may be closed with a mention of one or two matters not strictly included in the conditions of service, but affecting the Colonial Service as a body. Reference has been made above to the lack of educational facilities for officers' children in most Colonies; and the problem of education is one which concerns many officers. The cost of keeping children at boarding schools and during the holidays is a serious item in the family man's expenditure. It is therefore pleasant to be able to record that, thanks to the munificence of His Highness the Rajah of Sarawak, a fund has been established for the express purpose of assisting higher civil servants of the Colonial Service, and their widows, with financial grants towards the cost of children's education. The fund is administered in accordance with the donor's intentions by trustees.

A further generous gift to the Service from the Carnegie Corporation has taken the form of grants to enable selected officers to enjoy, without expense to themselves, a "refresher year", to be spent in study or travel in accordance with a programme approved by the Secretary of State, with a view to giving them a change of work and surroundings and an opportunity of enlarging their experience. For this beneficent purpose the Corporation placed a sum of 60,000 dollars at the disposal of the Secretary of State, to be distributed in grants to officers over a period from 1932 to 1935; and a further sum of 48,000 dollars was made available for the three years beginning with 1936.

A particularly valuable innovation in 1937 was the "Summer School of Colonial Administration" organised by the University of Oxford. About 150 members of the Colonial Service attended this two weeks' course, and had the benefit of hearing lectures on many aspects of Colonial administration by eminent authorities, both British and foreign. It may also be observed here that the British Broadcasting Corporation organise special series of talks in their Empire programmes for listeners in the Colonial Service.

Finally, a few remarks may perhaps be added on the subject of honours. In common with the other public services, the Colonial Service receives it share of honorary recognition, and every New Year and Birthday Honours List contains the names of numerous members of the Service whose work and devotion His Majesty has been graciously pleased to reward by the grant of an appropriate honour. The Order of Chivalry especially associated with the Service is that of St Michael and St George, which is reserved for the recognition of services rendered in connection with the Dominions and Colonies and in connection with foreign affairs. The Chancery of the Order is located in the Colonial Office, and the Secretary of State for the Colonies has a certain allocation of vacancies in each class for which he is privileged to submit names. The Companionship of the Order (C.M.G.) is available for officers of all branches of the Service, and is usually conferred on selected senior officers of the administrative and professional branches. The dignity of Knight Commander (K.C.M.G.) is usually reserved for Governors, but is sometimes conferred on other high officials; Governors who have rendered especially distinguished service may be created Knights Grand Cross (G.C.M.G.). The Secretary of State has also the privilege of submitting the names of officers of the Service for other honours, including those of Knight Bachelor, all classes of the Order of the British Empire, the Companionship of the Imperial Service Order and the King's Police Medal.

CHAPTER X

THE COLONIAL ADMINISTRATIVE SERVICE

HAVING thus briefly examined the conditions of employment which are common to all officers of the classes with which we are concerned, we now turn to a more detailed description of the various branches of the Service. The branch which calls for first consideration, both on the ground of historical priority and on that of numerical importance, is the Colonial Administrative Service.

In relation to the Colonial Governments, the Colonial Administrative Service performs functions broadly corresponding to those associated in this country with the Administrative Class of the Home Civil Service—the Class which used to be known as the First Division. The correspondence is only a rough one, however, since the sphere of action of an administrative officer may in some ways be much wider, and in others more restricted, in a Colony than at home.

The work of the Colonial Administrative Service may conveniently be considered under three heads:

    (i)   The Secretariat;

    (ii) Other headquarters departments;

    (iii) Provincial and district administration.

(i) All Dependencies, except the very smallest, such as for example Seychelles, have a central Secretariat, the head of which is the Colonial, or Chief, Secretary. He is the chief executive officer under the Governor, and the officer who normally acts for the Governor when the latter is absent. The Colonial Secretary is a member of the Colonial Administrative Service, and he has as many junior members of that Service to assist him in the Secretariat as the size and circumstances of the Colony concerned may call for. The Secretariat is the central office of the Government, and the clearing office for interdepartmental correspondence, the channel of communication between the Governor and the other departments or the general public. It deals with the work of the Executive and Legislative Councils, and with the preparation of the annual Budget. It assists the Governor in the conduct of his correspondence with the Secretary of State. In short, *mutatis mutandis*, the work is not dissimilar from that of a Government department at home, though on a smaller scale. The Secretariat officer is engaged, like his Home Service colleague, in dealing mainly with matters of correspondence, minuting files, and drafting replies to letters and despatches, though much work is, of course, dealt with by interview and discussion. It is, perhaps, advisable to make it clear that it is only the more responsible work upon which Administrative officers are employed; the routine functions of the Secretariat are performed by a clerical staff, usually recruited in the Colony itself.

A Colonial Secretariat is not as a rule a very large department. In Kenya, for instance, which is one of the larger and certainly one of the more important Colonies, the Administrative staff of the Secretariat, under the Colonial Secretary, numbers seven. It is the general policy that Secretariat officers should be freely interchangeable with other Administrative officers employed in the Colony concerned. While, therefore, it may be assumed that officers with an aptitude and liking for Secretariat work will in all probability have some opportunity of doing it, at any rate at some stage of their careers, and while it cannot be gainsaid that experience of this work is of the utmost value to an officer, wherever he may be employed, it would be inadvisable for anyone to enter the Service with the idea of taking up Secretariat work exclusively. There is no separate recruitment for Secretariat duties, and officers are rarely posted to a Secretariat on first appointment: the junior Secretariat posts are normally filled by the selection of officers who have acquired some experience of general administration. Such officers often return after a time to district work.

An important development has taken place during the last few years in the employment of Administrative officers on financial work. In the past, the general tradition has been for the Colonial Treasury to be regarded as a separate department of government, whose relations with the Secretariat, while perhaps more intimate than those of, say, the Public Works Department, remained those of an exterior organisation. The Treasurer was in charge of all the financial business of the Government, in the sense that he was responsible for the proper management of the public funds, for bringing to account the revenue and controlling the disbursements in accordance with the authority of the Legislature, and so forth. But, except in so far as he might be consulted in his personal capacity, or in his capacity as an Executive Councillor, he was not concerned with financial policy in the broader sense. Recently, a growing realisation of the fundamental importance to Colonial Governments of sound economic and financial planning—a realisation sharpened by the serious effects on many of the Colonies of the financial crisis of 1931—led to a movement in the direction of strengthening the position of the Treasurer as the accredited chief financial adviser of the Government. Later, as a result of further experience, and of consideration of the best means of fitting financial posts into the unification scheme, it was decided to adopt a policy based to some extent on Indian practice, and already familiar in the Eastern Dependencies where Indian models had been more closely followed in the organisation of the civil services than elsewhere. This policy, which is explained in detail in a memorandum circulated to the Colonial Governments by Mr Ormsby Gore in 1936, and reproduced in Appendix I, is, in brief, to bring economic and financial matters into the central Secretariat, and to provide means for equipping the Secretariats with administrative officers trained and experienced in this kind of work. This important development has much enlarged the scope of the Colonial Administrative Service, and has opened up a field for the employment of officers with special interests in finance and economics. Not only may such officers look forward to an attractive career on the financial side—the posts of Financial Secretary in the larger Colonies are of high status and carry substantial salaries—but the possession of financial as well as of general administrative experience will be a valuable qualification for promotion to the senior Secretariat posts in those Colonies where the establishment is not on such a scale as to allow of the employment of specialist officers on financial work alone. Here, again, however, it is necessary to make it clear that there is no marking off of the Service into a financial branch, a general Secretariat branch, and so on. The key-note of the system is flexibility, with the double object of providing opportunity for the utilisation of the particular gifts of the individual officer to the best advantage, and at the same time of avoiding the dangers inherent in over-specialisation.

(ii) The employment of Administrative officers on departmental work outside the Secretariat is tending to become more widespread, expecially in the more developed Colonies, but, taking the Service as a whole, it cannot be said that the practice is as yet common. As was stated in Chapter VIII, the normal Colonial organisation is based on the principle of technical departments being staffed by technically qualified officers. In the Eastern Dependencies, however, it has been quite common for posts such as the headships of Education, Postal and Customs Departments, which elsewhere would be filled by specialist officers, to be occupied by members of the administrative staff. In Kenya, again, we find posts of Commissioner of Local Government and Commissioner of Lands and Mines filled by Administrative officers. There is also discernible a tendency for junior officers to be attached to technical departments in a secretarial capacity, so as to assist the technical heads in their correspondence and office work. Labour Departments, staffed by specially selected Administrative officers, have existed in the Eastern Dependencies for some time, and the growing complexity and importance of labour questions is leading to the development of similar organisations in several African and other Dependencies.

(iii) Some two-thirds of the officers of the Colonial Administrative Service are employed in the work of provincial and district administration in Tropical Africa. The total strength of the Service may be taken at about 1,500, and over 1,000 of these are engaged on this class of work. In Kenya, there are about 100 officers so engaged; in Tanganyika some 150; in Nigeria some 300; in Northern Rhodesia, Uganda and the Gold Coast about 70 or 80 each.

But, while district work absorbs and will no doubt continue for some time to come to absorb the energies of the numerical majority of the Colonial Administrative Service, the whole trend of development in the Colonial Empire from the simple and primitive towards the civilised and complex brings with it a constant broadening of the range of the district officer's responsibilities, and the need for an ever closer co-operation between the central Government where the economic, financial, social and political affairs of the Colony as a whole are being dealt with, and the representatives of the Government in the districts. Mr Ormsby Gore referred to this need in his address to the Corona Club in June 1937, pointing out, first, that there must be no divorce between the central Secretariat and the district administration; and, secondly, that in modern conditions, the Colonial Administrative Service must become more and more a real civil service, equipped to deal not only with problems of local administration, but with the whole range of Government activities.

The basic principle of provincial and district administration in the Dependencies where the system exists is that within his particular sphere of administration the Administrative officer, whether he be a Resident, a Provincial Commissioner, or a District Officer, is the representative of the Government in all its branches. This doctrine, already familiar in the Eastern Dependencies, was formulated in Nigeria, some years ago, by that great administrator, Sir Hugh Clifford, and it has been adopted, either explicitly or implicitly, elsewhere. The Colonial Office Conference of 1930 stated that the doctrine was fundamentally sound and had not been seriously challenged. They observed that it implied two things; first, that the Administrative officer must consider the bearings of whatever he may do upon the work of the technical departments, and must take the available technical officers into close and constant consultation; conversely, technical officers must keep the Administrative officer informed of whatever they are doing, and must not take independent action without his knowledge and concurrence. "Such a system", said the Committee of the Conference from whose report these remarks are extracted, "necessarily calls for tact and sympathy on both sides; but we are convinced that the system is sound, and that given good will there is no reason why it should not be perfectly workable in practice." [1]

This, then, is the system which the majority of the members of the Colonial Administrative Service are called upon to work. Each Dependency is divided regionally into areas, usually called Provinces, under a senior Administrative officer usually described as Provincial Commissioner or Resident, who is the head of all Government activities in the area. The area is, in its turn, divided into districts, under District Officers, who again are responsible for all Government activities in their respective spheres. Associated with them are Assistant District Officers, in such numbers as circumstances may dictate. The Assistant District Officer takes his instructions from the District Officer, the latter his from the Provincial Commissioner, and he his from the Governor *via* the Secretariat.

In the region of policy, the general principle which is now generally if not universally followed in the Dependencies with "native" populations is that which is known rather loosely as "Indirect Rule", but which, as Mr Ormsby Gore has pointed out, should more properly be described as native local self-government. This is not the place for a discussion of administrative policy, even if I were competent to undertake such a discussion, but it may be stated briefly that the conception of its position as that of a trustee for the indigenous populations of the Dependencies is one to which the British Government has for many years been committed. The object, then, of the Administration, over and above the obvious duty of maintaining law and order, is primarily educative. It aims at training the people to assume responsibility for their own affairs, so far as

[1] Cmd. 3628, pp. 106–7.

that may be practicable without undue sacrifice of their interests and those of their fellow-citizens. It is not assumed that a mere copying of Western institutions will necessarily meet the needs of non-European peoples; on the contrary, a constant effort is made to seek out and to develop the best in the natural institutions of the peoples themselves. Wherever possible, the form of government natural to the tribe or community concerned, whether it be the rule of a Chief, of a Council of Elders, or of a popular assembly, is retained, strengthened if need be, and supported. The function of the British administrator is rather to guide by influence and advice than to rule by direct command.

There are, of course, many gradations of "indirect rule" to be met with in practice; and many instances in which for one reason or another the administrator must rule directly. But in general it is to the furtherance of this policy that a man entering the Colonial Administrative Service may expect to be asked to dedicate himself. It may fairly be suggested that the object is not an unworthy one.

Apart from Tropical Africa, to which most officers are posted on first appointment to the Service, Malaya is the principal field to which new officers are likely to be assigned. A certain number of opportunities also occur in Hong Kong, the Western Pacific region (Fiji, etc.), Ceylon, Cyprus, Palestine and the South African Protectorates. Though the last-named are administered under the supervision of the Dominions Office, it is the practice to provide their administrative staffs from the cadre of the Colonial Administrative Service. In the rest of the Colonial Empire, the employment of Administrative officers is as a rule confined to Secretariat staffs or special appointments, and vacancies are usually filled by transfer or promotion from within the Service, and not by the appointment of new recruits from outside.

As has already been made clear, the appointment of new candidates to the Service is made by selection. No rigid standard of qualifications is specified. The official recruiting pamphlet states that a high standard of general education is essential, and goes on to point out that, whilst a University degree is not an absolutely indispensable qualification, most of the candidates who are actually successful in the selection do possess such a degree, usually with honours, and that the exceptions relate to persons who have special qualifications or experience fitting them for Colonial administrative work. Selections are made annually, in July or August, and applications must reach the Director of Recruitment at the Colonial Office by the end of April. Candidates must not be less than 20½ years of age on 1 August in the year of selection, and should generally not be more than 30, though provision exists for extending the upper age limit in relation to certain appointments if this is considered for special reasons to be desirable. On the whole, however, it may be said that the aim of the recruiting authorities is mainly to staff the Service by University men who have just taken a good degree, and who possess, in addition to a high academic qualification, those personal qualities of leadership, adaptability and strength of character which are essential to the successful Colonial administrator.

The number of new candidates taken in each year must necessarily vary. On the basis of past experience, a fair average figure is in the region of 70 or 80. Every effort is made by the Colonial Office to keep recruitment as stable as possible, but inasmuch as vacancies depend upon so many incalculable factors, spread over so many separate administrations, anything like absolute steadiness is obviously impracticable.

The candidates approved by the Colonial Service Appointments Board and the Secretary of State are allocated to the available vacancies, any personal preferences which they may have expressed being taken into account as far as possible, and, the formalities having been completed, they are then, in practically all cases, sent to attend the Colonial Administrative Service Course at Oxford or Cambridge. This course runs concurrently at the two Universities, and lasts for a full academic year. The instruction given falls into three main groups: (i) subjects of practical utility, such as tropical hygiene, first aid, surveying, field engineering, and the Colonial system of accounts; (ii) civil and criminal law, Islamic law, native languages (with special reference to the territory to which the candidate has been allocated); (iii) anthropology, tropical agriculture and forestry, the history and geography of the Colonial Empire. The fees for the course are paid by the Government, and the candidate receives an allowance of £75 at the beginning of the course, £50 at the beginning of each of the two subsequent terms, and a final grant of £50 at the conclusion of the course; all this being naturally conditional on satisfactory work and conduct. During and at the end of the course examinations are held, at which a certain standard of proficiency must be reached, or the candidate's selection is liable to be cancelled. The seniority of candidates amongst themselves in the services of their respective Colonies is determined by the results of this examination.

It will be seen that the course, during which the candidate is under close supervision, and the concluding examination, form a legitimate and valuable check upon the selection machinery. On passing out from the course, the candidate proceeds, after a few weeks, to his Colony to take up his appointment. In practically every case his early years are spent in a district, where he gains practical experience and studies for the examinations in law and languages which he has to pass before he can be confirmed in his appointment. His subsequent career opens up numerous possibilities. He may continue in the district administration, and graduate in due course as a District Officer or perhaps as a Provincial Commissioner within the Dependency to which he was first assigned, where his knowledge of local conditions and languages will be of special value. There are, however, increasing opportunities for the inter-Colonial transfer of officers of this class. Or he may take to Secretariat work, in which event he may in time be offered a transfer, possibly with promotion, to another Colony. The "plums" of the Service are, of course, the more important Colonial Secretaryships and the Governorships; and for these some Secretariat experience at some stage of the officer's career is an almost essential qualification. The system of interchangeability between the junior Secretariat and general administrative staffs is, however, meant to secure (amongst other things) that as far as possible there is reasonable equality of opportunity for all.

As the machinery of Colonial administration becomes more complex, increasing scope for specialisation may be expected to present itself. Finance, municipal government, land settlement, co-operation, labour questions: in all these fields there are growing opportunities for the officer who desires to make a special subject his own, and increasing openings for officers to carry from one Colony to another the experience which they have acquired.

Attachment for a time to the staff of the Colonial Office at home offers to a limited number of officers a valuable opportunity of gaining experience of a more general nature than is afforded by the service of any one Colony. These attachments have for some years past been worked on a regular system. About ten officers of the Colonial Administrative Service can be accommodated in the Colonial Office at a time. The normal period of attachment is 2 years, and officers with from 5 to 10 years' seniority are usually taken, being selected by the Secretary of State from lists of suitable candidates which the Governors supply. The salaries and passage expenses of the seconded officers are shared by the Home Government and the Colonial Government concerned, the salaries being fixed in accordance with a standard scale.

It is now time to give some account of the remuneration and prospects offered by the Service. I do not propose, in this and the succeeding chapters, to attempt more than a general outline of the conditions as presented to new entrants to the Service. Full details of the salary scales and of the establishments of the various grades in each Colony are given in the Dominions Office and Colonial Office List, and in the series of Colonial Service Recruitment pamphlets which are issued to any interested enquirer who may apply to the Director of Recruitment at the Colonial Office. As these sources of information are readily available and are annually brought up to date, anyone requiring detailed particulars would be well advised to have recourse to them. I shall, however, try to give, in connection with each branch of the Service, enough information regarding the salary scales and the opportunities for advancement to enable the reader to gain a fair impression of the career afforded.

There is at present no uniform scale of salary for the Colonial Administrative Service, but there is a fair correspondence amongst the various scales in force in the Dependencies where most of the Service is employed. In East Africa probationers (Cadets) begin at £350 a year during the two years of probation. On confirmation they rise to £400 in the third year, £450 in the fourth, and £500 in the fifth. They then proceed by annual increments of £25 to £600 a year, at which point there is an "efficiency bar". Provided that the officer is certified as efficient, his next increment takes him to £660, whence he proceeds by annual increments of £30 to £840, and subject to a further "efficiency bar" by £40 to the maximum of £1,000. The whole scale covers a period of twenty years; thus every officer who maintains his efficiency may count on reaching a salary of £1,000 a year soon after he is 40, assuming that he enters the Service at the normal age. (It will no doubt be recollected that, as explained in the preceding chapter, all these salaries are supplemented by the grant of free quarters.) But it should be understood that, while no more than this can be *guaranteed* to any individual, it represents only a minimum. In special cases officers may be allowed to pass an "efficiency bar" before they would reach it on the normal time-scale. Nor will an officer necessarily have to wait until he reaches the maximum before he secures promotion to a "super-scale" post. These chances are, however, obviously incalculable, though they should not be ignored.

Before dealing with the higher appointments, I will proceed with the description of the time-scales in force in other parts of the Colonial Empire. In West Africa, the scale is similar to the East African, except in the following respects. The commencing salary is £400 for two years, rising to £450 in the third year and £500 in the fourth. The probationary period is 3 years. The first "efficiency bar" occurs at £630, and is followed, as in East Africa, by a double increment, the scale being resumed, after passage of the bar, at £690. The general effect is that the West African officer is the equivalent of one increment ahead of his

East African colleague throughout his career, until he reaches the maximum of the time-scale, which he accomplishes in 19 years. This differentiation is designed to reflect in some degree the difference in amenities and climatic conditions between the East and West coasts, with special reference to the fact that the West African officer is more likely to have to incur expense in maintaining two establishments.

In turning to Malaya, we must bear in mind that it is not the practice to allow free quarters to officers there, apart from Cadets under training, who are paid at the rate of £490 a year.[1] On passing his examinations the officer is known as a Passed Cadet, and receives a salary of £560. At the end of three years' service, the Cadet, if he is confirmed in his appointment, is placed on a time-scale of £630, rising by annual increments of £42 to £1,400, subject to efficiency bars at £756, £966, and £1,190. (The increment following the efficiency bar at £966 is £56 instead of £42.) The scale, it will be seen, runs for a period of 22 years, and the salaries are throughout somewhat in advance of those ruling in Tropical Africa, even when allowance is made for the non-provision of free quarters. On the other hand, the cost of living in Malaya is high, especially in the larger towns, where Administrative officers are expected to maintain a certain position.

In Hong Kong, Fiji and the Western Pacific the revision of the salary scales is under consideration at the time of writing, and it is not, therefore, possible to give details.[2] In Cyprus an adaptation of the East African scale is in force, the chief differences being that free quarters are not provided, and there is a promotion bar at £840. Ceylon has its own time-scale, running from £400 to £1,200 (without quarters), and Palestine also has its own scale, constructed on somewhat different principles.

[1] For the sake of convenience salaries are given in "pounds a year" and not (as they strictly should be) in "dollars a month".
[2] Since this was written, the new Hong Kong scale has been promulgated. It runs from £400 to £1,150 a year, with efficiency bars at £700 and £950. Free quarters are not provided (except for Cadets on probation), but a "residential allowance" is paid, beginning at £50 a year in the sixth year of service, and rising to £100 after the passage of the first efficiency bar and £150 after the second.

While it is the lot of most officers to serve through the normal time-scale of the Colony to which they are assigned, there are a certain number of openings for comparatively junior officers in the Secretariats of the smaller Dependencies. In the West Indian Colonies, and other places such as Gibraltar, Malta, the Falkland Islands, Secretariat vacancies occur from time to time at salaries varying from £600 or £700 to £1,000 a year. Sometimes such vacancies are filled by local promotion, but it is the practice to consider for them any officers serving on the time-scale in the larger Colonies who may be suitable and willing to exchange their existing appointments for those in question, with a view to acquiring experience. The experience to be gained in this way is, in fact, very valuable, since an officer who in a large Colony would be occupying a comparatively junior position may, in a smaller administration, find himself called upon to act as Colonial Secretary or even as Governor.

Turning now to posts which represent definite promotion to time-scale officers, we find that these fall into two fairly well distinguished classes. First, there are the posts which as a rule will be filled by the promotion of officers already serving in the Dependency in question; secondly, there are the posts for which all officers in the Service can be considered on a more or less equal footing. Theoretically, in a unified Service, all posts should be in the latter category, and it is, in fact, the policy to make this category as wide as is practicable. But, as has already been pointed out, in the realm of provincial and district administration, local knowledge and experience is an almost essential qualification in the senior as well as in the junior officer. The endeavour is therefore made so to organise the administrative departments of the various Dependencies that each provides in itself a satisfactory career for its own staff.

In East Africa, the posts in the first category are those of Deputy Provincial Commissioner, Provincial Commissioner or Senior Commissioner. The salaries vary from £1,000 to £1,350 (plus quarters). The number of posts in this category naturally depends upon the organisation and requirements of each Dependency: the present number in Kenya is 9; in Uganda 6; in

Tanganyika Territory 12; in Northern Rhodesia 5. In West Africa the salaries range from £1,200 to £1,600. There are over 30 posts of the category now under consideration in Nigeria; 7 or 8 in the Gold Coast; 3 in Sierra Leone. In Malaya there are some 50 posts above the time-scale, most of which are normally filled by local promotion; the salaries range from £1,470 to £1,960.

In the second category, that of "open" posts, may be placed all senior Secretariat appointments, and certain Administrative offices, such as Chief Commissioners in Nigeria and the Gold Coast, Resident Commissioners in the Western Pacific, and the Administrators of St Lucia, St Vincent, St Kitts-Nevis, Dominica, etc. Selections for these posts are made by the Secretary of State from the general cadre of the Service, due regard being had to the claims of any local candidates recommended by the Governors, and to any special requirements in the way of qualifications or experience which may be attached to the vacant post. The salaries of these appointments vary considerably. In the larger Colonies there are usually Secretariat appointments parallel to the Administrative "super-scale" posts already described. In a large Secretariat there will be a number of posts of similar status to those of Provincial Commissioner, Resident, etc., and in many cases these are interchangeable with the latter. Elsewhere, salaries are fixed *ad hoc* according to local circumstances, and short of cataloguing them in detail it is difficult to describe them. Broadly speaking, there is a considerable range of posts carrying from £1,000 to £1,500 a year. This range includes second and third posts in large Secretariats, and a number of Colonial Secretaryships and semi-independent commands such as the Administratorships in the West Indies and Resident Commissionerships in the Western Pacific. Above the £1,500 a year mark there are some fifty appointments in the Colonial Administrative Service as a whole, but at least half of these must properly be regarded as falling within the first category, that is to say, they normally call for previous experience of local conditions. The remainder comprise the important Colonial or Chief Secretaryships, such as those of the Straits Settlements, Ceylon, Nigeria, Kenya, the Gold Coast, Hong Kong and Tanganyika, all with emoluments ranging between £2,000 and £3,000 a year; and a number of other posts (including several Financial Secretaryships) with salaries up to £2,000.

Finally, we may legitimately include the Governorships in the list of posts to which members of the Colonial Administrative Service may aspire. There are some thirty of these important offices open to members of that Service, and although Governors may be and are appointed on occasion from other sources, that Service is the normal field from which they are selected. Information regarding the salaries and other circumstances relating to the employment of Governors will be found in Chapter XVI, and a list of the posts in Appendix V.

Enough has been said to show that a career in the Colonial Administrative Service possesses all the charm of incalculability. The very fact that the Service is spread over so many administrative units, each with its differing circumstances and requirements, prevents the possibility of a uniform and machine-like organisation. Every member of the Service carries a Governor's cocked hat in his knapsack; and, although spectacular promotion cannot, in the nature of things, come the way of all, each Colony, so far as may be, offers, within the scope of its own administration, a reasonable career for those whom inclination or circumstance may direct to the straightforward course of service under a single Government, rather than to the uncharted seas of inter-Colonial transfer.

The Colonial Administrative Service List was the first of the unified service lists to be issued by the Colonial Office, and is published periodically. It is an undemonstrative document, containing merely the Special Regulations for the Service, and brief biographies of serving members; but a glance at it is sufficient to indicate the great variety of opportunity open to officers of this Service—a variety which cannot surely be matched by any other public service in the world—and also the extraordinary range of the qualifications and experience which this body of men can place at the disposal of the Colonial Empire.

CHAPTER XI

THE COLONIAL LEGAL SERVICE

ESSENTIAL legal principles are universal: and while in a number of Colonies, for historical reasons, French, Roman-Dutch, Mohammedan and tribal laws have important places in the system, the principles of English law are generally applied throughout the Colonial Empire. For judicial and legal work in the Colonies, a sound practical knowledge of the Law is more important than experience of local conditions. The Colonial Legal Service might therefore be expected to be a more freely interchangeable Service than the Administrative, and the published lists of transfers do in fact indicate that there is considerably more movement amongst legal and judicial officers than amongst Administrative officers, or indeed any other class.

The functions of the Colonial Legal Service may be regarded as falling into three divisions. First, there is the judicial division. Except for a few of the smaller Colonies (for example, St Helena, the Falkland Islands and Somaliland), where the Governor acts as Judge, each Dependency maintains a regularly constituted Court, with one or more professional Judges, as circumstances may require. In a large Colony there will be found a Chief Justice and a substantial number of Puisne Judges. Practically all Colonies also possess subordinate magisterial Courts, and although much of the minor magisterial work is performed by Administrative officers, or lay Justices of the Peace, professional magistrates are employed wherever the volume and complexity of the work calls for the services of such officers.

The second division concerns the legal work of the Government. The usual title of the Government's Legal Adviser is Attorney-General. He is a highly important official, and invariably a member of the Executive and Legislative Councils. His functions are: to advise the Government on all matters having a legal aspect; to draft Bills for submission to the Legislature; and, when necessary, to undertake prosecutions or civil cases in the Courts on behalf of the Crown. He is the leader of the local Bar. According to the size and requirements of the Colony, he is provided with professional assistance: most of the larger Colonies have a Solicitor-General, and a number of Crown Counsel who are members of the Attorney-General's department.

In the third place, there are a number of posts not very uniformly dispersed throughout the Colonial Empire, the holders of which deal with special aspects of legal work. Such posts include Court Registrars, Public Trustees, Land Officers, Crown Solicitors, etc. The nature of the functions is sufficiently indicated by the titles. Many of these posts are filled by solicitors, whereas for the two previous classes the qualifications of a barrister are practically essential.

Apart from these special posts, officers normally enter the Colonial Legal Service as Magistrates or Crown Counsel. The declared aim of the Colonial Office is to secure for these appointments candidates who, preferably after taking a University degree, have been called to the Bar and have had about four years' practical professional experience. Importance is attached to this point, since, once he is in the Government Service, the officer cannot in the ordinary course hope to acquire the same practical experience of Court work in all its aspects that he can gain in good Chambers at home. Many of the Colonies possess a strong local Bar, with which the Government lawyer, whether as advocate or as judge, must be able to hold his own; and, while it may be admitted that the need for a wider practical experience is more obvious in relation to the senior than to the junior appointments, it must be remembered that it is the latter which form the field from which the former will in due course be filled. It is with a view to the strengthening of this field that the tendency has grown, since the formation of the unified Service, to fill by the appointment of practising lawyers even some of the junior Magistracies which in the past were quite commonly held by Administrative officers who had been called to the Bar in their spare time. It has now been laid down by the Secretary of State that such officers will only in exceptional cases be appointed to posts included in the schedule of the Colonial Legal Service. But in some Dependencies the arrangements in regard to junior appointments are still in a transitional stage.

At present, it is mainly to Malaya and the African and West Indian Colonies that officers are likely to be posted on first appointment to the Service. In the West Indies, the openings are for Magistrates, and for Attorneys-General in the smaller Colonies. The salaries are usually non-incremental and in the region of £700 to £800. Such posts as these afford a most valuable training ground for any officer during the early years of his service. In Tropical Africa, there is a standard time-scale based on that for the Administrative Service which was described in the preceding chapter. The initial salary for Magistrates and Crown Counsel is £600 in East Africa, and £630 in West; but officers are allowed one increment in the scale for every year of practical professional experience between their reaching the age of 25 and their first appointment to the Service, subject to a maximum of 5 increments. Thus a practising barrister selected at age 26 would start at £630 in East Africa and £660 in West; and so on. The increments are of £30 up to £840 and then, subject to an efficiency bar, of £40 to £1,000; all, of course, with free quarters. The scale for junior legal officers in Malaya runs from £700 to £1,400, with similar provision for experience additions.

More important, however, in the case of the Colonial Legal Service, than the question of initial salary is that of prospects. It has already been pointed out that there is more movement of officers within this Service than in other branches. It is also fair to claim that there are exceptional opportunities of promotion for the really well qualified man. The proportion of senior to junior posts is distinctly high. To some extent, "wastage" is reduced by the fact that Judges are not normally called upon to retire before reaching the age of 62; but even so, there is a very constant and substantial flow of promotion from the junior to the senior legal and judicial posts, and while promotion goes by merit and cannot be claimed or promised, there is no reason why an officer who enters the Service should anticipate that he will remain indefinitely in a junior appointment. Actually, out of the 300 or so posts which are normally filled by members of the Colonial Legal Service, nearly half carry emoluments exceeding £1,000 a year.

The present tendency is for the Magistrates and Crown Counsel to be treated as to a large extent interchangeable, and for officers in the early years of their service to be given, as far as possible, opportunities of acquiring experience on both sides. At a later stage, the aptitudes and tastes of individuals may lead to specialisation, but there is no hard and fast line between the legal and judicial sides, and officers frequently pass from one to the other in the course of their careers.

After a shorter or longer period, spent in gaining experience of Colonial conditions in one or more junior appointments, the officer may hope to receive promotion to one of the higher posts. It is not possible to classify these except in a very rough way, since they are scattered throughout the Colonial Empire in small groups or as isolated posts, and cannot conveniently be sorted out into grades. Nor, in the circumstances, is it possible to indicate any typical line of advancement, since in the case of each individual his career must to a great extent depend upon the actual working out of vacancies at particular times. The kind of post which is likely to be offered to an officer who has served for a reasonable time and with satisfactory reports in a junior appointment is one of the less important judgeships, that of Attorney-General of a medium-sized Colony, or that of Solicitor-General of a large Colony. The salaries of such posts may be taken as ranging from £1,000 to about £1,400 a year. The next stage of promotion would probably be to a Puisne Judgeship or Attorney-Generalship in one of the larger Colonies, or to the Chief Justiceship of one of the smaller. The salary range of this class of post may be taken as from £1,400 to £1,800. The "plums" of the Service are the more important Chief Justiceships and, on the legal side, the Legal Secretaryship of Ceylon, and the Attorney-Generalships of the Straits Settlements, Hong Kong, Kenya and Nigeria. There are about 20 appointments in all in this class, with emoluments ranging from £1,800 to about £2,500.

While, therefore, the topmost heights naturally cannot be attained by all, the Colonial Legal Service offers excellent prospects to lawyers of ability. The rewards may not compare favourably with those of a successful private practice at the Bar, but they are substantial. The Law Officers of a Colonial Government are rightly regarded as personages of considerable importance in the local scheme, and have the opportunity of carrying considerable weight in the counsels of the administration. As for the judiciary, nothing is spared to preserve its dignity and its traditional independence. The Chief Justice and, in their several degrees, the Judges are regarded with all the respect due to their high office. The Chief Justice of a Colony normally ranks as second only to the Governor in official precedence, and is customarily addressed as "His Honour". A Birthday or New Year's Honours List rarely fails to contain the notification of the conferment of the honour of knighthood upon one or more senior members of the Colonial Legal Service.

I have already mentioned that Judges are not normally called upon to retire before reaching the age of 62, but it should be understood that they are at liberty if they so desire to retire on pension on or at any time after reaching whatever is the usual retiring age laid down for civil servants in the Colonies in which they are employed. In a few Colonies special provision still exists for granting pensions at enhanced rates to Judges (and in some cases to Law Officers); but the present tendency is for such special provisions to be abolished, and for the ordinary pension rules to apply. In other matters of conditions of service, legal and judicial officers are treated in the same way as the members of other unified Services. It is, however, perhaps worth while to mention that Judges hold office by virtue of Letters Patent, issued in His Majesty's name under the Public Seal of the Colony. They hold "during Pleasure", but the Secretary of State has given a pledge that they shall not be dismissed unless His Majesty in Council is so advised by the Judicial Committee of the Privy Council. What this means in practice is that a Judge is protected in the tenure of his office except in the event of proved misconduct. It has also the minor consequence that the ordinary rule of a unified Service with regard to the liability of the individual officer to be compulsorily transferred by the Secretary of State does not apply to Judges.

It will have been appreciated that the majority of the posts dealt with in this chapter require the qualifications of a barrister, and it must be admitted that the Colonial Service does not offer the same opportunities to the other branch of the legal profession. At the same time, there are certain openings of a not unattractive character for solicitors. Some Magistracies are open to solicitors, but they are in general ineligible for the judicial and law officer posts which have been described. There are, however, a fair number of posts, both junior and senior, for which solicitors are not only eligible but may actually be indispensable. Such posts are broadly speaking of three kinds: Registrars of the High Court; Administrators-General; and Land Officers. Practically all the larger Colonies have one or more Court Registrars, but in some cases the office is combined with another. The salaries vary considerably but do not as a rule commence at less than £550 a year with free quarters and may rise by annual increments to £720 or even £840. There are also a few posts of Chief Registrar in the largest Colonies, which carry higher salaries and are available to be filled by promotion from the Service generally.

The Administrator-General is the usual title in a Colony of the officer who deals with such matters as the administration of the estates of deceased persons and the business of a Public Trustee. There are local variations of title and also of the duties entrusted to this officer. There are also plenty of variations in the salaries, but in the larger Colonies these work out at about £1,000 a year, more or less, and the junior posts (Assistants in the large Colonies and the Administrators-General themselves in the smaller) are on incremental scales.

Lastly, in a few Dependencies (especially the Gold Coast and the Tanganyika Territory), there are certain posts in Land Departments for which solicitors with a knowledge of conveyancing are required.

CHAPTER XII

THE COLONIAL MEDICAL SERVICE

SOME account has been given on earlier pages of the origin and growth of the Colonial Medical Service, which at the present day consists of about 600 professionally qualified men and women. Until comparatively recent times, the function of the medical services in the Colonies was primarily that of "garrison" services, which existed mainly for the purpose of looking after the health of Government officials. But during the last 30 or 40 years, the medical departments have developed into highly organised State public health services, devoted to the prevention and cure of disease and the preservation of health amongst the general populations of the Colonies. It must be remembered that in these territories the Governments must perforce undertake tasks which in this country are carried out by voluntary organisations, by private enterprise, or by local and municipal authorities. In many areas of the Colonial Empire it is the Government alone which is in a position to erect and maintain hospitals and to organise public health activities. Not only this, but in all except a comparatively few centres, where there are sufficient inducements for private practitioners to establish themselves, there would be no medical attention available for the public were it not for the presence of the Government medical staff.

The professional scope of the Service is extraordinarily wide. An official pamphlet puts the matter thus:

"Throughout nearly the whole of the Colonial Empire such diseases as malaria, yaws, leprosy and hookworm disease menace the health of the indigenous people and retard the progress of development. In Equatorial Africa sleeping sickness and plague persist, in West Africa yellow fever has not yet been eradicated, and in the Near and Far East outbreaks of cholera and plague occur from time to time. But in addition to tropical diseases, those maladies usually met with in this country occur throughout the Empire. An officer in the Colonial Medical Service thus has unique opportunities for the practice of his profession in general medicine and surgery as well as in the special branch of tropical diseases."

The greatest importance is attached both by the Imperial Government and by the several Colonial Governments to the medical services, and a substantial proportion of the revenue of every Colony is devoted to them. In every part of the Colonial Empire, Government hospitals are to be found, many of them equipped with every modern facility. In the larger Colonies, too, there are important teaching schools for the training of native practitioners, up-to-date laboratories, maternal and child welfare clinics, research institutes and indeed every kind of modern medical organisation.

I have observed in an earlier chapter that candidates for admission to the Service must possess a full medical qualification entitling the holder to be registered in this country. In addition, the Colonial Office seeks to secure, as far as possible, candidates who have held hospital or public health appointments, or who have special knowledge of some particular branch of medicine or surgery. Great importance is attached to post-graduate experience, as a quite junior officer may often be placed in the position of having to deal with serious emergencies on his own responsibility, without the opportunity of consultation. Over and above his professional qualifications, he needs to have a personality such as to command the respect and trust of the native inhabitants of a Colony (who in some cases require much tactful persuasion before they will accept the ministrations of a European doctor in place of their own traditional medicine), as well as the confidence of the European community.

Candidates are usually recruited for general service in the first instance as Medical Officers, the great majority of first appointments being to the Tropical African Dependencies and Malaya. The selected candidate usually begins by attending a course of from 3 to 6 months at the London, Liverpool or Edinburgh School of Tropical Medicine. This is the course leading to the

Diploma in Tropical Medicine and Hygiene, which practically all members of the Colonial Medical Service are expected to acquire either on their first appointment or at the first opportunity thereafter. Subject to satisfactory work, the candidate's fees for the course are paid by the Colonial Government, and he is given an allowance of £25 a month for his expenses. The Government also refunds the fee for a diploma examination if the candidate is successful.

On reaching his Colony, the new Medical Officer is normally posted in the first instance to one of the large hospitals, where he spends some time in getting to know local conditions and the particular problems which the Colony presents. Later, he will probably be given a spell of work in the districts. Here he may find himself in charge of his own hospital, and of the general medical and sanitary work of a considerable area, in addition to being responsible for the medical care of his official colleagues at the station. Stations of course vary a great deal in conditions and amenities, but a Medical Officer is not likely in the ordinary way to be posted anywhere where there is not a fair number of European officers and some social life with opportunities for recreation.

After the early stages have been passed, there is plenty of variety in the careers open to members of the Service. They may carry on with general district work; or they may specialise in public health or pathology, in a particular branch of medicine or surgery, or in departmental administration. The Colonial Governments are generally very willing, by payment of fees, by the grant of allowances, and by giving extensions of leave for study purposes, to assist members of their medical staffs to improve their qualifications and efficiency by taking approved courses in special subjects, or the courses leading to additional medical or surgical degrees and diplomas. In some cases attendance at such courses is a condition of passing an "efficiency bar".

The "time-scale" for Medical Officers in West Africa is £660 for three years, then £690 rising by annual increments of £30 to £840 and, subject to an efficiency bar, by further increments of £40 to £1,000; in East Africa the scale is similar, except that it commences at £600 for two years, rising to £630 in the third and £660 in the fourth. All these salaries are, in accordance with the general practice, supplemented by free quarters. In Malaya, the time-scale is equivalent to £700 rising by annual increments of £35 to £1,120, with an efficiency bar in the fifth year; free quarters are not provided. There is thus a very fair degree of uniformity as regards the Dependencies in which the great bulk of the Service is employed. Elsewhere the scales vary considerably, and at the time of writing some of them are under revision. Generally speaking, however, while the initial salaries are of the order of £500 or £600, the scales end at an earlier point than those already described; but it should be observed that within the unified Service it is often possible to arrange for officers who have reached the maximum of one of the lower scales to be transferred to a Dependency where the scale runs higher.

Above the time-scales, the Dependencies where most of the members of the Service are employed have a grade of Senior Medical Officer, or the equivalent, which is filled by promotion. Usually, but by no means necessarily, promotions to this grade are made from the staff of the Colony in which the vacancy occurs, or at any rate from the Colonies in the same group. In this class may also be placed the headships of the smaller medical departments. In West Africa, the posts of this grade include Senior Medical Officers who are employed at the larger stations; Senior Health Officers, responsible for the sanitation of the large towns; Specialists of various kinds. The standard salary of this grade in West Africa is £1,200 a year. In East Africa, the designations and functions are similar, but the ruling salary is £1,100. In Malaya, the corresponding class is on an incremental scale of £1,190 to £1,400.

The highest posts in the Service are the Directorships and Deputy Directorships of Medical Services in the more important Colonies, and a certain number of senior specialist appointments. The salaries naturally vary considerably, according to the duties of the posts and the general schemes of salaries for heads of departments and other senior officers in the different

Colonies. In Nigeria and the Gold Coast there are appointments of Assistant Director at £1,400, of Senior Specialist at £1,500, and of Deputy Director at £1,700 (Nigeria) and £1,600 (Gold Coast). The Director in Sierra Leone also receives £1,600; the Directors in Nigeria and the Gold Coast £2,000 and £1,800 respectively. In all, about 25 posts in West Africa come into this range, and there are indications that this number may be increased. On the East coast, following the normal practice, the salaries of corresponding appointments are somewhat lower. £1,200 is the usual salary for Deputy Directors, £1,300 for the Directors in the smaller Dependencies, and £1,500 for those in the larger. There are a dozen or so posts in the range at present.

In Malaya there is a good number of posts above the £1,400 mark. 12 posts carry a salary of £1,470, and 4 a salary of £1,540; while the Director of Medical Services draws £1,890. There are posts at £1,000 and upwards also in Ceylon, Hong Kong, Palestine, Jamaica, Trinidad, British Guiana, Fiji, Cyprus and Gibraltar.

We may therefore summarise the material prospects offered by the Colonial Medical Service as follows. A candidate who is accepted for the Service after having held a hospital or similar appointment at home for a year or two following qualification may expect an initial salary of £600, more or less. Provided that he is reasonably efficient in the performance of his duties, he may normally count on reaching, within from 13 to 15 years, a salary of £1,000, plus allowances and, in many cases, some private practice. Promotion beyond this mark must necessarily depend upon various uncertain factors, but even the average officer may legitimately aspire to reach at least the Senior Medical Officer grade, and there are reasonable chances of rising higher still, while, as has been observed, there are paths of advancement open in all branches of the profession.

It is obviously necessary to give some account of these material conditions, since "bread and butter" has to be considered; but it would be unjust and absurd to suggest that they constitute the main attraction of the Service. Its principal attraction must lie in the unequalled opportunities which it offers for the exercise of professional skill not only in the fields covered by ordinary medical work but in fields as yet still but partially explored; and for the application of scientific knowledge to the alleviation of suffering and distress amongst vast populations sorely in need of medical assistance. In few other branches of human activity can the work so surely be its own reward.

The Director of Medical Services in a Colony is one of the most important officials. He usually has a seat on the Executive and Legislative Councils, and is the Government's chief adviser on all matters connected with the public health. At the same time he is responsible for the organisation and administration of his department. His work is thus primarily, if not entirely, of an administrative character, and he is not called upon to perform specifically professional duties. There is therefore no question of the avenue of promotion being confined to any one branch of the profession, and in practice Directors have been selected freely from all branches, some having worked up through the medical branch, some through the sanitary, others as surgeons or as research workers.

The Colonial Medical Service does not comprise all the medically qualified personnel of the Colonial Medical Departments, but only that element which is employed on a whole-time basis and is interchangeable amongst the various Colonies. In addition, many of the Colonial Governments employ comparatively large staffs of doctors who are locally recruited and do not in the ordinary course seek employment outside their home countries, and some who are to a substantial degree private practitioners, paid a retaining fee by the Government for official work. Officers in these categories are not as a rule included in the Colonial Medical Service, though they can be considered, if they so desire, for posts in that Service.

I must here venture some observations on the question of private practice. It has already been pointed out that the Colonial Medical Service is envisaged primarily as a Service of whole-time officers. The salaries paid are generally based on the assumption that they will not be substantially supplemented by private earnings. But the medical facilities available for the general public vary a great deal from Colony to Colony. It may be said that the Government has two objects in view: first and most important to see that the best possible medical advice is at the disposal of the greatest possible proportion of the population; secondly to see that the Government medical staffs do not overlap into the proper sphere of the private practitioner. The problem has to be dealt with in different ways in different circumstances. In a few places in the Colonies there are ample numbers of private practitioners available to meet the needs of those members of the public who are in a position to pay fees. In such cases the natural policy of the Government is to restrain its officers from undertaking private practice except as consultants, leaving them free to devote their whole time to strictly official duties, including the gratuitous treatment of persons not in a position to pay fees who attend at Government hospitals and dispensaries. This is substantially the situation which exists in Malaya and Hong-Kong.

In some of the smaller Dependencies a somewhat different position is found. It may be that neither the Government work nor the private practice in a particular area would in themselves provide sufficient justification for the maintenance of a doctor, however desirable his presence might be from the point of view of the population; but that the two in combination are sufficient. In such a case the Government will probably appoint a Medical Officer, but will naturally not reckon to pay him at the full scale appropriate to whole-time employment. Posts of this kind are often filled by local recruitment, and for this reason as well as on account of the obvious restriction on the mobility of officers who have substantial private practice, are (as already explained) not as a rule included in the Colonial Medical Service. In a Colony where this situation exists, probably only the Directorship and perhaps one or two senior posts would be so included.

The Tropical African Dependencies present yet another aspect of the matter. Here, apart from a few of the larger centres, there are no private practitioners, but in most places there is a certain amount of private practice to be had. The Governments acknowledge the claim of the general native population to receive free medical treatment from the Government medical staff, in so far as it can be made available, and this work, together with the care of Government officials, European and non-European, must take precedence of any other. But, in the interests of the unofficial communities, Government medical officers, with the exception of those employed in administrative or public health duties, are permitted to undertake private practice, provided that it does not interfere with their official work, and subject to some control in the matter of the fees which they may charge. The Governor may at any time prohibit officers from engaging in private practice in any particular station or area, if he is satisfied that the needs of the community (apart from those entitled to free treatment) can be adequately met by unofficial practitioners.

The present rules of the Colonial Medical Service with regard to private practice may then be summed up as follows:

(i) No officer has a right to private practice.

(ii) All officers may undertake consulting practice, that is to say, they may receive fees for giving an opinion when called into consultation by another medical man.

(iii) Heads and Deputy Heads of Medical Departments, Health Officers and officers employed in laboratories are not allowed private practice.[1]

(iv) Other officers are generally allowed private practice if their duties admit of it and if the needs of the public cannot adequately be met by unofficial practitioners. On this principle, private practice has been withdrawn in Malaya and Hong Kong, and it may be withdrawn elsewhere if circumstances make this desirable.

(v) Officers who are allowed private practice may retain the fees earned, provided that these are in accordance with an approved scale. (In some cases a proportion of the fees paid by members of the public for operations, X-ray examinations, etc., is retained by the Government in consideration of the use of Government premises and appliances.)

(vi) While in a few cases the remuneration obtainable from

[1] In West Africa, time-scale officers not allowed private practice are granted "staff pay" at the rate of £150 a year.

private practice may be substantial, in most instances it is not large, and in any event no officer can claim to be posted to a station at which private practice is available. Unless, therefore, an officer is serving in one of the appointments which I have described as being within the category of "subsidised" posts, he will do well to assume that any remuneration which may come his way from this source will be a fortuitous rather than a regular addition to his official income.

It will perhaps be of interest if, in concluding this sketch of the Colonial Medical Service, I give some particulars of the machinery which exists for co-ordinating the work of the Service and for making the experience gained in one Colony available for others. Although the appointment of a Director-General had been advocated by distinguished authorities in connection with earlier schemes for the unification of the Colonial Medical Services, the introduction of an executive head has formed no part of the Colonial Office plan of unification, as eventually adopted. Executive control, in the medical as in other spheres, has been retained in the hands of the Secretary of State and the Governors. At the same time, it is the well-established policy that the executive authority should avail itself freely of the best professional advice that can be obtained. In 1909 an authoritative Committee was set up as a standing body to advise the Secretary of State on medical and sanitary matters in relation to Tropical Africa, and in 1922 the functions of this Committee were enlarged to cover the whole Colonial Empire. In 1926 the Secretary of State appointed a Chief Medical Adviser on the staff of the Colonial Office, and this post, at first experimental, is now a permanent feature of the Office organisation. The Chief Medical Adviser is assisted by an Assistant Adviser who is also an experienced medical man, and he is Vice-Chairman of the Advisory Medical Committee. His advice, and when necessary that of the Committee, is sought on all Colonial medical questions and on all matters affecting the Colonial Medical Service. By this means co-ordination is secured, and ample provision is made for the professional point of view to be represented and taken into account when technical matters are under consideration.

Much also is done by means of the exchange of reports between the medical departments of the various Colonies, and a special Bureau of Hygiene and Tropical Diseases is maintained in London for the purpose of summarising and circulating throughout the Service all new information which is obtainable from these reports or from other publications, whether British or foreign, as it becomes available. In the sphere of research, close co-operation is maintained with the Medical Research Council through the Chief Medical Adviser. Through the same officer the Service is kept in touch with the international sanitary work dealt with by the League of Nations and by the International Office of Public Health at Paris. In these and in all other possible ways, every effort is made to maintain the Colonial Medical Service as a fully equipped organisation, abreast of modern progress, worthy, both as a corporate body and as a combination of individuals, to discharge the high task to which it is called.

The future development of the Service must be a matter of speculation; but if the premise be conceded that the ultimate aim is to bring the resources of modern medical science within the reach of the whole population of the Colonial Empire, it is difficult to resist the conclusion that this aim is unlikely to be achieved by so vast an expansion of the European medical staffs as would be necessary if they were to be called upon to accomplish the task by their own unaided efforts. Considerations both of expense and of policy would preclude such a solution of the problem. In the long run, it must fall to the indigenous peoples themselves to supply the need not only of money but of manpower. Nor, we may assume, would they wish it to be otherwise. While, then, we may confidently predict a certain expansion of the unified Service, we may legitimately at the same time envisage the functions of the Service as evolving more especially, in the advisory and educational directions, the practical application in the field of the principles laid down in the school and the laboratory being more and more entrusted to trained staffs drawn from the local populations. Already in several parts of the Colonial Empire medical schools have come into being. In Ceylon and at the Hong-Kong University and the King Edward

VII College of Medicine, Singapore, a full medical training is given, and the local medical staffs are largely recruited from the graduates of these institutions. In East Africa the most advanced training school is that at the Mulago Hospital in Uganda, where a fairly comprehensive course is available for native medical students. In West Africa somewhat similar facilities are available at Yaba in Nigeria and at Achimota College in the Gold Coast. While the training locally of fully qualified African medical men and women cannot be said to have developed as yet beyond an early stage, a good deal has been done throughout the African Dependencies to train a staff of partially qualified native dressers, dispensers and assistants, and the provision of fuller facilities for medical education is clearly only dependent upon time, money and the development of secondary education as a foundation.

NURSING SERVICES

Some account of the Nursing Services may appropriately be appended to this chapter on the Colonial Medical Service. As yet there is not a Colonial Nursing Service, but there would appear to be no reason why one should not be created in due course. Nearly all Colonies employ a number of European Nursing Sisters, recruited from home. These are usually employed in supervisory or training work, the actual nursing being carried out largely by locally recruited personnel; but conditions vary according to the circumstances of the Colony. Most home-recruited nurses serve as matrons or sisters at the larger hospitals, but some are employed as health visitors and in maternity or welfare work. There is therefore plenty of variety and scope for the nurse who chooses the Colonial Service as a career. In the past, it was usual for nurses to be engaged on fairly short agreements, with the idea that they should return to work at home before they had been absent long enough to lose touch, and should be replaced by fresh recruits; but of late the tendency has been to offer a permanent career in the Colonial Service, and to retain on the pensionable establishment such nurses as after a reasonable period of trial have proved themselves to be suited to Colonial conditions. This arrangement is believed to be more satisfactory from the nurse's point of view, as experience has shown that it may not be altogether easy for her to resume work at home after some years abroad.

The recruitment of nurses from this country for posts under Colonial Governments is carried out by the Overseas Nursing Association, who recommend candidates for the Secretary of State's approval. Candidates are normally required to be qualified both in general nursing and in midwifery and to have been trained in surgical technique and theatre work. In some cases special qualifications may be called for. Preference is given to nurses who have been trained at one of the larger teaching hospitals.

In all, the European nursing establishments of the Colonial Governments total more than 600. In West Africa a regional unified Service has been set up, known as the West African Nursing Staff. Like the former West African Medical Staff, this Service covers the four West African Colonies, and the members are on a common list for promotion. Nurses are engaged in the first instance on a temporary agreement for one tour of service, and if at the end of it they wish to remain permanently in the service and are recommended by the local authorities, they are placed on probation. If confirmed at the end of three years' service in all, they are admitted to the pensionable establishment, and serve on the same footing as other permanent officers, except that their retiring age is 45. The standard salary scale is £350 to £480, plus allowances, and about 90 Nursing Sisters are employed on this scale. There are 15 senior posts carrying a salary of £500 to £600, and one at £700 a year.

Nearly 150 Nursing Sisters are employed in the East African Dependencies, the standard scale being £240 to £300, with allowances; there are about a dozen higher posts at various salaries between £300 and £550. These figures do not include Northern Rhodesia, where the nurses are usually recruited from South Africa. Malaya employs over 150; the salary scale, excluding allowances, is £294 to £448, and there are 24 senior posts with salaries between £462 and £630. The salaries elsewhere are generally on somewhat lower levels; but it should be remembered that the value of an appointment depends not only on the actual salary but on the allowances, which, in the case of Nursing Sisters, are usually on a reasonably generous scale.

As has been observed above, the present tendency, at any rate in the Colonies whose salary scales have been quoted, is to offer a permanent career with a pension on retirement. Many Colonies have, however, adopted, either in lieu of or as a supplement to the ordinary pension scheme, an arrangement by which a nurse can receive a retiring allowance in respect of service which would not normally be pensionable, provided that she has served for a minimum of three years under the Government concerned and a minimum of fifteen years (not necessarily continuous) in public hospitals to which she obtained appointment through the Overseas Nursing Association.

The Colonial Service, then, makes substantial demands on the nursing profession at home for staff, and offers a career rich in interest and, for the most part, attractive from the point of view of remuneration and amenity. As is the case in other branches of the Service, one of the chief attractions to the candidate who is enthusiastic about her profession is the fact that the opportunity of doing really responsible work is likely to come her way at an earlier age in the Colonies than at home. This, after all, must be the most valuable guarantee that the peoples and officials of the Colonial Empire may rely, in the future as in the past, on a continuous succession of nurses of the highest professional attainments being available for the care of the sick and for the promotion of the welfare of the mothers and the children.

DENTAL SERVICES

Government Dental Surgeons are employed for hospital work and for the dental care of officials in several of the larger Dependencies, such as Malaya, Nigeria, Gold Coast, Tanganyika and Uganda; also, on a part-time basis, in some small Colonies, like the Falklands and St Helena, where there are no private practitioners. The conditions of employment are generally similar to those of medical officers.

CHAPTER XIII

THE COLONIAL FOREST SERVICE, THE COLONIAL AGRICULTURAL SERVICE, & THE COLONIAL VETERINARY SERVICE

THESE three Services may fittingly be grouped together, for in their respective spheres they illustrate the application of the biological sciences to the problems of the Colonial Empire. Mr Ormsby Gore, the present Secretary of State, has said that all these problems are basically biological. The Services with which this chapter is concerned have to do with the economic, that is to say with the material welfare of the Colonial communities; but it is a truism that economic development and material progress are necessary conditions of those communities' ability to realise the social, moral and spiritual benefits which we claim are made available for them within the framework of the British Empire.

The Colonial Forest Service is a comparatively small and highly specialised Service. Increasing importance has been attached of recent years to the function of forestry in the economic life of a country, and those Dependencies in the Colonial Empire in which forests exist have paid a good deal of attention to their conservation, development and exploitation. The objects of a forest department are twofold. In the first place it must study the forest needs of the locality in relation to questions of water supplies, fuel and soil erosion, and must see that a proper policy of conservation and, where necessary, afforestation is pursued in accordance with properly worked out plans. If necessary, the forests must be guarded against human and animal depredations. In the second place, it is the duty of a forest department to take such steps as may be possible for the utilisation of the forest products in the interest of the community. In this sphere it must deal with such matters as the relative economic values of timbers, methods of extraction, and the problems of marketing both locally and overseas. Thus the work of a forest officer is varied in character, and involves not only scientific knowledge but the ability to deal with native tribes, to handle labour, and generally to conduct administrative duties of a responsible kind. In addition, he may need to exercise a business sense, and to deal with problems of a directly economic nature.

The head of a Colonial forest department is usually termed Conservator of Forests, and his professional staff Assistant Conservators. In some Colonies there are special posts such as Silviculturist and Utilisation Officer.

As has been stated in an earlier chapter, candidates for admission to the Colonial Forest Service are required at present to possess a degree in Forestry of a British University, involving not less than three years' university study, such study to have included not less than two years at forestry subjects; followed by an approved course at the Imperial Forestry Institute. This course is normally taken after selection, as will appear below. Candidates who possess the necessary degree are required in the first instance to pass a test in regard to their technical knowledge, applied by a Board of forest experts appointed annually to advise the Secretary of State. This test includes the submission by the candidate of documentary evidence relating to his professional studies, and oral examination at an interview. A candidate who is provisionally selected after the test is then appointed to a Probationership of one year, to be spent at the Imperial Forestry Institute at Oxford (the present Director of which is, incidentally, an officer with long experience in the Colonial Service). During this period of probation the candidate, besides receiving instruction at the Institute in the special problems of Tropical and Colonial Forestry, is sent on tours of the Continental forests during the vacations. He receives a grant of £75 at the commencement of his training, and three further grants of £50 each, making £225 in all; he also receives a grant of £50 for the expenses of his Continental tours. On the satisfactory completion of the training course, the candidate proceeds to take up appointment as an Assistant Conservator of Forests in the Colony to which he has been assigned.

It will be observed that this programme of recruitment and training is based on the presumption that the Colonial Forest Service can and should be staffed by officers who have in the first instance graduated of their own initiative and at their own expense at one of the University Schools of Forestry. In 1930–31 a Committee, under the Chairmanship of Sir James Irvine, Principal of the University of St Andrews, investigated the recruiting problem and advised that this field should be supplemented by providing facilities for the selection and training of candidates with honours degrees in Natural Science. Moreover, a considerable body of expert opinion favours the view that the post-graduate training at the Imperial Forestry Institute can more profitably be given to an officer who has seen something of the actual surroundings in which he will have to practise what he has learnt, than to one who has not done so. It has accordingly been suggested that a system of scholarships should be introduced, in order to enable Natural Science graduates to be selected and assisted to obtain post-graduate qualifications in forestry. Under this proposal, recruits of this category would be sent for a year's preliminary training at the Imperial Forestry Institute, and would then go to the Colony for about two years. At the end of this so-called "apprentice tour", they would return to this country for a final year at the Institute. On the other hand, candidates already possessing a degree in forestry would proceed straight to the Colony for the "apprentice tour", but would similarly return in the third year for the Institute course.

The salary scales in the various Colonies' forest departments are now as a rule based on the general plan of Colonial Service salaries which has already been described. In Africa, the scales are similar to those of the Administrative Service, except that the initial salary is somewhat higher, in consideration of the extra professional training required, and that the higher "efficiency bar" is replaced by a "promotion bar". That is to say, the scale is divided into a lower and an upper grade, the latter being attainable only by specific promotion, and not merely on a certificate of efficiency. The objects of this arrangement are

≪ 164 ≫

twofold: to provide a means of accelerated advancement for the best officers and so to afford a stimulus to good work; and to provide a point at which interchange of officers on promotion between Colonies can conveniently be effected when the interests of the Service render this desirable. It is the intention that, taking the Service as a whole, the establishment of posts in the higher grade shall be sufficient to ensure that all efficient officers have a reasonable prospect of reaching the maximum of the scale without undue delay.

The salary scale in West Africa is: £450 for two years, then £475 rising by annual increments of £25 to £600. The next increment takes the officer to £630, at which point there is an efficiency bar. On passing the bar, he proceeds to £690, and thence by increments of £30 to the promotion bar at £840, which is reached in the fifteenth year of service. The higher scale (Senior Assistant Conservator) is £880 by £40 to £1,000. Posts on this scale may be filled by lower-scale officers from anywhere in the Service, and conversely any lower-scale officer is eligible for such posts not only in the Colony in which he is serving but in any other. In East Africa the corresponding scales are: for Assistant Conservators, £400 for two years, then £450 by £25 to £600, and, subject to an efficiency bar, £660 by £30 to £840, the promotion bar being reached after sixteen year's service; for Senior Assistant Conservators the scale is the same as in West Africa. In Malaya, Assistant Conservators are on the usual "professional" scale of £560 by £35 to £1,120, with an efficiency bar at £840. (It will be recollected that free quarters are not provided.) The posts corresponding to Senior Assistant Conservator are on a fixed salary of £1,260.

Forest departments are also maintained by Ceylon, Trinidad, British Guiana, British Honduras, Cyprus, Mauritius and Palestine. In Ceylon the junior posts are normally filled by locally recruited staff, and are not included in the Colonial Forest Service. The departments in the other Colonies mentioned are mostly small in numerical strength and the salary scales vary considerably in detail.

The number of officers in the Colonial Forest Service is

rather more than 150, and five-sixths of these are employed in Tropical Africa and Malaya. While the bulk of the Service naturally falls within the salary classes which have been described, there is a fair number of superior posts to which members of the Service can look for promotion. The headships of the smaller departments fall rather within the Senior Assistant Conservator grade, but the highest posts in Kenya, Tanganyika Territory, Uganda, Sierra Leone, Ceylon and Palestine, together with the Deputyship in Nigeria, carry emoluments ranging from £1,000 or so up to £1,200 with or without quarters; above these, so far as salaries are concerned, are the chief posts in Nigeria (£1,600 plus quarters), the Gold Coast (£1,400 plus quarters), British Guiana (£1,200 by £50 to £1,500 plus quarters) and Malaya (£1,680), together with the second post in the last-named (£1,470).

No special organisation has been created for co-ordinating forestry policy in the Colonial Empire as such, but a valuable part is played by the Empire Forestry Conferences which are held periodically and at which representatives of the Colonial forest departments attend. A measure of co-ordination is also secured by the fact that all members of the Service undergo instruction at the Imperial Forestry Institute prior to appointment, and many visit it again for "refresher" courses. In the sphere of marketing, the Colonial Office maintains a Colonial Forest Products Development department in London. Finally, mention should be made of the fact that Professor R. S. Troup, when Director of the Imperial Forestry Institute, visited many of the Colonies and reported on their individual forest problems.

The operations of the Colonial Agricultural Service are, of course, on a much larger scale. The basic industry of nearly the whole of the Colonial Empire is agriculture in one form or another, and the vital importance of agriculture to the economic life of the Dependencies is reflected in the numbers and variety of the technical staffs which they employ. The total strength of the Service is rather more than 300. This represents the professionally qualified staffs, principally recruited under the

Colonial Agricultural Scholarship scheme, to which reference has already been made; the various agricultural departments also include considerable numbers of officers, some with professional qualifications and some without, who are not members of the unified Service.

As has been stated on an earlier page, admission to the unified Service is confined to persons who possess a University degree in Agriculture or Natural Science, or a diploma of an Agricultural College of University status, the acquisition of which involved at least a three years' course of study in agriculture or horticulture, coupled with not less than two years' post-graduate training in agricultural sciences or two years' approved post-graduate experience. In practice, the normal method of entry is by way of a Colonial Agricultural Scholarship.

Selections for Scholarships are made annually, the number at present granted in any one year being limited to ten. Candidates may apply either for a Scholarship in General Agriculture, or for one in some particular branch, such as Agricultural Chemistry or Agricultural Entomology. The normal period of tenure is two years, the first year being usually spent on approved post-graduate study in this country, the next nine months at the Imperial College of Tropical Agriculture in Trinidad, and the remainder of the period in such manner as the Secretary of State may consider most suitable in the individual case. The Scholarship scheme provides for the payment of the scholar's tuition fees and travelling expenses, and of an allowance at the rate of £200 a year while he is in this country and £225 a year while he is abroad, together with a grant of £5 for books. These payments are conditional on satisfactory work and conduct, and they are made on the understanding that the candidate will accept a post in the Service if offered to him within six months of the termination of his scholarship period. Should he decline to accept such an offer, he is under obligation to refund a stated sum. On the other hand, the Government does not bind itself to offer him a post, since the availability of one must necessarily depend on the occurrence of vacancies, which is to some extent fortuitous; but in practice the demand for trained scholars tends to exceed rather than to fall short of the supply, and it would be only in exceptional circumstances that a scholar who had successfully completed his course would not be offered an appointment. If this were the case, the person concerned would be free to take up other work, and no claim would be made for the cost of the training which he would have received at Government expense.

The organisation of the Colonial Agricultural Service follows the lines of the other unified Services, and is therefore much less formal than that envisaged by the Lovat Committee (see Chapter IV). No attempt has been made to divide the Service into general and specialist "wings", or to introduce any strict system of classification and grading. Whether anything of the kind may prove desirable in the future remains to be seen; at present the indications are that such standardisation as may be necessary and practicable will come about naturally as the Service develops.

A Colonial Agricultural Department usually contains both general and specialist staff, the former being in the majority. The official description of the duties of a general Agricultural Officer is as follows: to investigate native methods of agriculture and to discover what is useful in them; to stimulate the improvement of the indigenous methods of cultivation or the adoption of new methods; to give advice to owners; to instruct native subordinate staffs; to supervise Government experimental stations; and generally to assist in the work of the department. Specialists are of various kinds, and are employed according to the needs of the different Colonies. They include Botanists, who deal with the improvement of economic plants by selection, hybridisation or other means; Chemists, comprising soil chemists, agricultural chemists and biochemists; Entomologists for work in relation to insect pests; Plant Pathologists for dealing with the study and control of fungus and other diseases of crops; and specialists in various types of crop, such as tobacco, coffee, cacao or sugar.

The salary scales are generally similar to those described for the Colonial Forest Service earlier in this chapter, and need not be detailed here. It will, of course, be realised that the

Agricultural Departments are generally larger than the Forest Departments, and exist in practically all Colonies. There is a correspondingly higher number of "super-scale" posts. Particulars of some of these may be given, in order to afford an idea of the prospects open to members of the Service:

East Africa

Director of Amani Research Station, £1,350 to £1,500.
Director of Agriculture, Kenya, £1,500; Deputy Director, £1,200.
Director of Agriculture, Tanganyika Territory, £1,350; Deputy Director, £1,000.
Director of Agriculture, Uganda, £1,350; Deputy Director, £1,000.
Director of Agriculture, Zanzibar, £1,200.
Director of Agriculture, Nyasaland, £1,100.
Director of Agriculture, Northern Rhodesia, £1,000.

West Africa

Director of Agriculture, Nigeria, £1,750; two Assistant Directors, £1,200.
Director of Agriculture, Gold Coast, £1,400; Deputy Director, £1,100.
Director of Agriculture, Sierra Leone, £1,100.

Eastern Dependencies

Director of Agriculture, Ceylon, £1,400 by £50 to £1,550.
Director of Agriculture, Straits Settlements, and Adviser, Federated Malay States, £1,680; Chief Field Officer and Chief Research Officer, £1,330 each.
Director of Agriculture, Mauritius, £1,250 (approximately).

West Indies

Director of Agriculture, Jamaica, £1,000 by £50 to £1,200.
Director of Agriculture, Trinidad, £1,200.
Director of Science, etc., Barbados, £1,000.

Other Dependencies

Director of Agriculture, British Guiana, £1,100.
Director of Agriculture, Cyprus, £1,000
Director of Agriculture, Palestine, £P1,200 plus expatriation allowance £P200.

Free quarters are attached to all the above-mentioned posts, except those in Malaya, Ceylon, Cyprus and Palestine.

Reference has been made more than once to the Imperial College of Tropical Agriculture in Trinidad. This most important institution is supported by His Majesty's Government and by the Colonial Governments, but is managed by an independent Governing Body, on which the supporting Governments are represented. The College is open to unofficial as well as to official students, and provides Diploma courses, including a special course in sugar technology, as well as post-graduate and refresher courses.

Research activities are carried on by the various Colonial agricultural departments, according to their resources and necessities, and also by a number of special research organisations, some within the Service and others of an unofficial or semi-official character. Amongst the former may be mentioned the East African Agricultural Research Station at Amani in the Tanganyika Territory. This Station was instituted by the pre-War German administration, and since the War has been carried on by the East African Governments in conjunction. Amongst non-Government organisations, reference may be made to the Empire Cotton Growing Corporation, the Rubber Research Institute in Malaya, and several special crop research schemes in Ceylon, the West Indies and elsewhere.

The Colonial Veterinary Service is much smaller in numbers than the Agricultural Service. In some of the Colonies no separate veterinary department has been considered necessary, but in general more attention is being given to veterinary matters now than in the past, and the Service is one in which a tendency to expansion may be looked for.

The work of officers of the Colonial Veterinary Service differs markedly from that of the ordinary veterinary practitioner at home. It is concerned less with the actual treatment of disease in individual animals than with the prevention and control of epidemic disease, and with research into animal diseases as met with more especially under tropical conditions. The problems connected with such diseases as, for example, rinderpest have to be dealt with on a large scale. Apart from questions relating to disease, the Service is concerned with the many important matters which arise in connection with animal husbandry and the improvement and management of live stock in the Colonies.

In these circumstances, much importance is necessarily attached to post-graduate experience, and in selecting candidates for the Service preference is given as far as possible to those who have received training as Colonial Veterinary Scholars, or who have obtained other suitable post-graduate training, such as that acquired in the course of studying for a university degree in Veterinary Science, or for a Diploma of Veterinary State Medicine. The Colonial Veterinary Scholarships, through which entry to the Service is normally obtained, are similar in their general features to the Agricultural Scholarships already described, but the application of the general principles is different, on account of the difference in the methods of professional training. There are two kinds of Scholarships: the first is designed for candidates who have not acquired a veterinary qualification, but have obtained a university science degree after a course of biological study. Such a candidate may be awarded a Scholarship for four years, while qualifying for the Diploma of Membership of the Royal College of Veterinary Surgeons. The second class of Scholarship is designed to allow candidates who have already a veterinary qualification to obtain the post-graduate experience necessary to render them fully qualified for Colonial work. Such a Scholarship may last from one to three years, the time being spent either in research work under supervision at an approved institution, or in reading for an additional degree. The value of a Scholarship in either case is £200 a year, plus tuition and examination fees and a grant of £10 for books.

As in the case of the Agricultural scholars, the Government does not guarantee the scholar an offer of appointment at the end of his study, but in practice it is very unlikely that a scholar whose work had been satisfactory would not receive an offer. On the other hand, the scholar is bound, under penalty of refunding a stated sum, to accept any appointment in the Colonial Veterinary Service which may be offered to him within eighteen months (in the case of the first-mentioned class of Scholarship), or six months (in the case of the second class), of the termination of the Scholarship. At the end of these periods, the scholar is released from any obligation and is free to take up other employment.

The only Dependencies in which extensive veterinary services exist at present are: Kenya, Tanganyika Territory, Uganda, Northern Rhodesia, Nigeria, the Gold Coast and Malaya. Veterinary services are also provided in Nyasaland, Hong Kong, Ceylon, Fiji, Cyprus and Palestine and in a few other Dependencies.

In Kenya the Veterinary Services are divided into an administrative and a research division, each with its own head, both until recently under the administrative control of the Director of Agriculture. This arrangement had been adopted in view of the close relation of agricultural and veterinary problems in a country largely devoted to mixed farming, but the Veterinary and Agricultural Departments have now been separated, as a result of recommendations made by Sir Alan Pim. In the other Dependencies of the first group, the Veterinary Department is an independent organisation, field and research work being under a single Director.

The standard salary scale for veterinary officers in East Africa is £500 for two years, then £550 by £25 to £600 and by £30 to £840, subject to an efficiency bar at £720. There is a higher grade, reached by promotion, at £880 by £40 to £1,000. In other words, the scale is similar to that in force for agricultural and forest officers, except that it begins at a higher point, in consideration of the additional time which a veterinary officer must spend in acquiring the necessary professional training. On the other hand, the adoption of an initial salary somewhat lower than that assigned to members of the Medical and Legal Services reflects the fact that the veterinary officer, unlike those, has normally received substantial help from the Government in equipping himself for his professional duties.

In West Africa the salary scale differs from the East African only in commencing at £550 for two years, following the general principle to be observed throughout these schemes of placing the West African scales approximately one increment in advance of the East African. In Malaya the scale in force is £560 by £35 to £1,120, with an efficiency bar at £840. Free quarters are provided in the African Dependencies, but not in Malaya. The scales in the scattered posts which exist elsewhere vary considerably.

The number of "super-scale" posts is naturally not large, the Service itself containing only about 110 officers. Two Deputy Directors of Veterinary Services in Kenya, and the Director of Animal Health in Northern Rhodesia receive £1,000; the Chief Veterinary Research Officer, Kenya, the Directors of Veterinary Services in Tanganyika, Uganda, the Gold Coast, and the Deputy Director of Veterinary Services, Nigeria draw £1,100; the Veterinary Surgeon, Hong Kong £1,000 by £50 to £1,200; the Director of Veterinary Services in Kenya £1,200; the corresponding officer in Nigeria £1,400; the Director of Veterinary Research and Veterinary Adviser, Malaya £1,470.

While most of the biological appointments in the Colonies are included in one or other of the unified Services described in this chapter, there are a few which are not so included. These are posts the holders of which are specialists employed on work limited to a particular field, such as medical entomology, or of interest only to a particular Colony or group of Colonies. Such officers cannot readily be brought within the scope of an inter-Colonial Service, but in practice their conditions of employment are as far as possible assimilated to those of the unified Services, and they would certainly be considered for promotion to any posts in other Colonies which might become available and for which they were qualified.

The co-ordination of policy with regard to agricultural and veterinary questions in the Colonies is effected by the Colonial Advisory Council of Agriculture and Animal Health. The Chairman of the Council is the Parliamentary Under-Secretary of State, and the Vice-Chairman the Secretary of State's Agricultural Adviser. The personnel of the Council consists of distinguished experts in the agricultural and veterinary sciences. The Agricultural Adviser and the Assistant Agricultural Adviser are both whole-time officers with extensive experience of agriculture in the Colonies, and their advice is available both to the Colonial Office and to the Colonial Governments. The Agricultural Adviser spends a considerable amount of his time in visiting the Colonies and discussing their problems with the officials on the spot.

CHAPTER XIV

OTHER UNIFIED BRANCHES OF THE COLONIAL SERVICE

W E have seen that, following the lead given by the Warren Fisher Committee, the Colonial Office have worked out the policy of unification in practice by creating, within the larger whole of the Colonial Service, a series of separate Services, each based on certain unifying factors: a common standard of qualification, a similarity of function in a substantial number of Dependencies, a need for recruitment from outside the Colonial Empire itself. In the preceding chapters I have dealt in some detail with the organisation of some of the principal branches to which the process of unification has been applied; I propose now to mention rather more briefly the other main branches in regard to which, whether or not at the time of writing they have been formally unified, the same principles and considerations may be said to hold good.

(i) THE COLONIAL AUDIT SERVICE

Historically, the Audit Service may be considered the forerunner of the unified Services. Up to 1910, the audit of the accounts of the Colonial Governments was undertaken by a Colonial branch of the Exchequer and Audit Department. In that year it was decided to set up a separate organisation, under a Director of Colonial Audit, responsible to the Secretary of State. With a few exceptions, the audit of Colonial Government accounts is carried out by this organisation. While the Auditors and their staffs in the various Colonies are paid by the local Governments and are subject to the local regulations, they work under the supervision of the Director in London, and the audit which they carry out is, in principle, carried out on behalf of the Secretary of State, on the one hand, and, on the other hand, on behalf of the

Governor and the Legislative Council, where one exists. Thus it is necessary that the staff should be not only qualified in accountancy but generally capable of taking their proper place in the official community of the Colony in which they are employed. A good general education, preferably at a university, and a high standard of character and ability are regarded as essential qualifications for appointment, in addition to a natural aptitude for figures and accounts.

Officers of the Audit Service are appointed by the Secretary of State, on the recommendation of the Director of Colonial Audit, and with the advice of the Colonial Service Appointments Board. They are liable to be transferred at any time from one Colony to another or to or from the central establishment in London, on the recommendation of the Director; but as a rule and subject to the exigencies of the service, such transfers are not made without consulting the wishes of the individual. On first appointment new officers normally undergo a short course of training at the London office.

The establishments of audit departments in the Colonies vary according to circumstances. The largest local establishment is that of Nigeria, with a staff of 19 officers; at the other end of the scale, many of the smaller Colonies have only one Auditor. The whole Colonial Audit Department is divided into classes. Class IV, the lowest, consists of the junior Assistant Auditors in the Colonies or in the Central Office. There is no fixed scale of salary, the scales in each Colony being arranged in relation to those of other officers of comparable status serving there. We may select as typical the West African scale, which is £400 for two years, then £450, £500 by £25 to £600, £630, £660 by £30 to £810; or the East African scale, which is similar, except that it begins at £350, rising to £400 in the third year, and £450 in the fourth, with a double increment at £600 and the maximum fixed at £780; or the Malayan scale, which is equivalent to £560 rising by increments of £35 to £980.

Class III consists of Senior Assistant Auditors in the larger Colonies, and of the Auditors of the smaller, such as Gibraltar, Gambia, British Honduras. In Africa the Senior Assistant

Auditors are on incremental scales rising to £920. Some of the Auditors in this class are actually paid lower salaries than Class IV officers on the time-scales already mentioned; their compensation lies in the fact that they are in a higher class for purposes of ultimate promotion. Class II contains the Auditors of several Colonies, the Assistant Director, Central Office, and the Deputy Auditors of the largest Colonies, the Auditors of which are included in Class I. The range of salaries in Class II may be taken as from about £900 to £1,100, and that in Class I as from £1,100 to £1,400. The Auditor in Malaya draws £1,680. It should be noted that the above particulars relate only to the superior establishments. Each local audit department has its own subordinate personnel, who are recruited locally, and are not members of the unified Service.

The total strength of the superior establishment is about 100, about 50 officers being included in Class IV, about 20 in Class III, 15 in Class II, and 8 in Class I. The Director of Colonial Audit and his Deputy are not included in the interchangeable staff, and their conditions of employment are assimilated to those of the Home Civil Service. The Directorship was held by the late Sir Edward Stephenson from the establishment of the Department in 1910 until his death in 1928, when he was succeeded by the present Director, Sir John Harding, who was transferred to this appointment from the Colonial Office.

(ii) THE COLONIAL POLICE SERVICE

Every Colony maintains a police force, small or large according to its needs. There are now no strictly military Colonial police forces, but all are organised on semi-military lines, and are capable of operating as armed forces should the preservation of law and order render such a course necessary. At the same time, the general development of the Colonies has led to an increasing emphasis upon the civil side of police work, such as the utilisation of modern methods of criminal detection and the problems which arise out of the growth of motor traffic. A few Colonies have mounted sections, but in general the forces are dismounted.

The rank and file are for the most part locally recruited; but in Hong Kong, Kenya, Palestine and some few other places there are substantial numbers of European non-commissioned officers and constables. These do not rank as members of the Colonial Police Service.

The duties of a police officer in a Colony are very varied, and there is increasing scope for the keen officer who is prepared to specialise. Legal and linguistic ability, aptitude for games, physical smartness, and the characteristics of initiative and courage, are all highly desirable qualifications.

A certain number of vacancies in the Colonial Police Service are filled by the promotion of specially selected men from the ranks of the Palestine and other forces in which European rank and file are employed; but the normal method of recruitment is by the selection of candidates from outside the Service by the ordinary appointments machinery of the Colonial Office, supplemented, in the case of some of the West Indian forces, by the appointment of a proportion of local candidates on the nomination of the Governors. Officers are usually recruited at a fairly early age and trained in the Service; until lately there was no arrangement for central training, but a start has now been made with the training of cadets at the Metropolitan Police College. The larger Colonies, moreover, have well-organised local arrangements for the training of young officers during their probationary years.

At the present time, most of the appointments made from outside the Service seem to be to the Eastern and the West Indian Colonies. As the Malayan Police Forces form the largest group within the Colonial Police Service, we may begin with a short description of their organisation and conditions of employment. The Straits Settlements and the Federated Malay States each possess a police force under its own head, but the officers are on one combined seniority roll. There are about 100 officers on the time-scale, which runs from a commencing salary of £350 to a maximum of £1,120. Above the time-scale there are some 15 posts with salaries ranging from £1,120 to £1,540. At the head are the Inspector-General, Straits Settlements, and the Commissioner, Federated Malay States, who each draw £1,680. The "other ranks" of the combined forces number about 8,000. Candidates are required to be under 22 years of age on 1 January in the year of selection. They must be unmarried, and must have passed the School Certificate or an equivalent examination. The selected candidate, after a short course in the Malay language held in London, goes out as a Probationer. While on probation he is required to live in a mess, and is under supervision and instruction. On passing the prescribed examinations he receives an increase of his pay to £420 a year; and if at the end of three years he is confirmed in his appointment he enters the incremental scale of £490.

The general conditions in the Ceylon and Hong Kong police forces are similar to the above, but the salaries vary in detail.

The West Indian group contains three important police forces, which are recruited on similar lines to those in the Eastern Colonies, except that candidates are accepted up to 26 years of age, and a proportion of vacancies is reserved for local candidates. The three forces referred to are those of British Guiana, Trinidad and Jamaica. Their present establishments of officers are respectively 16, 19 and 23. The salaries (apart from those of the head posts) are considerably lower than those paid in the East, ranging from £200 or £300 to £500 or £600; but they are supplemented by various allowances and are in line with the general range of salaries in the Dependencies concerned.

In the Tropical African police forces rather more than 200 officers are employed, the largest forces being those of Nigeria, the Gold Coast, Kenya, Tanganyika Territory and Uganda. In filling vacancies importance is attached to previous police or military experience, and candidates from outside the Service are expected to have had some experience in the regular or territorial forces, or at least to possess the Officers' Training Corps "A" certificate. While no specific educational test is prescribed, it is required that a candidate should produce evidence of a standard of general education comparable to that demanded of candidates for the Malayan Police. Salary scales are: in West Africa, £400 for two years, then £450 to

£810, with an efficiency bar at £600; in East Africa, £350 for two years, then £400 to £780, with an efficiency bar at £550. Officers on these scales are usually called Assistant Superintendents; there is a higher grade of Superintendent, reached by promotion, at £840 to £920 in West Africa, and £810 to £920 in East. The heads of the forces in the Gambia and Somaliland correspond to this grade, but elsewhere the heads (and the Deputy heads in the larger Dependencies) are super-scale officers. The Commissioner of Police in Sierra Leone and the Deputy Commissioner in Uganda receive £960; the Deputies in Kenya and Tanganyika Territory and the Commissioners in Nyasaland and Northern Rhodesia £1,000; the Commissioner in Zanzibar £1,100; the Commissioners in Tanganyika and Uganda and the Deputy in Nigeria £1,200; the Commissioners in Kenya and the Gold Coast £1,350; and the head of the Nigerian force £1,500.

While some Colonies have separate prison departments, in a good many the head of the police is also in charge of the prisons. This arrangement is convenient and economical in many cases, but it is recognised that it is open to certain objections in principle, and is out of accord with modern ideas of prison management. Proposals for the establishment of a separate Colonial Prison Service are under consideration.

(iii) THE COLONIAL CUSTOMS SERVICE

With few exceptions, the Colonial Governments depend largely upon customs and excise duties for their revenue, and employ substantial staffs on the collection of these duties. The work of a customs department is responsible and complex; the senior officers are expected to study the trend of trade and to advise the Government on economic matters within this sphere.

The largest customs department in the Colonial Empire is that of Malaya, with a superior staff of nearly 100 officers. These officers are recruited and paid on very similar lines to the Malayan Police, whose conditions of service have been described in the preceding section. Their duties are many and varied, comprising not only customs work as ordinarily understood but the super-vision of distilleries, the repression of smuggling, especially that of opium, and the prosecution of offenders. The preventive work, in particular, is full of interest and, on occasion, of ex-citement.

In the African Dependencies the customs departments are not large, the routine work being done by locally recruited staffs, and there being as a rule no serious preventive problems like those of Malaya to be dealt with. The posts filled by European officers have often been offered to experienced officers from the Home Customs Service, or to officers who have obtained some customs training in the West Indies or elsewhere; there has been little direct recruitment. Salaries are as a rule similar to those of the police. In the other Colonies, apart from the head-ships of departments, which are filled by the promotion of officers serving in the same or another Dependency, the staffs are mostly locally recruited.

(iv) THE COLONIAL POSTAL SERVICE

Every Colony maintains a Postal department, which, in the larger Dependencies, with a considerable volume of traffic, is an important part of the Government organisation. All normal postal, telegraph and telephone business is conducted, and in several Colonies broadcasting has lately come into the field.

The Colonial Postal Service is regarded as a professional branch, recruitment in the lower grades being carried out in one of two ways, according to the circumstances of the different Colonies: (i) by the secondment of trained staff from the Home Postal Service, usually for a period of three years, at the end of which the officer either reverts to home employment or is per-manently transferred to the Colonial Service, as he and the Government may desire; or (ii) by the local engagement of "learners", who receive their training in the department itself. At one time the former method was more widely used than it is to-day, but it is still employed, especially in connection with the more technical branches of the work, such as telegraph engineering. Most of the senior postal appointments in the Service are at present held by officers with home training, but the coming generation partly consists of locally recruited personnel who have received their training in the Colonial departments. In most Colonies the head of the Postal Service, usually called the Postmaster-General, is an officer whose career has been spent in postal work; but in Malaya, Ceylon and Hong Kong it is traditional that the head should be an administrative officer.

In the large Colonies considerable postal staffs are employed, and there are many senior and responsible posts, carrying substantial salaries. In Malaya there are nearly 50 Superintendents and engineers, on the usual professional "time-scale" of £560 rising to £1,120. Above, there are about a dozen "super-scale" appointments, including a Director of Posts and a Director of Telegraphs; each of the two last mentioned is on a salary of £1,470. Kenya, Uganda and the Tanganyika Territory maintain an amalgamated Postal Service under a Postmaster-General whose headquarters are at Nairobi. He draws a salary of £1,600. Formerly, the junior ranks of this Service were regularly recruited from home, but now they are mainly recruited locally, the senior posts being filled by promotion from the lower ranks or from other Colonies. These senior posts include a Senior Deputy Postmaster-General and an Engineer-in-Chief at £1,120 each; a Deputy Postmaster-General and a Chief Accountant at £1,000 each; and about 20 posts at varying scales between £600 and £840.

Another important Postal department is that of Nigeria. Here the Postmaster-General is at £1,450, the Controller of Posts and the Chief Engineer each at £1,200, and the Chief Accountant at £1,050. Surveyors are in two grades, with scales of £400 to £810 and £840 to £920; and Engineers likewise in two grades, with scales of £475 to £840 and £880 to £1,000. While it is true of the Postal as of the other branches of the Service that inter-Colonial transfers are more common in the higher than in the lower ranks, it is of interest to note that several of the present Surveyors in Nigeria have obtained their appointments on transfer from East Africa.

Apart from the strictly postal aspect of the work, there is a considerable philatelic interest about anything connected with Colonial stamps. Many Colonial issues are justly celebrated for their beauty of design, and in general, as collectors well know, a high standard is maintained, while, at the same time, "stunts" are deliberately avoided. The business connected with the manufacture and supply of stamps is managed by the Crown Agents for the Colonies, working, of course, in close touch with the Governments which they represent.

(v) The Colonial Survey Service; the Colonial Geological Survey Service; the Colonial Mines Service

Most Colonies possess a Survey department, whose duties are to map the country and to execute the location of boundaries, roads, etc. A certain amount of office work is involved, but most of the work of the Colonial surveyor is field work, calling not only for special professional qualifications but for personal endurance and the tact necessary for successful co-operation with other departmental officers and for the handling of subordinate staffs. In some Colonies the actual surveying is carried out by unofficial licensed surveyors, but generally the Government employs its own survey staff for official work. About 200 qualified surveyors are employed in the Colonial Survey Service, some of these being locally engaged or recruited from the Dominions, but a fair proportion being recruited from this country.

Persons desiring to enter the Service from this country are generally required to possess an Honours degree in Mathematics, Physical Science, Engineering or Geography, or alternatively a recognised Surveying Diploma or Licence. Persons not possessing these qualifications may in some cases be admitted as candidates on passing a qualifying examination in Mathematics and the use of surveying instruments. The selection of candidates takes place in the summer, and those selected are sent on a course of at least six months' duration at the

Ordnance Survey Office, Southampton. In addition, candidates for certain appointments are given a course of one year at Cambridge University, either before taking up their appointments or during their first leave.

The salaries paid to surveyors are generally similar to those in force for members of the Colonial Forest Service and the Colonial Agricultural Service, as already described. Malaya has the largest Survey department, with over 50 officers, some of whom are recruited from Australia and New Zealand. Above the time-scale there are 2 posts at £1,190, 8 on salaries ranging from £1,260 to £1,400, a Deputy Surveyor-General at £1,470, and a Surveyor-General at £1,680. Ceylon also has a large department, with 27 time-scale posts and 12 super-scale; the Surveyor-General is on a scale of £1,400 by £50 to £1,550, and the Deputy on one of £1,150 by £50 to £1,200. In Africa, Kenya, Tanganyika Territory, Uganda, Northern Rhodesia, Nigeria and the Gold Coast have survey establishments of substantial size; each has one super-scale post at £1,000 or thereabouts, and in addition Tanganyika, Uganda, Nigeria and the Gold Coast have one post each on salaries from £1,250 upwards, the best-paid post being that of Commissioner of Lands and Surveyor-General in Nigeria, which carries a salary of £1,600.

While Meteorology does not strictly come under the heading of Survey, it may be convenient to include some mention of this as yet comparatively small, but not unimportant, branch of the Colonial Service in this section. The employment of trained meteorologists in the Colonies is a fairly modern development, but one which is likely to increase with the growth of aviation and wireless telegraphy and telephony. At present, apart from the Government observatories at Colombo, Hong Kong and Mauritius, there are meteorological stations in West and East Africa, Malaya and Bermuda. There should be, as time goes on, increasing opportunities in this line for officers possessing the requisite scientific equipment combined with a taste for research and the power of organisation.

Finally we come to two comparatively small and highly specialised Services which have only recently been unified. The

Colonial Geological Survey Service consists of the professional staffs of the Geological Survey departments which are maintained in Malaya and in some of the East and West African Dependencies. For admission to the Service the possession of an Honours degree in Geology, or an equivalent qualification is necessary. Salaries are on normal lines, commencing at £500 in East Africa, £550 in West Africa, and £560 in Malaya. The Directors of Geological Survey in Nigeria and the Gold Coast receive £1,400, those in Sierra Leone and Uganda £1,100, and those in Tanganyika and Nyasaland £1,000. The corresponding post in the Federated Malay States is on a scale of £1,190 to £1,330. The principal duty of the departments is to survey and map the geology of selected areas, with a special view to economic possibilities and to questions of water-supply.

The Colonial Mines Service covers a number of Mines departments in the larger African Dependencies, Malaya, Trinidad and Cyprus. The departments are not large, and there is a good proportion of super-scale posts. Except in the case of Trinidad, where the work is concerned with the oil-fields, the members of the Service are mainly employed in connection with metalliferous mining, their duties including the inspection of mines, the enforcement of mining legislation and mediation in mining disputes. Entrants to the Service are normally required to possess the Diploma of a recognised School of Metalliferous Mining.

CHAPTER XV

BRANCHES NOT AS YET UNIFIED

(i) EDUCATIONAL SERVICES

AT the time of writing preliminary action has been taken with a view to the establishment of a Colonial Education Service, and it is probable that before long such a Service will have been created. The conditions precedent to the formation of a unified Service already exist; the only substantial question awaiting consideration is that of defining the posts which should be included in the schedule of offices normally to be filled by members of the Service, and those which should be excluded.

It is scarcely necessary here to enlarge upon the immense importance of education as the foundation of all true progress in the Colonial Empire as elsewhere. Nor need we, in these days, echo the cautious phraseology of the "Colonial Office List" of 1897, which, after referring to the schools in existence in some half-dozen of the older Colonies, can find nothing further to say except that "secondary education is not neglected in some of the others". In fact, no aspect of administration has of recent years received more continuous study and stimulation on the part of the Colonial Governments and of the Colonial Office authorities than the educational responsibility of the Government. At the centre, a standing Advisory Committee on Native Education in the Colonies is constantly at work guiding and coordinating policy; while in each Colony the local education department is carrying the general policy into practice and adapting it to the varying demands of local circumstances.

This policy has been officially defined as having for its object the provision of an education that will be: "adapted to the mentality, aptitudes, occupations, and traditions of the various peoples, conserving as far as possible all sound and healthy elements in the fabric of their social life, adapting them where necessary to changed circumstances and progressive ideas, as an agent of natural growth and evolution. Its aim should be to render the individual more efficient in his or her condition of life, whatever it may be, and to promote the advancement of the community as a whole through the improvement of agriculture, the development of native industries, the improvement of health, the training of the people in the management of their own affairs, and the inculcation of true ideals of citizenship and service. It must include the raising up of capable, trustworthy, public-spirited leaders of the people belonging to their own race."[1]

The successful application of such a policy, the keynote of which is adaptation to local needs and local circumstances, calls for different methods in different conditions; yet much can be gained from a reasonable amount of interchange of staff, enabling the experience of problems in one Colony to be made available for dealing with related, if not precisely similar, problems in another. Again, in the educational no less than in the other Services unification will have the advantage of publicly affirming the principle that the Service is Empire-wide, and that the worker even in the smallest Colony and the most isolated post is a part of a larger system and need not feel that his task is a solitary one, or that he himself will necessarily be cut off from the opportunities of change and advancement which present themselves to officers serving in Colonies where the work is wider in its scope.

The work of the Educational Services in the Colonies falls into two divisions—administration and teaching—but the two functions may often be exercised by the same officers. Primary teaching is mainly in the hands of both men and women either locally trained and engaged or recruited from this country under special arrangements with the Board of Education. The conditions of employment of these staffs vary considerably, and it would not be practicable to deal with them here in detail. The staffs to which any scheme, of unification would apply are mainly those engaged on secondary education and on the organisation of educational arrangements in the Colonies.

[1] Cmd. 2374 of 1925.

On the administrative side, a Colonial Education department is organised on normal departmental lines, with a Director of Education at the head, and probably, in a large Colony, a Deputy Director to assist him. He ranks with other heads of important departments and is usually, though not invariably, a professional educationist. He is responsible not only for the administrative control of the department but for advising the Government on all matters connected with the educational policy, for administering any system of grants to non-Government schools which may be in operation, and for arranging for the inspection of such schools. In several Colonies there is a local Board of Education, or other similar Committee, over which the Director would normally preside, and with which he must take care to work in co-operation.

In some cases there is a separate Inspectorate, while in others the inspection of schools is carried out by officers detailed for the purpose from a general list of "Education Officers" who are employed from time to time on teaching, inspectorial or other duties at the discretion of the Director. The latter system is that generally in force in the African Dependencies where, with the exception of certain staffs definitely allocated to particular schools and colleges, the personnel of the departments comprises a single cadre of interchangeable officers. These officers, often termed Superintendents of Education, are recruited from much the same field as the members of the Colonial Administrative Service, and are on the same salary scale, except that there is a "promotion", instead of an "efficiency", bar at £840; that is to say, in order to reach the higher scale of £880 to £1,000 the officer must not merely be certified as efficient but must secure promotion to a definite vacancy, either in his own Colony or in another. Candidates for these appointments must have a degree, usually with honours, and either possess a Diploma in Education or attend a year's course at the University of London Institute of Education. In the case of those who attend the course, the fees are paid by the Government and the candidate receives an allowance at the rate of £20 a month.

EDUCATIONAL SERVICES

The duties of an education officer in an African Dependency are very varied. He may be employed in teaching at one of the Government intermediate or secondary schools, in the training of native teachers, in inspection work or in the organisation of the teaching of a particular subject, such as handicrafts, over a wide area. While comparatively junior in service he may have a school of his own, with native assistants, and be called upon not only to teach in the upper forms but to interest himself in the stimulation and organisation of every form of school activity. At a later stage he may advance on the teaching side to the headship of one of the large colleges, or on the administrative side to a Deputy Directorship or Directorship of Education.

Outside Tropical Africa, the demand is primarily for teaching staff, most vacancies occurring in Malaya, but some also in Hong Kong and the West Indies. In these Dependencies the work of most of the educational staff consists of teaching in the secondary or grammar schools. In these schools the medium of instruction is English, and the curriculum is designed to enable pupils to prepare for such examinations as the Cambridge Locals and the London Matriculation. The schools are arranged on lines corresponding as nearly as possible to those of an English public school. In Malaya the salary scale of European masters is equivalent to £560 rising by £35 to £1,120, subject to an efficiency bar at £840. Elsewhere the salaries are too various to be shortly described.

While secondary schools of the type referred to above are now found in a large number of Colonies, there are as yet few institutions of university standard in the Colonial Empire. The only Government institution of this kind is the Ceylon University College; the Raffles College at Singapore and the Hong Kong University are not Government institutions, though from time to time members of the Colonial Service may have opportunities of serving on their staffs. In Africa, Makerere College in Uganda and Achimota College in the Gold Coast promise in time to develop into universities for East and West Africa respectively. The former is at present managed by the Government of Uganda, but its future has lately been the subject of enquiry by an authoritative Commission under the presidency of Earl De La Warr. Achimota has an independent Board of management; the Government of the Gold Coast, however, retains certain powers of control, and interchange between the staff and the Colonial Service is a recognised feature of the system.

Education is one of the branches of the Colonial Service in which women have an important part to play. Considerable numbers of women are employed as primary teachers throughout the Colonies, many of these being recruited locally, but many also recruited from home through the Board of Education. There are also several women employed in different Dependencies in secondary and higher education. Malaya, Hong Kong, Nigeria and Palestine may be cited as Dependencies in which the employment of women in this field is on a substantial scale.

In concluding this very brief survey of the Educational Services in the Colonies, I should perhaps mention that most of the Colonial Governments have taken advantage of the provisions of the Teachers' Superannuation Acts which enable them to make reciprocal arrangements with the Board of Education at home, whereby a teacher transferred from pensionable employment at home can preserve his home pension rights, and receive, on his retirement from the Colonial Service, the pension for which he has contributed at home as well as the pension earned in his Colonial employment.

(ii) RAILWAY, MARINE AND PUBLIC WORKS SERVICES

All railways in the Colonial Empire, with the exception of those operating in Nyasaland and Northern Rhodesia, are managed by the respective Colonial Governments. They vary from great systems like the Kenya-Uganda Railway, the Nigerian Railway, the Tanganyika Railway and the Federated Malay States Railway, to comparatively small organisations. The competition of road transport is creating a problem for many of these systems, especially those in island Colonies, but the very considerable developments which have taken place during recent years in the railways of the African mainland are a clear indication that the railway maintains its traditional superiority to other methods of transport where conditions are suitable to its full economic exploitation.

The Kenya-Uganda Railway, with its associated harbours and lake-steamer services, is a separately constituted administration, with the Governors of Kenya and Uganda as High Commissioners for Transport, and a Railway Council, on which the interested Governments are represented. It has a separate budget, and its own establishment of officers. The other Colonial railways are usually in form departments of the Government, but it is customary for them to be managed on semi-commercial lines, and the conditions on which the staffs are employed frequently differ in some respects from those applicable to ordinary civil servants. A railway often has to engage temporary staff for construction works, and even when no new construction is in progress it is necessary to preserve a certain elasticity in the staff arrangements, in view of the inevitable fluctuations of the traffic.

For this reason, it is not uncommon for the subordinate staffs, at all events, not to be pensionable in the ordinary way, but to be employed on provident fund terms. The Government and the officer each make regular contributions into a fund, where these deposits accumulate at compound interest; and the amount standing to an officer's credit is available for him on his discharge or retirement, or for his estate in the event of his death. The system has certain evident advantages from the point of view both of the Government and of the employee; but it is generally considered that the normal pension system is to be preferred for superior staff recruited from overseas for permanent employment.

In the past, skilled drivers and artisans, as well as "uniformed" staff were to a large extent recruited from the home railways; but there is a growing tendency for such staff to be trained and recruited locally. Most Colonial railways still, however, look to the home country to provide them with the higher traffic and engineering staffs. The recruitment of railway personnel from home is entrusted to the Crown Agents for the Colonies, who engage officers for service in the first instance on an agreement for a specified period—usually a tour of service, or, in West Africa, two tours. While serving on agreement the officer is not pensionable, though he may be contributing to a provident fund, if one exists in connection with the railway on which he is employed. When the period covered by the agreement comes to an end, neither the officer nor the Government is bound to renew it, but it may be renewed by mutual consent. If, however, the officer's services have been satisfactory and it appears that he will be permanently required, the usual course is for him to be placed on the pensionable establishment after a reasonable period of service on agreement; in which event he is in exactly the same position as any other civil servant, as regards security of tenure and general conditions of employment.

No attempt has as yet been made to create a unified Colonial Railway Service, and it may be that no such attempt will be considered desirable, in view of the special necessity of considering each separate railway as a separate economic unit, whose capacity to pay must to some extent dictate the conditions of employment of its staff. Again, the interchange of officers presents difficulties, since different railways are differently organised on account of variations in the local conditions, and General Managers must be conceded a considerable amount of freedom in picking their own staffs to suit the special duties for which they are required. In the filling of the higher posts, however, it is the practice to proceed on very much the same lines as in the case of other branches of the Colonial Service; that is to say, the Secretary of State, in selecting officers for appointment, reviews the whole field of the Colonial Service, and officers on every railway have an equal opportunity of reaching the highest ranks.

The differing methods of organisation also preclude any close standardisation of railway salaries, and without going into the question at considerable length it is difficult to give any idea of the prevailing rates. It must suffice to say that the salaries in force are generally in scale with those of other branches of the Service which have already been or will hereafter be described.

Many of the higher appointments carry very substantial emoluments. The General Managers of the larger systems receive salaries of £2,000 a year or more; while the heads of departments on these railways (Superintendents of the Line, Chief Engineers, Chief Accountants, etc.), along with the General Managers of the smaller lines, may draw anything from £1,000 upwards.

In Nigeria and on the Central African lakes, Marine Services are associated with the railways; while the ports with which the Colonial Empire abounds call for the services of marine officers as harbour masters and pilots. For the floating staffs, officers with Mercantile Marine experience are usually required; for some of the shore appointments ex-Naval officers are preferred. The Nigeria Marine, Kenya-Uganda Marine, and Tanganyika Marine offer good careers to officers with Masters' or Engineers' certificates; and there is always keen competition for the various harbour appointments, especially those at the big ports, such as Singapore or Gibraltar.

Road transport in the Colonies is mostly in the hands of private enterprise, but in some Dependencies experiments are being made in Government management, the General Manager of the railway or the Director of Public Works usually being in charge of the arrangements.

The main business of the Public Works departments is, however, the construction and maintenance of roads, Government buildings, water-supply schemes and development works generally. In some Colonies, where private contractors have established themselves, the actual work may often be done by contract, the duty of the department being to supervise it in the interest of the Government; but in a large number of cases the department must be its own contractor, and all Colonies find it necessary to retain a certain permanent staff for day-to-day work. For important or special works the advice and assistance of recognised firms of Consulting Engineers are obtained, through the agency of the Crown Agents for the Colonies, who also act as purchasing agents for the Colonial Governments for necessary stores and material.

Staffs for Colonial Public Works departments are recruited

by the Crown Agents in the same manner as those for the railways, that is, on agreement in the first instance. There is, however, no question of the Public Works establishments being in any way separated from the rest of the Government Services, and, apart from those who are engaged for special pieces of work, whose employment terminates on the conclusion of that work, it is usual for the Public Works staff to serve on similar conditions to other civil servants and to be admitted to the pensionable establishment after a reasonable probation. It is not usual for staffs of the Public Works Services to be employed on provident fund terms.

The superior Public Works officers are mostly engineers, but a few architects are employed in some Colonies. For most appointments civil engineering qualifications are required, but for special posts hydraulic, electrical and other engineering qualifications may be specified, according to circumstances. The Crown Agents endeavour as a rule to secure for first appointment to the Service young engineers who after qualifying have had a few years' practical professional experience with one or other of the important engineering firms. Under the related salary schemes in force in Tropical Africa, engineers start at £450 for two years, then proceed by annual increments of £25 to £600; then to £630, and, subject to an efficiency bar, by £30 to £840. There is a higher grade (Executive Engineers) on £880 by £40 to £1,000. This is the scale for East Africa; that in West Africa is similar, except that it begins at £475, and the efficiency bar occurs at £660. In Malaya, engineers are on the usual "professional" scale of £560 by £35 to £1,120, with an efficiency bar at £840. The salaries elsewhere vary. For those who are fortunate enough to be promoted above these scales, there are numerous well-paid posts in the shape of Directorships and Deputy Directorships of Public Works, as well as a number of specialist appointments. Thus the Colonial Service offers good prospects of a career to members of the engineering professions, and the great developments which are taking place in many parts of the Colonial Empire afford considerable scope for the employment of engineers in important and interesting professional work.

(iii) OTHER TECHNICAL SERVICES

There are few professions which do not have some representatives in the wide field of the Colonial Service, but this survey is necessarily confined to those branches which are of substantial size and of reasonably general distribution. In this category mention should be made of Analytical Chemists, of whom some thirty are employed in the Service as a whole. Malaya and Hong Kong have comparatively large Analytical departments, with ten and five professional officers respectively. Nigeria, the Gold Coast, Ceylon, Jamaica, Trinidad and British Guiana each employ two such officers; Kenya, the Tanganyika Territory, Uganda, Cyprus, Mauritius and Palestine one each. The conditions of service vary considerably, but are similar to those of other professional officers in the Colonies concerned. The duties cover a wide range, including all kinds of analytical and medico-legal work and the supervision and training of subordinate staff.

Another small but specialised section of the Colonial Service is that comprising the officers responsible for Government printing. Most Colonial Governments maintain their own printing presses for the production of estimates, reports, blue books, forms, circulars and the Government Gazette. In the larger administrations the volume of such work is considerable, and in general a high quality of production, combined with speed, is demanded and obtained from the Printing departments. While the actual labour is normally carried out by locally recruited personnel, it is common for the Government to employ one or more technically qualified European officers to instruct and supervise, and generally to be responsible for the management and business of the department.

(iv) ACCOUNTANCY SERVICES

Considerable numbers of accountants are employed, both on the general financial business of the Colonial Governments and on the more specialised accounting work of Railway, Postal and Public Works departments. The holders of some posts are required to possess a recognised qualification in accountancy, but this is not a general rule. As might be expected, many accounting posts are filled by local recruitment, but there is a fair demand for European officers to fill the higher grades in the African and some other Dependencies. Postal Accountants are included in the Colonial Postal Service, and are interchangeable with officers on the "traffic" side of postal work; but there is as yet no Colonial Accounting Service covering the accounts staff of the other departments.

Accountants, when not recruited locally, are usually engaged by the Crown Agents for the Colonies in the same way as other technical personnel. They may be employed either in specific posts or as part of a cadre of accountants in one of the larger administrations. Some of these cadres, as for example those attached to the Nigerian Railways, the Kenya-Uganda Railway, or the Malayan Corps of Accountants, are of considerable size and afford within themselves scope for advancement to posts of substantial responsibility and commensurate remuneration. Apart from the opportunities of local promotion in the large Services, there are the more general possibilities opened up by the new policy with regard to the management of the financial affairs of the Colonial Governments described in Appendix I. Whether or not a unified Accounting Service is formally created, it may be assumed that the new posts of Accountant-General, like other senior posts in the Colonial Service, will be filled by selection from the general field of duly qualified serving officers.

This is being written at a time when the new policy has not been fully worked out in practice, and it is therefore difficult to speak in more detail of the conditions and prospects of accounting officers in the Colonial Service. In Tropical Africa the salary scale on which such officers are initially engaged usually rises to a maximum of £720, with a senior grade (reached by promotion) on a scale rising to £920. In Malaya the time-scale for officers of the Corps of Accountants is £560 to £1,120. Amongst the higher posts open to accountants, mention may be made of the new posts of Accountant-General in Nigeria and the Gold Coast, the salaries of which have been fixed at £1,300; those of Accountant-General in Uganda and Tanganyika, with salaries of £1,100 and £1,000 respectively; and the posts of Chief Accountant on the Nigeria, Kenya-Uganda and Federated Malay States Railways, carrying respectively salaries of £1,300, £1,350, and £1,470.

(v) Miscellaneous Posts

This brief survey has by no means exhausted the list of activities carried on by the Colonial Service, but the remaining posts do not easily lend themselves to classification. The particular needs of different Dependencies at different times call for the employ-ment of special staff who do not fall into any of the categories hitherto mentioned. Thus, in Eastern Africa there are specialist officers employed on game preservation and tsetse fly control; in places such as Palestine and Cyprus experts are employed in archaeological research and the care of antiquities. From time to time, as circumstances may require and as officers with the necessary qualifications are available, special appointments such as that of Government Anthropologist are made; but in general anthropological study is carried out in the field by the adminis-trative officers who are in direct contact with the people and who, as already remarked, receive a grounding in anthropology as part of their preliminary course of training. Many important contributions to anthropological knowledge have been made by members of the Colonial Service, as a result either of researches specially commissioned by a Colonial Government, or of obser-vations gathered in the course of the daily work of administration.

CHAPTER XVI

GOVERNORS

"THE GOVERNOR", say the Colonial Regulations, "is the single and supreme authority responsible to, and representative of, His Majesty. He is, by virtue of his Commission and the Letters Patent or Order in Council constituting his office, entitled to the obedience, aid, and assistance of all military, air force, and civil officers."

In each Dependency the Governor is the head of the executive administration and he is also, in most, the President of the Legislative Council. To him is delegated the exercise of the Royal Prerogative of mercy. He is the sole channel of communication with His Majesty's Government: all official correspondence between His Majesty's Government and the Colonial Government is conducted by means of written or telegraphic despatches passing between the Secretary of State and the Governor personally. In addition to his official functions, the Governor is the leader of the social life of the Colony.

Heavy and responsible burdens are therefore laid on a Governor, and it is not to be assumed that in a small Colony the task is necessarily less exacting than in a large one. The problems of the smaller administration, where much may have to be done with comparatively few resources, may well prove as exacting to the Governor himself as those of a larger place, where there is a highly organised departmental system to dispose of the bulk of the work, and a wealth of experienced counsellors upon whose wisdom he can draw. It is no wonder, then, if, as has appeared at various points in this narrative, the endeavour to select the best available persons to discharge these important duties has been a constant preoccupation of successive Secretaries of State.

A Governor is appointed by the King, and holds his appointment by virtue of a Commission from His Majesty; the Secretary of State for the Colonies is the Minister constitutionally responsible for submitting the names of candidates to the King, and advising His Majesty in his choice. Three Colonial Governorships—those of the "fortress" Colonies of Bermuda, Malta and Gibraltar—are by tradition held by distinguished military officers; apart from these, the choice of Governors is entirely unrestricted, but although, in special cases, Secretaries of State have not hesitated to look to the Home Civil Service, to the fighting Services, to the political world and elsewhere, for suitable Governors, the normal and natural field of selection is the Colonial Service itself, and in particular the Colonial Administrative Service. Promotion to a Governorship is naturally and rightly looked upon as the culmination of a successful career in the Colonial Service.

Some reference has already been made to the position of the Governor in the constitutions of the Colonial Governments; the main purpose of the present chapter is to give some account of the special terms and conditions on which Governors are employed, since these differ in many respects from those applicable to the ordinary civil servant. It should be noted that while the powers and duties of the Governor devolve in full upon any person appointed to administer a Government in the Governor's absence, the conditions of service about to be described apply only to substantive Governors.

The salary of the Governor is paid from the funds of the Colony, and its amount in each case is a matter of arrangement between the Secretary of State and the local legislature. No attempt is made to fix a scale of Governors' salaries: each has to be determined individually, the responsibilities of the post, the resources of the Colony, and the social obligations imposed on the Governor being taken into account. It may readily be supposed that these factors vary considerably, even as between neighbouring territories. On the whole, the rates of remuneration are necessarily substantial, and except in the case of one or two of the smaller Colonies the emoluments range from £2,000 or £3,000 to as much as £8,000 a year. Even so, it is generally recognised that, in view of the expenses which a Governor's position requires him to meet, few, if any, Colonial Governors are paid more than the necessities of the case demand.

It is usual for the Governor's emoluments to be divided into salary and duty allowance. The latter is drawn only while he is on duty in the Colony; when he is absent it is drawn by the officer who administers the government. This arrangement takes into account the fact that in some degree the Governor's emoluments represent not so much remuneration for official services as reimbursement for expenditure incurred in the interests of the community. Colonial society looks to the King's representative as its leader, and imposes certain obligations on him in this capacity. Again, the Governor is the natural person to extend the hospitality of the Colony to distinguished visitors, and entertainment of this kind may assume considerable proportions, especially in places where visitors are frequent, or where ordinary facilities for their temporary accommodation are not highly developed. Expenditure of this description naturally does not fall on the Governor when he is not in residence in the Colony, but it then falls on the Acting Governor, and it is clearly appropriate, therefore, that he should draw the allowance.

It would not be justifiable, however, to suggest that this division of the Governor's emoluments represents a hard and fast distinction between remuneration and reimbursement, or that the duty allowance is an entertainment allowance pure and simple. Circumstances vary too greatly to enable any general and categorical statement to be made. We are concerned here only to observe that the normal terms upon which a Governor's emoluments are arranged are such as to secure him a substantially larger amount while he is on duty and subject to the full responsibilities of his position than while he is on leave of absence. In this respect he differs from the ordinary civil servant, who normally receives the same salary when on leave as when on duty.

The Governor's salary, then, is paid by the Colony. The Colony is not, however, called upon to bear any expense in connection with his passages or pension, it being an established tradition that the Imperial Exchequer undertakes these expenses on the Colony's behalf. The underlying principle is, no doubt, that, inasmuch as the Governor is the person sent by His Majesty to represent him in the Colony, it is proper that His Majesty's Government should make themselves responsible for the Governor's transport to the Colony at the beginning of his term of office and from the Colony at its end; also for any pension which it may be considered proper to grant to him when his connection with the Colony has ceased. But it rests with the Colony to be responsible for his remuneration while he is actually its Governor.

A Governor is appointed for a certain and limited term of office. In the regulations in force until lately the maximum term was specified as six years, but the Secretary of State recently decided to reduce this to five years. On his appointment, the Governor receives a lump sum grant from the Imperial Treasury to cover the passages of himself, his family and his staff, together with incidental expenses such as the purchase of uniform. The amount of the grant is fixed in relation to each Colony by the Secretary of State and the Treasury, and the amounts in force are published in the Colonial Regulations. They vary from £210 (in the case of Gibraltar) to £740 (in the case of Fiji), the distance of the Colony from England and the cost of passages being an important factor.

At the completion of a Governor's term of office, a grant of similar amount to that paid on his appointment is made. If he retires or is transferred to another Governorship before completing the full term for which he was appointed, an *ad hoc* grant is made according to the circumstances. A Governor proceeding on leave has to pay for his own passages.

Somaliland is an exception to these rules. As the normal tour of service there is from 12 to 15 months, owing to the climatic conditions, the Governor must take leave several times in the course of his term of office. For this reason, coupled with the fact that the administration is subsidised in any case by the Exchequer, it has been thought most appropriate for the Governor's passages on appointment and on leave to be borne on the accounts of the Protectorate in the same way as those of ordinary civil servants; and the grant which he receives from the home Government on appointment and termination of office is limited to £100 for incidental expenses.

Governors' pensions are regulated by special Acts of Parliament, and are calculated on an entirely different system from those of other public servants. The arrangements at present in force are set out in three Acts, dated 1911, 1929 and 1936. These Acts apply also to Governors of Dominions; in fact their title is: "The Pensions (Governors of Dominions, etc.) Acts". The reason for having a special system is primarily that the normal method of assessing pensions on the basis of a fraction of retiring salary is difficult to apply in the case of Governors, inasmuch as they generally receive salaries higher than those of other officers in the public service who might be regarded as of comparable status, a proportion of these salaries being designed to enable them to keep up their position. The normal method of pension calculation would result in anomalies as between one Governor and another and as between Governors and other classes of public servants.

Special Parliamentary provision for Governors' pensions dates back to 1865, when the first of the series of Acts was enacted. Under this Act (which was somewhat modified by a further Act of 1872), pensions were granted at flat rates depending partly on the salary of the Governorship, and partly on the length of the Governor's service. The arrangement was found to be defective in practice, and the wording of the law excluded the Governors of Protectorates from its scope. No alteration was, however, effected until 1911, when, as a result of recommendations by the interdepartmental Committee on pensions, to whose work reference was made in Chapter II, the old Acts were repealed and a new system introduced. After the War, it became clear that amendments were required, both to improve the pension rates, which were no longer adequate, and to enable provision to be made for Governors of Mandated Territories; and the whole matter was reviewed, during 1927 and 1928, by a Committee presided over by the late Earl Buxton (himself an ex-Governor-General), and including representatives of the three political parties and of the Treasury. The recommendations contained in the report[1] of this influential Committee were accepted by the Government, and formed the basis of the Act of 1929. By this Act considerable improvements were effected and most of the existing anomalies removed; but one anomaly remained, affecting the numerous class of Governors appointed from the Civil Service (Home or Colonial).

The system embodied in the 1911 and 1929 Acts provided that the special scale of Governors' pensions should apply only to persons who had actually served for ten years as Governors before retirement. This rule is clearly fair and reasonable in the case of the Governor appointed from outside the public service, but the only alternative provision made for the ex-Civil Service Governor was that, if he retired before completing ten years' service as a Governor, he should receive, in respect of his service as Governor a pension calculated under the Superannuation Acts on the basis of his last Civil Service salary. In other words, although his service as a Governor earned him a pension, it was (broadly speaking) no better a pension than that which he would have earned if he had remained in his last Civil Service post and had never received promotion to a Governorship. In many cases this rule involved appreciable hardship, since age or ill-health might often prevent a Governor who had worked his way up in the Colonial Service from completing ten years in Governorships, while the salary of his last Civil Service appointment was not invariably of such magnitude as to secure to him a pension adequate to his services and his position. This consideration was bound to be present to the mind of the Secretary of State when selecting officers for submission to the King for appointment to Governorships, or arranging for changes in Governorships; and to an appreciable extent restricted his freedom to deal with such important matters on the sole basis of the public interest. Lord Swinton, when Secretary of State, initiated further discussion of this question, which eventually resulted in the passage of the amending Act of 1936.

[1] Cmd. 3059.

By this Act the qualifying period for earning the special rates of pension was reduced, in the case of the ex-Civil Service Governor, to three years as a Governor. The opportunity was taken at the same time to provide for reciprocity with the Anglo-Egyptian Sudan, so that, if occasion should arise, a Governor could be transferred from, or appointed to the Sudan, without loss of pension rights.

As was observed above, the necessity for these special provisions in respect of pensions for Governors arises from the impracticability of applying the usual methods of pension computation to their case. The arrangement sanctioned by Parliament aims at solving this problem as equitably as possible by dividing Governorships into four classes, and attaching to each class a flat rate of pension in respect of each month of service as a Governor. In assigning Governorships to classes it is possible to take into account not merely salary but the importance and relative responsibility of the various posts (which may not invariably correspond to the relative salaries), and also differences in climatic conditions.

The pension rates are: for Class I, £6 a year for every month of service in the Class; for Class II, £5; for Class III, £4; and for Class IV, £3. Thus a Governor who had had five years' service in a Class II Governorship, followed by another five years in a Class I Governorship, would have qualified for a pension of £660 a year. The actual allocation of Governorships to Classes is not laid down in the Acts, but is arranged administratively by the Secretary of State and the Treasury in consultation, and may be varied from time to time in the light of changes in circumstances.

The grant of pensions is subject to the fulfilment of certain conditions, and these differ according to whether the Governor concerned was promoted from the Civil Service (Home or Colonial), or appointed from outside. In the latter case, no pension can be paid unless the Governor completes ten years' service. In the former case, the Governor will, of course, be eligible on his retirement for the pension which he has earned in the Civil Service up to the time at which he becomes a

Governor. In addition, he will be eligible for a pension in respect of his service as Governor, but this will not be at the special Governor's rate unless his service as Governor amounts to at least three years. If he should retire in circumstances rendering him eligible for pension before completing three years' service as Governor, he is pensioned, not at the special rate, but, in effect, as if he had remained in his last Civil Service appointment and had not become a Governor.

Subject to his having completed the necessary qualifying period of service, a Governor is eligible for pension on retirement at an age of not less than 60, or on account of ill-health or abolition of office. There are also special provisions under which a Governor who is physically fit and has not attained the age of 60 may be given a pension if the Secretary of State is unable to find him further appropriate employment. In such a case, the pension is reduced by an amount depending on the number of years by which his age falls short of 60.

The total pension which a Governor may receive from all sources must not exceed £2,000 a year; but in practice this figure is not very often reached. There are a number of other provisions in the Acts, but these are of minor interest, and enough has probably been said to give a fair picture of the main features of the system.

The only other points which it seems necessary to mention in connection with the conditions of employment of Governors are, first, that it is usual for the Governor to be statutorily exempted from the payment of local income tax, where such a tax is in force; and secondly, that in some cases, but not all, the Governor is granted exemption, under somewhat varying conditions, from the payment of customs duties on goods imported for his use in the Colony.

A list of the Governorships, and other posts of corresponding status, open to officers of the Colonial Service, is given in Appendix V.

CHAPTER XVII

THE COLONIAL OFFICE

No description of the Colonial Service would be complete which did not include some mention of the organisation and functions of the Colonial Office in London, with special reference to its arrangements for dealing with matters affecting the Service. Some remarks on this subject have been made in earlier portions of this book, but it will be convenient to allot a chapter to dealing with the whole question more comprehensively. Numerous references have been made in these pages to the position of the Secretary of State for the Colonies in relation to the Colonial Service; and while the part played by Ministers is a real and personal one, and of paramount importance, they must have staffs to assist them, and a certain amount of responsibility must, in the nature of things, be delegated to the permanent officials of the Department. While, then, the Colonial Office staff, which is a part of the Home Civil Service, is not interchangeable with the Colonial Service, it has close relations with that Service, and some description of its activities is strictly relevant to our theme.

The office of Secretary of State for the Colonies has had a curious history, which can only be touched upon here. Actually, Colonial affairs have been dealt with by a Secretary of State only since 1768, and then for some time but partially. In the seventeenth and eighteenth centuries, the control of what then existed of the present Colonial Empire fluctuated between a Committee of the Privy Council and a separately constituted "Council of Trade and Plantations", consisting of selected Members of Parliament. Towards the end of the eighteenth century, after a brief interlude during which Colonial affairs were dealt with by the Home Department, the Secretaryships of State for War and for the Colonies were combined, and this apparently incongruous association lasted up to as late as 1854, when the two departments were finally separated. Thenceforth the Secretary of State for the Colonies continued to deal with both what are now the Dominions and the Colonial Empire until 1925, when a separate Secretaryship for Dominion Affairs was created; but this post continued to be held by the same Minister as the Colonial Secretaryship until 1930, since when, apart from a short period in 1931, the Colonial Office has had its own Secretary of State.

Physically, the Colonial Office has since 1875 occupied the north-eastern corner of the block of Government buildings which houses also the Home, Foreign and India Offices. The old Colonial Office was at No. 12, Downing Street, a house similar in general appearance to the still existing Nos. 10 and 11, and standing across the end of the street on space now covered partly by the one-storied Whips' Office and partly by the steps leading from the street to the Park. The building was evidently in very bad condition at the end of its life, for minute books have been preserved in which a mournful picture is drawn of the discomforts with which the staff had to contend: rain poured through the roof, smoke and draughts coursed along the corridors, the sky was visible through cracks in the walls. But the house must have possessed some fine rooms, and some excellent eighteenth-century chimney-pieces were preserved and incorporated in the new building, that now in the Secretary of State's room having a particularly attractive carving. One of these fireplaces came from the waiting-room of the old building, which witnessed the only meeting of Nelson and Wellington, who chanced to wait upon the Secretary of State at the same time. Wellington records that Nelson evidently did not know to whom he was talking, and had to slip out and ask a messenger for enlightenment.

The old building also witnessed the labours of the future Cardinal Manning, who served as a Supernumerary Clerk from 1830 to 1832, and of Sir Henry Taylor, the poet, whose services were so valuable that, although he was prevented by ill-health from attending at the Office during the thirteen years preceding his retirement in 1872, he was permitted to remain on the establishment and to have his work sent to him at home.

The story of the designing of the new Offices by Mr (afterwards Sir) Gilbert Scott is well known. Mr Scott had prepared designs in the Gothic manner which he loved, but Lord Palmerston would have none of it, and peremptorily ordered the architect to submit a fresh design in the Italian manner. Protests and attempts at compromise were ignored, and at length, "shuddering with horror", as Lytton Strachey said, Mr Scott constructed the Offices in Renaissance style. It must be admitted that the resulting edifice is one of some dignity, and it even achieves beauty in certain atmospheric conditions. The view of the block from the bridge in St James's Park is one of the sights of London. Unfortunately, exterior appearance has taken precedence of interior comfort and convenience; though many of the rooms are of imposing proportions, a much larger number are badly planned for office use, and indeed expansion of staff has necessitated the employment as offices of several rooms which were originally meant only as store-rooms. This is not remarkable when it is considered that the administrative staff of the Colonial Office numbered about 40 in 1915, and that twenty years later the administrative staffs of the two Offices were twice that figure, while accommodation had to be provided for two Secretaries of State with their personal staffs and assistants, and for increased executive, clerical, typing and other staffs proportionate to the increased administrative complement. In the meantime, the physical boundaries of the Office have remained unaltered, except for the most welcome loan of a suite of rooms in the Home Office; and it has been necessary not only to strain the internal resources of the building to the utmost, but to transfer the Appointments, Accounts and Printing departments to outside accommodation, and also to house several of the Secretary of State's professional Advisers away from the main Office. These arrangements, while the best that could be made, have inevitably proved a severe handicap to the convenient working of the Office, and it is to be earnestly hoped that some more satisfactory solution of the problem will present itself.

It is only right, however, that a tribute should be paid to the Office of Works, who have not only worked wonders of late in improving the amenities and comfort of the building, so far as structural limitations will allow, but have done all that is practicable to minimise the inconvenience caused by the continuous pressure of the expansion of staff against the exigencies of space.

A few years ago, the internal distribution of the staff was reorganised so as to provide self-contained accommodation for the Dominions Office, which now occupies a compact block of rooms on the basement, ground and first floors on the Whitehall front of the building. Above this block lies the large and well-stocked Library, which is shared by both Offices and is open to the public for the purpose of research into Dominion and Colonial questions. Practically everything published with reference to such questions, as well as official reports, etc., is there available for consultation, together with a complete set of the Colonial and Dominion laws. The remainder of the building houses the Colonial Office, with the exception of those portions of the staff which, as already explained, are at present accommodated outside.

The usual entrance to the two Offices is by way of a small doorway in Downing Street itself; there is, however, a more imposing entrance from the inner quadrangle, leading to a pillared hall on the ground floor. From this hall a massive spiral staircase leads up as far as the second floor. On the basement, ground and first floors, as stated above, the rooms overlooking Whitehall are occupied by the Dominions Office; thus on these floors the Colonial Office has a comparatively small number of rooms grouped round the spiral staircase. The principal department housed in the basement is the Telegraph Section (which serves both Offices). On the ground floor are the rooms of the Parliamentary Under-Secretary of State and the Chief Medical Adviser, together with the Conference Room.

The first floor contains two admirable rooms, assigned respectively to the Secretary of State and the Permanent Under-Secretary. The Deputy Under-Secretary and certain other administrative officers are on this floor, also the Legal Advisers.

On the second floor, the Colonial Office penetrates deeply into that part of the building normally assigned to the Home Office. In the rooms borrowed from that Department the Tropical African Division is housed. Most of the rooms grouped round the top of the spiral staircase have been incorporated in the Colonial Office Registry, this being the most centrally accessible portion of the building. Here the operations of filing, indexing and despatching correspondence are carried out for the whole Office. The Eastern, West Indian and Economic departments are also accommodated on the second floor. The third floor houses the General department and the Personnel Division.

For some years No. 2, Richmond Terrace, on the other side of Whitehall, accommodated some of those members of the staff for whom there has not been room in the main building, but this house was recently requisitioned for other purposes, and the Appointments Department was moved to No. 8, Buckingham Gate. The Agricultural and Financial Advisers, the staff of the Advisory Committee on Education in the Colonies, the Accounts and Printing departments are housed at Caxton House, Tothill Street.

For the history of the Colonial Office as an institution, the reader must be referred to Sir George Fiddes's standard work on the subject. I propose here to deal only with the more recent developments and with the organisation of the Office as it exists to-day. It is, perhaps, desirable that it should be clearly stated at the outset that, while it is common and indeed inevitable that the Colonial Office should be spoken of as if it were a corporation, the Office, strictly speaking, can have no policy and take no action. Every decision, every action, is the Secretary of State's. All despatches to Colonial Governments go over his signature; every letter which issues is written by his direction. Being subject to human limitations, he must of necessity delegate his responsibilities in minor and even in some important matters; but they remain his responsibilities.

I have already, in Chapter v, indicated very briefly the modern trend towards the establishment, alongside the traditional geographical organisation of the Office, of an organisation designed to facilitate the handling of matters which affect the Colonial Empire as a whole. The number, the importance and the complexity of such matters continually increase with the improvement of communications and the growing interdependence of the various component states of the British Empire and of the world. While, then, the Office still requires its Geographical departments, in which the affairs of each Colony are dealt with as a whole by officers who make a special study of its individual circumstances, modern conditions have been found to demand also a series of departments in which particular subjects are treated with reference to the Colonial Empire as a whole. The two organisations are strictly complementary: their existence side by side ensures that neither shall a policy be adopted in regard to one Colony which would be inconsistent with, or even injurious to that adopted for the Colonies generally; nor shall general policies or rulings be laid down without regard to the individual differences and varying circumstances of the several Colonies in which they are to be applied. Close co-operation between the geographical and the general sides of the Office is, therefore, an essential feature of the everyday conduct of business.

The head of the Office staff is the Permanent Under-Secretary of State. He is assisted by a Deputy Under-Secretary and three Assistant Under-Secretaries. The first-mentioned and one of the Assistant Under-Secretaries divide between them the supervision of the General Division and the non-African Geographical departments; the other two Assistant Under-Secretaries preside respectively over the Tropical African Division, and the Personnel Division.

The Geographical departments are at present seven in number, and each is under an officer with the Civil Service rank of Assistant Secretary. This title is more appropriate in Offices such as the Treasury or the Ministry of Health, where the permanent head is styled Secretary, than in one in which there are Under-Secretaries of State; it is important not to confuse the Assistant Secretary, who is the head of a department, with the Assistant Under-Secretary of State, who is his official superior.

Under the Assistant Secretary, the Colonial Office department normally consists of two or three officers with the rank of Principal, and one or two Assistant Principals. The place of some of the Assistant Principals is taken by officers of the Colonial Administrative Service temporarily attached to the Office for the purpose of acquiring experience of the "home front".

Each Geographical department is responsible for the business of a group of Colonies. While the basis of grouping is mainly regional, considerations of the volume of work connected with particular Colonies, or of similarity of problems affecting Colonies not geographically contiguous, have to be taken into account, and, where necessary, practical convenience takes precedence over purely geographical considerations. For example, the East African Dependencies, though presenting many common problems, are too large a group to be satisfactorily handled in a single department, and two departments are allocated to them: one deals with Kenya, Uganda and Zanzibar, and the other with the remaining Dependencies, that is to say, Tanganyika Territory, Northern Rhodesia, Nyasaland and Somaliland. One department, however, suffices for the four West African Colonies and St Helena. These three departments constitute the Tropical African Division.

On the non-African side, the Eastern department deals with Ceylon, Malaya, Hong Kong and Aden; the West Indian department with British Guiana, British Honduras, Bermuda and Bahamas, as well as with the West Indian islands properly so described; the Middle East department with Palestine and Trans-Jordan; and the Pacific and Mediterranean department with the Dependencies implied in its name, together with Mauritius, Seychelles, and the Falkland Islands.

While, apart from differences of detail, the organisation of the Geographical departments has not changed greatly since the end of the War, remarkable developments have taken place on the general side of the Office during the past decade. Up to 1928, the General department, as previously mentioned, was a single department about equivalent in strength to one of the Geographical departments. It dealt with the internal establishment of the Office, with promotions and transfers in the Colonial Services, and with a certain amount of largely formal business concerning the Colonies as a whole, such as the interpretation of Colonial Regulations, the administration of postal and copyright conventions, uniforms, flags and so forth. It was only to a very limited extent an organisation for the formation or execution of general policy. The reorganisation of 1928, referred to in Chapter v, resulted in the division of the one department into two, roughly but not exactly on the basis of one department to deal with "subject" questions and one to deal with "personnel" matters. In 1930, as we have seen, a further step was taken by the creation of the Personnel Division, in which that side of the General department which was concerned with questions relating to personnel in the Colonial Service and in the Office itself was absorbed. The General department continued to function, and to develop its activities, in the sphere of "subjects", until the work outgrew the capacity of a single department, and it was necessary once more to subdivide, this time by setting up a separate Economic department.

At the present moment, then, the General Division consists of two departments. The original General department continues to deal with matters not primarily of an economic character, such as defence, international relations, mandates, labour, education, public health, postal affairs, aviation, broadcasting, currency, etc. The Economic department, as its name implies, is concerned with the development and marketing of Colonial products, the study of world trade with particular reference to the commodities produced by the Colonial Empire, and questions arising out of international and inter-Imperial trade treaties and agreements.

This development has been accompanied by a considerable increase in the employment of qualified professional Advisers to assist the Secretary of State and his Office in dealing with the many technical matters which arise from day to day under modern conditions. The day is long past when each Colony can be expected to rely on its local resources, and when general matters can be left to *ad hoc* or periodically meeting Committees. These still have their place, but it is now well established that there is need in many directions for the continuous presence at headquarters of professional officers whose attention is constantly focused upon the requirements of the Colonial Empire, and whose experience is always at the disposal of the Office or of any Colonial Government which may have occasion to consult them.

The post of Legal Adviser goes back to 1867. The present legal advisory staff consists of four officers, whose services are at the disposal of both the Colonial and the Dominions Offices. On the Colonial side, their duties are to advise the Secretary of State on the legal aspects of any matters referred to them, to examine Colonial legislation submitted for the Royal Assent, to draft Orders in Council and other legal and constitutional instruments. They also maintain close touch with the members of the Colonial Legal Service, many of whom come into the Office to work in association with the Legal Advisers for the purpose of gaining experience. The Legal Adviser himself has, during the last few years, visited the East and West African Colonies to study and report upon the judicial arrangements.

The appointment of Chief Medical Adviser dates from 1926, when it was decided that such an officer was required to advise the Secretary of State on medical and public health matters in the Colonial Empire. The functions of the Chief Medical Adviser have been remarked upon in Chapter XII.

An Advisory Committee on Native Education in Tropical Africa was set up in 1923, with a distinguished ex-Colonial Director of Education as Secretary, whose functions were virtually those of an Adviser. In 1928 the scope of the Committee was extended to cover all educational problems in the Colonial Empire, and a Joint Secretary was provided. Thus there are, in effect, two whole-time Educational Advisers at the disposal of the Office.

The Agricultural Adviser was appointed in 1929, and an Assistant Adviser in 1936. A Veterinary Adviser was appointed in 1930, but the appointment was not renewed after the death of the officer in question in 1932.

The Financial Adviser, whose appointment in its present form dates from 1930, advises the Secretary of State on major questions of financial and economic policy, and on such matters as the international schemes for the control of rubber and tin production, in which certain Dependencies are closely concerned.

Advice on technical financial and accounting questions is given by another officer called the Officer of Colonial Accounts, who is attached to the General department.

While these Advisers are at the service of all departments of the Office, they must be regarded as essentially part of the general side. In the sphere of policy their normal contact with the Office is through the General or Economic departments, while in matters affecting the personnel of the technical Services they are in close touch with the Personnel Division. We must now proceed to discuss the organisation of that Division in somewhat more detail than the other parts of the Office, inasmuch as it is the part most intimately concerned with the Colonial Service.

The Personnel Division, which, as has already been noted, is presided over by an Assistant Under-Secretary of State, is made up of two departments. One of these, the Appointments department, is concerned with all questions of recruitment and training; the other, known as the Colonial Service department, deals with all matters relating to conditions of employment of officers in the Service, as well as with the internal economy of the Colonial Office.

The Assistant Secretary in charge of the Appointments department has the title of Director of Recruitment (Colonial Service). The department is a fairly large one, consisting of four Principals, three Assistant Principals and a clerical staff, with a self-contained Registry. The main business of the department is, naturally, to provide recruits for the various branches of the Colonial Service, the vacancies available and the terms attaching thereto being notified to the department by the different Geographical departments as occasion arises, on the basis of requisitions received from the Colonial Governments. Many kinds of vacancies, for example those in the Administrative, Agricultural, Police and Forest Services, are filled by selections held at stated times of the year, usually in the summer; others, in which recruitment is less regular, are dealt with *ad hoc*, as they occur. While, therefore, the work of the department is continuous, it is apt to be especially heavy during the months preceding the principal selections.

The department issues a series of booklets for the information of candidates, containing particulars of the various branches of the Service with which it deals. There is one booklet on Colonial appointments in general, and separate booklets on the following heads:

The Colonial Administrative Service; with particulars of financial appointments, and an introductory section regarding educational appointments.

The Colonial Medical Service.

The Colonial Agricultural, Veterinary and Forest Services; with particulars of other appointments of a biological nature, and of appointments for Analytical Chemists.

The Colonial Legal Service.

Survey, Meteorological, Geological and Mining appointments.

Police and Customs appointments.

These booklets contain the fullest possible information with regard to their respective subjects, and are issued to any enquirer who may ask for them; they are also circulated to universities, schools and other likely sources of candidates. The department maintains a close relation with the various University Appointments Boards.

The booklets also include full instructions as to the method of making application for appointment. Applications must be submitted on the proper forms, which are supplied on request, and must be addressed to the Director of Recruitment. In the case of candidates who are *prima facie* qualified for the posts for which they have applied, the Director and his staff proceed to take up references, to make enquiries, usually to interview the candidate, and so eventually to collect the material necessary for enabling the Colonial Service Appointments Board to select from the available field the candidate or candidates who in their opinion will most satisfactorily meet the requirements of the appointment under consideration.

The Colonial Service Appointments Board was constituted as a result of the recommendation of the Warren Fisher Committee to which reference was made in Chapter v. In accordance with that recommendation, the Board consists of the Civil Service Commissioners and certain other experienced persons, the First Commissioner being Chairman. The members of the Board are appointed by the Secretary of State, on the nomination of the Civil Service Commissioners. The Board is, therefore, independent of the Colonial Office. The Board considers the material collected for it by the Appointments department of the Office, and decides at its discretion whether to interview any or all of the candidates for a vacancy. The final selection is made by the Board, and submitted to the Secretary of State for his personal approval. Unless the selection is subject to attendance at a training course, the candidate then ceases to be a concern of the Appointments department, and his affairs are subsequently dealt with by the Colonial Service department.

The Appointments department, however, deals not only with the recruitment of candidates but with their training; and since it is evidently convenient that one department of the Office should handle matters relating to courses of instruction of all kinds, this department is in charge of work connected with courses attended by serving officers as well as with that connected more specifically with courses attended by officers prior to taking up their posts. This arrangement is convenient, too, from the point of view of the universities and training institutions, as it means that they deal with the same officials at the Colonial Office over all questions relating to courses.

The chief standing courses are those attended by the Administrative probationers, the Agricultural and Veterinary Scholars, Educational and Medical officers. The department is in charge of all these, and of a variety of other courses in languages, forestry, medicine, anthropology, police work, prisons administration and many other subjects.

The Colonial Service department has a wide commission, ranging over the whole field of the Service. It deals not only with general questions relating to conditions of employment, but with the matters that arise in connection with individual officers. It works, of course, in close co-operation with the Geographical departments. On the general side, it is this department which has been responsible for framing, subject to the direction of higher authority, and for putting into practice, the schemes of unification which have been described. It has also been responsible for working out the possibilities of establishing a standard of conditions of service, and for collecting the material on which the reports of the various Committees, such as the Plymouth and Watson Committees,[1] have been based. In the past, when the idea of a single Service was not recognised, questions relating to conditions of employment, as well as individual cases, were dealt with in respect of each Colony by the Geographical department concerned. Now it is the practice for the Geographical department to consult with the Colonial Service department, so that both the general Service aspect of the matter in hand and the local circumstances, in the light of which the general practice must be applied, are properly taken into account.

One main function, then, of the Colonial Service department is to advise on matters such as salary scales, pensions, leave and passage regulations and discipline, supplying information as to the general rulings and practice in force, drawing up model regulations, and enabling experience gained in connection with one Colony, or one particular case, to be used in connection with similar circumstances that may arise elsewhere. Another important function of the department relates to questions of promotion and transfer. It will be remembered that the Warren Fisher Committee urged that special attention should be paid to this aspect of the work of the Colonial Office; that promotions and transfers should be planned with the definite object of

[1] See Chapter VII.

making the best possible use of the available material; that the arrangements for noting the qualifications of officers and for bringing them up for consideration should be improved, and that a special staff should be employed on this work. It rests with the Promotions Branch of the Colonial Service department to carry out these recommendations. Careful arrangements are made for noting and indexing the officers of the various branches of the Service according to their qualifications and other relevant factors, and as each vacancy occurs, lists are prepared and the necessary material supplied to enable the Secretary of State to make his selection of the most suitable candidate. The actual recommendation to the Secretary of State is put forward, after such discussion and consideration as may be called for, by a Promotions Committee, consisting of the Permanent Under-Secretary and the Assistant Under-Secretaries, together with the Advisers and such other officers as may be summoned in an advisory capacity. In order to make the available information as full as possible, the officers of the Colonial Service department who are engaged on this work make a point of interviewing Colonial Service officers on leave, ana discussing with them their individual wishes with regard to the work they prefer and the Colonies in which they like to serve. Every effort is made to ensure that the officers of the Colonial Service are not merely names to the Colonial Office, and to give them the assurance that, in this instance, "out of sight" does not mean "out of mind".

While much of the work connected with the affairs of Colonial Service officers in this country, such as the issue of pay and pensions and the booking of passages, is performed by the Crown Agents for the Colonies, and not by the Colonial Office, the latter is responsible for dealing with any question which may arise outside the scope of the ordinary regulations, and for such matters as the arrangement of medical examinations or extensions of leave. The day-to-day work which has to be done on the cases of individual officers is in the hands of a special clerical staff attached to the Colonial Service department and operating under its supervision.

The head of the department is also Establishment Officer for both the Colonial Office and the Dominions Office, the staffs of which are interchangeable up to and including the rank of Assistant Secretary. In this capacity he is responsible to the Permanent Under-Secretaries for all matters relating to the staffing of the two Offices.

Great importance is attached to the maintenance of personal liaison between the Colonial Office staff and the personnel of the Colonial Service. Colonial officers on leave are encouraged to call at the Office, and to make acquaintance with the members of the Geographical departments dealing with their respective Colonies, as well as with the Colonial Service department. Senior officers are invited to call and discuss problems which are often handled more satisfactorily in this way than by correspondence. The system of interchange of officers provides another important link. All administrative officers joining the Colonial Office are under a liability to serve abroad for one or more periods, as the Secretary of State may direct; and a regular system has been evolved by which such officers, after three or four years' service as Assistant Principals, go out to one of the Colonies for about two years, and take up the ordinary duties of an officer of the Colonial Administrative Service. The Colonial Governments to which they are attached make a point of giving them the widest possible range of experience, not only at headquarters but in the districts; and the officer thus gains a practical knowledge of conditions in at any rate one Colony, and in addition makes for himself a valuable series of personal contacts in the Colonial Service. There is also in operation a converse arrangement, whereby selected officers of the Colonial Administrative Service are attached to the Office for two years at a time and work as Principals or as Assistant Principals. In addition to these regular arrangements, many occasional visits are paid by members of the Office staff to particular Colonies for special purposes. By all these means close and constant contact is preserved between the staff at home and the "men on the spot", and both parties work together, if not formally as members of one Service, at least as collaborators in a common cause.

The question of interchange between the Colonial Office staff at home and the Colonial Service abroad is one which has been kept constantly in view for many years. While suggestions that both should be amalgamated into a single Service have not found acceptance, it has long been a recognised principle that the interchange, in suitable cases, of individual officers is in the public interest. Thus, apart from the systematic exchanges for instructional purposes, referred to in the preceding paragraph, there have been several instances of transfer of individuals to substantive appointments in either direction. Sir Reginald Edward Stubbs went out from the Colonial Office in 1913 to become Colonial Secretary of Ceylon, and subsequently served as Governor of Hong Kong, Jamaica, Cyprus and Ceylon. More recently, Colonial Office Principals have been appointed to the Chief Secretaryship of Palestine, the Secretaryship of the East African Governors' Conference, and the Financial Secretaryship of Hong Kong. Conversely, Sir Samuel Wilson came from the Governorship of Jamaica to be Permanent Under-Secretary of State in 1925; and he would have been succeeded on his retirement by another Colonial Governor, Sir Graeme Thomson, but for that officer's untimely death. Sir George Tomlinson, the first head of the Personnel Division, had spent his previous official career in the Colonial Service in Nigeria; while in 1937 another of the Assistant Under-Secretaryships was filled by the then Governor of Sierra Leone, Sir Henry Moore. It may fairly be assumed that the policy of promoting interchanges of these kinds will continue and will develop, to the unquestionable advantage of both the Colonial Office and the Colonial Empire.

<h2>THE CROWN AGENTS FOR THE COLONIES</h2>

A note on the Crown Agents for the Colonies may conveniently be appended to this chapter. Up to 1833, it was the practice for each Colony to appoint its own London agent, but in that year the agencies were consolidated, except for those connected with some of the West Indian Governments, which, however, in due course joined with the rest. The Crown Agents are, as their name implies, the Agents in London of the Governments of the various Dependencies for the administration of which the Secretary of State for the Colonies is responsible. The Crown Agents themselves, at present three in number, are appointed by the Secretary of State, who fixes their salaries and pensions and lays down the conditions upon which their staff is employed. While the Crown Agents receive instructions directly from the Governments which they represent, they are subject to the general supervision of the Secretary of State.

The Crown Agents' office is at No. 4, Millbank, London, S.W. 1. The Crown Agents are financially self-supporting, the cost of maintaining the office and its activities being met by commissions and fees paid by the Colonial Governments for the work done. The staff, apart from technical officers, is mainly recruited from the ordinary Home Civil Service examinations (executive and clerical), and is employed on conditions analogous to those applicable to civil servants.

The Crown Agents perform many functions, amongst which the following may be mentioned:

(i) Purchase, shipment and inspection of stores of all kinds which the Colonial Governments may require to obtain from this country. By purchasing in bulk on behalf of so many administrations, whose collective requirements are very considerable, the Crown Agents are naturally in a position to secure the best possible terms.

(ii) Preparation of designs for bridges, buildings and other engineering works, and for locomotives, cranes and the like; the negotiation of contracts for large public works, and the provision of technical advice with regard to such matters, with the assistance of consulting engineers when necessary.

(iii) Issue and management of Government loans, and the investment of Government moneys.

(iv) Payment of salaries and pensions to officers in this country, and of widows' pensions.

(v) Booking of passages for officers.

(vi) Selection and engagement of certain classes of staff, mainly technical.

It will be seen that the Crown Agents hold a very important and responsible position in the economy of the Colonial Empire. At the same time it should be understood that they are strictly the commercial and financial agents of the *Governments*. It is no part of their duties, for example, to push the sale of Colonial products, or to advise intending settlers or investors. These functions are performed in respect of certain Colonies, but by separate agencies set up for the purpose, and not necessarily of an entirely official character. Thus there is a Malayan Information Agency, an East African Dependencies Trade and Information Office, etc., the functions of which are quite distinct from those of the Crown Agents. The West India Committee carries out a somewhat similar function in connection with the West Indies. There has also very recently been set up an official organisation known as the Colonial Empire Marketing Board, which deals on a wide scale with the task of promoting the successful marketing in this country of the many and varied foodstuffs, raw materials and other commodities produced in the Colonial Empire.

CHAPTER XVIII

RETROSPECT AND PROSPECT

IN this study we have seen the growth of the Colonial Service from small beginnings to its present position as one of the largest and most important of the British public services, and its development from a series of isolated components to a corporate body with a considerable amount of homogeneity. We have seen that it is still in a state of transition, but that the transition is taking place upon orderly lines and towards a fairly well-defined objective. It is quite in accordance with modern ideas that the doctrine of *laissez-faire* should have given place to the doctrine of planning; the latter is not without its dangers, but it may perhaps be reasonably claimed that in this instance there is no question of the new doctrine being pushed too far. The change of policy which took place in 1930 was revolutionary; but the change affected a strictly limited portion of the Service, and it has been put into force cautiously and gradually, and with due regard to the necessity for conciliating informed public opinion in the Colonies concerned.

If it be true that the ultimate object of British Colonial policy is the development of the various communities of the Colonial Empire into self-supporting and self-reliant partners of the British Commonwealth of Nations, each preserving all that is best in its individual culture and tradition, then it must be conceded that ultimately each shall provide and organise its own public service, allowing full scope to its own inhabitants to serve their own country and the Empire according to their abilities. The simple theory underlying the mechanism of the Services as they existed up to the beginning of the present century was that, in anticipation of this eventual development, the public service of each unit should be kept distinct and separate. No differentiation in terms of employment was as a rule made between staff recruited locally and any who might be recruited from outside. The terms in force were those which suited the circumstances of the Colony. If it was necessary to supplement the local resources by recruitment from overseas, the officers so recruited became part of the local service, and had no status otherwise than as members of that service.

This theory outlived the possibility of its continued application in practice. Fifty years ago the Colonial Empire (if we exclude what are now the Dominions) was a comparatively small affair, considered from the point of view of public service organisation. The Colonial administrations were on a small scale, they were well established, their local resources were sufficiently developed to meet most of their staff requirements, and their recruiting needs were not great. The conception of local and separate public services was consonant with public opinion, and suited the facts of the case as they then presented themselves to all not endowed with the prescience of a Chamberlain. Very different were the new administrations which were coming into being during the years between 1900 and the outbreak of the Great War. Not only were they on a much larger scale than all but a few of the older Colonies, but they had very little indeed in the way of local material upon which to draw. It was natural that the conception of Colonial organisation which had established itself in connection with the older Colonies should be applied to the new; it was also natural, in the circumstances, that it should be found inadequate. And this inadequacy affected the older Colonies, though to a less extent, as well as the newer Dependencies, since the former also experienced a growing need, in a more complex and more highly organised world, for administrative and professional staffs of similar type to those being recruited for the new Services.

Although the theory of separate Colonial Services was not officially modified until 1930, it had in practice to a large extent broken down long before then. A serious inroad upon it was made by the creation of the West African Medical Staff and the East African Medical Service; but more general and significant were the effects of the policy of inter-Colonial transfer and of admitting officers in any Colony as candidates for promotion in others. The result of this policy was to set up a Colonial Service in all but name, and in these circumstances the local diversities of conditions and of practice, while strictly consistent with the accepted theory, were not only inconsistent with the policy but positively inimical to it. The position as the Warren Fisher Committee found it was one in which the conception of separate services no longer fitted the facts, and yet the advantages of co-operation could not be properly exploited. It was the contribution of that Committee to point the way towards the more subtle and yet more accurate conception which the facts of the case and the needs of the Colonial Empire demanded.

If the proposition put forward at the beginning of this chapter be correct, that the ultimate objective must needs be the development in each Dependency of a fully efficient local public service, it follows that there can be no question of successfully adopting any scheme of unification which would lead away from that objective. The problem which up to 1930 evaded solution was to devise and to secure acceptance of some scheme that, without depriving the individual service of each Colony of its characteristic of being, as Mr L. S. Amery has expressed it, "autochthonous, racy of the soil", would combine with the advantages of that characteristic the equally significant advantages of Imperial co-operation for the general good. It would have been easy enough to produce a paper plan for creating a unified Colonial Service controlled from Downing Street; but such a plan would have been foredoomed to failure as being out of harmony with the general spirit and atmosphere of the Colonial Empire.

It seemed at one time as if a solution might be found in the creation of regional Services, as, for example, in Tropical Africa. At first sight such a solution might have been thought to have much to commend it, but the view taken by the responsible authorities was that in fact it would have been a retrograde step. As we have seen, the Colonial Services, though nominally separate, possessed in practice many of the characteristics of a single Imperial Service. Had they been formally broken up into regional groups, those characteristics would have been finally lost, and no regional group could have claimed the prestige which had accrued to the Services collectively. Moreover, a regional Service tends to become a closed Service, and the advantage of selection for the higher appointments from the widest possible field would have had to be sacrificed to the necessity for giving to officers serving in a region prior consideration for promotion within that region. Finally, geographical grouping does not necessarily correspond to community of interests or of circumstances, and there would inevitably have been cases in which Colonies would have had to be left in isolation, or associated with others with which they had little in common save the accident of propinquity.

The principles laid down by the Warren Fisher Committee, which have formed the basis of all subsequent developments, were threefold. In the first place, the existence of a single Imperial Colonial Service was to be recognised. Secondly, "within this larger whole", unified branch Services were to be organised on a professional, not a regional, system of grouping. Thirdly, these unified branches were to comprise the grades normally recruited from outside the Colonies themselves. These simple and rational propositions provided the resolution of the difficulties which the anomalies of the situation had presented. The first enabled all the advantages in prestige and *esprit de corps* of an Empire-wide Service to be realised. All officers could henceforth claim membership of the Colonial Service in addition to and without detraction from their membership of the Service of the Colony in which they were employed. The second article adumbrated the formation of a series of professional corps, the members of which, while sharing in the common loyalty to the Service as a whole and to the Colony of their employment, would also severally be linked to their professional colleagues engaged in similar work throughout the Colonial Empire. Finally, the restriction of practical measures of unification to personnel normally recruited from overseas left room for the fullest possible scope to be allowed to each Colony to develop its public service in the way best suited to the local conditions. Only so long as, and in so far as it should be necessary for a

Colony to import officers to supplement its local resources would that Colony be called upon to take into account conditions external to itself in arranging the terms on which that service should be employed. On the other hand, so long as, and in so far as a Colony should have to recruit from outside, it would be able to take advantage of the professional prestige enjoyed by the Service as a whole, provided always that it was prepared to offer the terms which experience should have shown to be required to attract and retain personnel of the stipulated qualifications.

The change effected in 1930 was not, then, one of merely nominal or sentimental importance. It was essentially practical. The picture of the Colonial Services before 1930 is one of a number of separate public services, some large and some very small, not associated with each other in any way, except for the fact that the administrations which they served were all dealt with by the Colonial Office; with marked and increasing divergencies in the conditions of employment, some arising out of differences in local circumstances but some merely fortuitous; officially precluded even from regarding themselves as a Colonial Service. The picture which we have endeavoured to present in the second part of this book is that of a Colonial Service which includes and transcends these local services without affecting their local flavour, and whose members, while remaining officers of the Colony in which they are employed, can also claim partnership in a great Imperial Service.

In a broad sense, then, unification affected the whole range of the former Colonial Services. The formal creation of professional branches, however, has so far covered only a limited field, and while the process is not fully complete, enough has been done to enable the limits of the scheme to be fairly closely envisaged. We may assume that the formation of unified branches on the lines of those already in existence will proceed until every section of the Service which is capable of being dealt with in this way has been covered. We may also assume that, if there should remain a residue of posts which on account of their small number or special character cannot be formed into unified branches, but whose holders nevertheless ought to serve on the same conditions and to occupy the same status as the members of the unified branches, means will be devised for securing this object. In these directions we may look to see a development of the practical side of the unification policy. But, as has already been emphasised, the development of the unified branches is complementary and not in opposition to the development of local services manned as far as may be possible from local resources. The object of creating a unified branch is simply to secure to each Colony the best possible chance of obtaining the best men by offering a career wider in its scope than any single Colony can offer. This implies two things: interchangeability of personnel amongst the participating Colonies, and a reasonable assimilation of the terms of employment in order that interchange may be facilitated. Again, interchangeability of personnel implies preparedness on the part of each Colony to accept officers from elsewhere for any post included in the scheme. Thus, as soon as it becomes normal in any particular Colony to fill any particular class of appointment by local recruitment, the advantage of retaining that class of post in a unified branch comes into question so far as that Colony is concerned. The system must therefore be an elastic one; and the plan which has been devised is, as we have seen, to constitute each unified branch on the basis of a schedule of offices, which, it is provided, shall normally be filled by members of the branch. If the published schedules be examined, it will be observed that they by no means cover all the appointments in the Colonies which are held by persons of the professions concerned. For example, although Ceylon has a large and important medical department, only two posts, those of Director of Medical and Sanitary Services and Director of the Bacteriological Institute, are included in the schedule of the Colonial Medical Service. The reason is that the other medical posts in the Island are not normally filled from outside but from the excellent field of recruitment afforded by the local population. There is no question of debarring officers of the Colonial Medical Service from appointments in Ceylon, should an appointment from outside be desired; nor is there any question of Ceylonese officers being debarred from appointment to scheduled posts, as is shown by the recent promotion of a Ceylonese officer to the scheduled office of Director of Medical and Sanitary Services. The point is simply that the majority of the posts are normally filled by locally recruited staff, who may be presumed not in general to wish for employment outside their own country and whose terms of service are naturally and properly related to local conditions rather than to the recruiting and other factors which must necessarily influence the terms to be attached to posts normally filled from outside the Colony.

In describing the conditions of employment, I have been obliged to confine myself almost entirely to those of officers of the unified branches and of corresponding status, that is to say, officers for the most part recruited from this country. It would scarcely have been practicable, within any reasonable limits, to give particulars of the conditions applying to all classes of officers in the Service. As I observed in the Introduction, the Service numbers some 200,000 members; of these perhaps about 7,000 are included in the unified or quasi-unified class, the remainder being locally recruited staff of all grades and descriptions. A few years ago, the task of describing the conditions under which even the 7,000 were employed would have been a very difficult one, owing to the differences not only in detail but in major matters between one Dependency and another; but, as I have shown, since the unification policy was introduced, considerable progress has been made in formulating general principles which could be taken as the basis for local rules devised to suit the requirements of different places. In his speech at the Colonial Service dinner of 1936, Mr Ormsby Gore pointed out that unification does not mean uniformity; but it does imply a common standard on which to work, and this was almost entirely lacking until comparatively recently. As a result of the investigations carried out by the Personnel Division of the Colonial Office, and by expert bodies such as the Plymouth Committee on Leave and Passage Conditions, such a standard has been established in regard to many of the more important aspects of the conditions of service, and, what is more, a good deal of progress has been made in assimilating the actual conditions to the standard when once established. There is no question of forcing all the Colonies into a common mould, and many diversities must remain. There has, however, been much elimination of those diversities which were without meaning or purpose but had arisen merely in consequence of the lack of an established standard; and the task of giving a reasonably clear and concise picture of the general conditions of employment in the Colonial Service has been immeasurably simplified, whether or not in the present instance it has been adequately performed.

Such a treatment of the subject as has been attempted in this book is not without its pitfalls. Every member of the Colonial Service is not only, or indeed primarily, a member of that organisation. He is also and in the first instance a member of the public service of one Dependency or another. Even of what may be called the interchangeable part of the Service the majority spend their whole official careers in a single Dependency, and only a very few serve in more than two or three. It would be misleading if the prominence given in this book to the development of the policy of unification were to suggest that unification is a factor of prime importance to the individual officer, whether he belongs to one of the specifically unified branches or not. For each officer it is his own job in his own Colony which claims his first interest and his principal loyalty. His membership of the general Service remains for the most part in the background, and it must depend upon circumstances whether in his particular case it brings any tangible result. But it is always there, offering the chance of new opportunities and the certainty of impartial and sympathetic supervision by the Secretary of State.

Whatever developments may take place, it may be confidently asserted that for very many years to come the Colonial Dependencies, individually to varying degrees, but collectively on a considerable scale, will need the services of the best material the Mother Country can supply in the administrative, educational and various professional fields. Nothing but the best is good enough; in many cases it is questionable whether the second-rate is worth employing at all. By "best" we must not, of course, be understood to signify an inhuman standard of perfection; but we must at least postulate the qualifications laid down by the Warren Fisher Committee, namely: "a liberal education, a just and flexible mind, common sense, and a high character." All these are needed in the professional and technical branches no less than in the administrative branch of which the Committee was particularly speaking in the passage quoted. In addition, the professional officer or the technician must possess the highest possible qualifications in his subject, and the power of adapting his knowledge to conditions which may be very different from those in which he was trained, and of imparting it to others.

The Colonial Service does not, then, offer an opening to those whose prospects of success in other walks of life would be problematical; it boldly seeks to attract some at least of the leaders of the younger generation in Britain and the Dominions to join in the task of administering and developing the dependent Empire as a trust held on behalf of the communities which comprise that Empire and of civilisation in general. Although the work of the Service by no means lies exclusively amongst native peoples, it does so to so large an extent that anyone who is not in sympathy with the aspirations of our non-European fellow-subjects could hardly be advised to adopt it as a career. Nor is the Service likely to appeal to the lover of comfort or the seeker after high financial prizes. But to those who combine intellectual ability with the spirit of adventure, and who hold the faith that there is something in our British civilisation which is worthy of being passed on to others for whose welfare and progress we have become responsible, the Colonial Service offers a career rich in opportunity.

While, as has been shown, a university education, or the equivalent, is necessarily stipulated as a qualification for most of the appointments filled from this country, there are not wanting chances of useful work for those who have not had the benefit of such an education. The Colonial Service is, however, by its nature prevented from offering very many openings to youths at the age of leaving school. Most of its appointments are in the tropics, and medical opinion is against the employment of Europeans in any but the more favoured tropical regions before they reach the age of 21 or so. Thus, in most cases a gap of some three years must intervene between the leaving of school and candidature for the Service; and in the ordinary course this gap will preferably have been spent in the acquisition, at a university or elsewhere, of additional qualifications for appointment to the Service.

Enough has been said in this book to indicate that there are few lines of study which may not fittingly lead up to a career in one branch or another of the Colonial Service. A certain distinction may perhaps be drawn between those which result in the acquisition of a definite professional qualification and those which do not. The student of medicine, or veterinary science, or chemistry, or engineering, or of the law, will in due course become a member of a profession, in which the Colonial Service is only one of many openings. He may or may not have taken up the profession with the possibility of appointment to the Service in mind; one of the objects of creating the unified Services is to enable that possibility to be implanted in the thoughts of suitable candidates at a comparatively early stage, in the hope that some, at least, will be prepared to work with the aim of joining the Service instead of considering it as an afterthought. The general science student is in a rather different position; he reaches a stage at which he must decide on a particular line of specialisation if he is to turn his knowledge into a marketable commodity. The Colonial Service offers him a wide choice. If his bent is in the direction of biology, the agricultural, veterinary and forestry scholarship schemes are provided to assist him in obtaining the necessary post-graduate experience; the survey, geological and educational services afford openings for the student of the physical sciences. Finally, the Arts course at a university may equip a candidate not only for the Administrative Service but for other branches such as the Colonial Audit department and various educational posts. The Colonial Office is, as we have said, anxious to interest potential candidates at an early stage, and to encourage them to study with appointment to the Service in view. But it is always careful to emphasise that the student should follow the line which best suits him, and which will be of most value to him if he should not be successful in securing an appointment. There is no special line to which preference is given, and no need for anyone to feel that he has wasted his time on unprofitable studies which he is obliged to undertake in order to be accepted as a candidate.

I have been careful not to burden these pages with statistics, but it seems necessary to give some idea of the scale of the demands made for staff for the Colonial Service. It is not altogether easy to do so, as the demands are apt to fluctuate over a rather wide range from year to year. This is not surprising, when one considers the number of different administrations concerned; the fact that vacancies often have to be forecast a year in advance, to allow for the attendance of the selected candidates at the probationers' courses; and the innumerable changes and chances which may upset the estimate after it has been made. In spite of these difficulties every effort is made to keep recruitment for the various branches as stable as is practicable, for it is undoubtedly true that a steady and regular recurrence of vacancies is one of the best stimuli to satisfactory recruiting, and that far better results can be secured by maintaining a steady average than by offering a large number of vacancies in one year and a few in the next. At the same time, each Colonial Government must necessarily look at its own requirements, and the system does not admit of anything in the nature of a central pool in which selected candidates would be placed and drawn out as required to fill vacancies. In a few instances, however, expedients have been devised: for instance, there was at one time a West African Medical Staff Reserve, consisting of selected candidates who were paid a retaining fee on condition that they would be prepared to take up duty if called upon to do so within a certain period. Again, in order to maintain forestry recruitment during the recent time of economic difficulty and general retrenchment, an arrangement was arrived at with the co-operation of the Colonial Development Fund Advisory Committee and the Forestry Commission, whereby a number of forestry probationers for whom no immediate vacancies could be foreseen were selected each year and promised employment for a limited time with the Forestry Commission in the event of its not being possible to offer them appointments in the Colonial Forest Service at the end of their probationary course. In actual fact, all the officers so far selected under this scheme were absorbed in vacancies which matured after their selection. The agricultural and veterinary scholarships have also been of considerable value in this connection, since a regular number can be awarded each year without the necessity of guaranteeing that a corresponding number of vacancies will mature at the exact moment at which the selected candidates become available.

I give in an appendix[1] the official figures of the actual appointments made by the Secretary of State to the main branches of the Service in the years 1920–36. It will be seen that recruitment has been subject to well-marked fluctuations during the post-War period. After the heavy demands for staff to fill the gaps made by the War had been met, there was a natural falling off for a year or two; but, from 1924 to 1930 inclusive, recruitment was substantial and fairly steady. The economic depression of 1931 onwards is reflected in the diminished recruitment in that and the next three years, but 1935 and 1936 show a return to what may reasonably be regarded as normal conditions. Thus, in the ordinary course, the Colonial Service may be expected every year to call for from 300 to 500 recruits of a high standard both of academic qualification and of personality.

This is no light demand, but hitherto it has been met, not, it is true, without effort, but with a success of which the Service to-day is the living testimony. Britain has not failed to supply the need of the peoples for whose welfare and government she has made herself responsible, and she will not fail. We have seen throughout the story the evidence of a double care on the part of the responsible authorities both at home and in the Colonies themselves: first, a care that the Colonies should have the men

[1] Pp. 248–9.

and women they need; secondly a care that the men and women who answer the call should serve under conditions of reasonable comfort and security.

I have said "men and women", for these pages have shown that the Colonial Service needs women as well as men for the complete fulfilment of its work. It is true that in existing circumstances the employment of women—that is to say, of women recruited from home—is limited to certain particular branches of the Service. While, for example, there are unquestionably some administrative posts which a woman could fill with success, it will have been clear from the description of the Colonial Administrative Service that that Service, taken as a whole, is not one in which a woman could be expected to perform the ordinary duties effectually, or to be available for free interchange with other officers. Room, no doubt, there will always be for the exceptional case, but the very fact that the name of Gertrude Bell, for instance, is exceptional in the history of British administration merely proves the rule. Genius will always make its way, but for everyday purposes we must deal with the average rather than the exception.

At the other end of the scale, there is little or no opportunity for the employment of women recruited from overseas in clerical or secretarial capacities, since work of this kind is now almost invariably carried out by officers, whether men or women, recruited locally. But, leaving aside the administrative and quasi-administrative Services, there remains in medicine, in education and in nursing, work of incalculable importance which not only can be done by women, but cannot be done so well, if at all, by men. As we have so often had occasion to observe in the course of this study, the ultimate future of the Colonial communities lies less with the administrator, however efficient and well disposed, than with those communities themselves. Lord Lugard was never tired of quoting to his staff in Nigeria the dictum that "good government is not a substitute for self-government". In the future development of the Colonies the women of the Colonies will have an essential part to play; the work of the schoolmistress, the lady doctor and the health visitor in preparing them for that part is not less important than the work of the administrator in creating the conditions in which development can take place. Moreover, it should not be assumed that the Government Service is the only or even necessarily the best channel by which the civilising and educative influence of women can be brought to bear on those communities whose development has not yet progressed far. The work of women attached to missions and other organisations, and the social service undertaken by many officials' wives is perhaps not the less valuable and influential for not being directly associated with the Government.

I am only too conscious that in this brief and inadequate review of the Colonial Service it has been necessary, for the sake of clarity, to simplify and generalise overmuch; to sketch in the picture with bold lines, ignoring half-tones and details. In dealing with the work of the Service I have perforce concentrated on those spheres of administration and those areas of the Colonial Empire in which for the most part are employed those sections of the Service which can most readily be isolated for description. If some historic and important Colonies have received little mention in these pages, it is not that their importance has been overlooked, but rather that this is a study of the Colonial Empire with special reference to the Colonial Service; and although we began by postulating that this term represented the aggregate of the public services of the Dependencies constituting the Colonial Empire, yet it is evident that the main work of the Service, considered as a Service, must lie in those regions in which a full development of local institutions has not as yet been attained. In many parts of the Colonial Empire that development has already been attained, and the public services, while remaining within the general definition of His Majesty's Colonial Service, have acquired special characteristics suitable to the circumstances and the individual genius of the country. An adequate study of them could be undertaken only against a background of the historical, political and economic conditions of the several Dependencies in which they have grown up, and would occupy many volumes.

My less ambitious task has been to set forth some facts regarding the Colonial Service in its Colonial, in the sense of inter-Colonial, aspects; and more especially to illustrate the contribution of personnel which the Mother Country has made and must still make to the advancement of the Colonial peoples. The extent of this contribution, and the need for it, are in inverse ratio to the capacity of those peoples to sustain the machinery of their own government. While, then, it would be entirely incorrect to imagine that the whole Colonial Empire consists of undeveloped or semi-developed communities, or that the work of the Service is concerned wholly with the tutelage and administration of such communities; yet, inasmuch as the description applies to a large proportion of the whole, if we are to generalise it must be on this basis, and we are safe in doing so, as long as we bear in mind the existence of the exceptions. Yet, even when we consider the exceptions, we must take into account the fact that the Service has its contribution to make to the life and welfare of even the most advanced Dependency. No Colonial territory is so placed that it cannot derive benefit from a system which permits of at least the most responsible administrative and technical offices in the public service being filled on occasion by selection from a wider field than that afforded by the resources open to local recruitment. It is true that the field may sometimes with advantage be wider even than the Colonial Service itself, as may be seen from the conspicuous success which in many cases has been achieved by Colonial Governors drawn from the fighting Services or from political life; but in the ordinary course the Colonial Service is the most natural and the most fruitful source upon which to draw. The problems confronting the most and the least developed of the Dependencies have, as we observed in the Introduction, much in common; and it is not only reasonable in theory but it has been proved time and again in practice, that experience gained in one Colony, so far from being a disability, is of great and positive value in assisting the possessor to grapple with the problems of another, even though the external circumstances may differ widely. The qualities of tact, common sense, ability, imagination and leadership, which make a man a successful native administrator, have repeatedly been found to make him no less successful in guiding the destinies of an advanced and politically conscious community. Thus, with all the variety of the conditions in which it has to work, the Colonial Service justifies its title and its integrity.

It is my hope that this book may in some degree help to interpret this great public Service to its members, to those whom it serves, and to readers in our own country, whose culture and whose liberties it is the duty and the privilege of the Colonial Service to carry abroad into the Empire which has been given into our trust.

APPENDICES

✳

APPENDIX I

THE FINANCIAL ORGANISATION OF COLONIAL GOVERNMENTS

[Extracts from Colonial Office Memorandum]

IN a circular despatch of 10 June 1932, the Secretary of State observed that he was impressed with the desirability of each Colonial Government having at its disposal some member of its staff charged with the special duty of advising the Government on all financial questions; he suggested that this duty might appropriately be assigned to the Treasurer, and that definite steps should be taken to stress that officer's functions in this respect, and to give him adequate opportunity for exercising them.

.   .   .   .   .   .

Nevertheless, the experience of the past few years, during which the Colonies have been exposed to the effects of the general depression, has created a strong impression that the machinery in most Colonies for developing a sound, progressive, and consistent policy in the financial and economic sphere is far from being as effective as it should and can be made. It has also drawn urgent attention to the fundamental importance of sound economic and financial policy as an essential basis of good government. In these circumstances, it has been found necessary to give the whole matter further consideration.

The word 'financial' has various connotations, and it is necessary to emphasise that in this discussion it is intended to relate to matters of policy and general control, and not to technical questions of accounting. The essential feature of the organisation now to be described is the inclusion, in the central machinery of the administration, of a financial officer fitted by training and experience to advise upon the whole financial and economic policy of the Government. It will be the business of this officer to indicate the measures necessary to maintain financial and economic policy on proper lines; to point out weaknesses where they exist; and to initiate improvements. He will examine all new proposals, and all matters coming up for decision, in which public funds might be involved, not merely with a view to estimating the expenditure which would be incurred or the revenue which might be expected, but also and more especially with a view to ensuring that the action taken is in conformity with sound financial and economic principles. Inasmuch as personal emoluments form a large part of the expenditure of a Colonial Government, he should be responsible for advising the Government on questions relating to the numbers, pay, and conditions of service of Government employees.

Under this conception the financial officer in a large Colony, whose position would be suitably indicated by the title 'Financial Secretary', will form, with his immediate staff, an integral part of the Headquarters establishment of the Government. He should be a member of both the Executive and Legislative Councils; he should be responsible for the preparation and presentation to the Legislative Council of the Annual Estimates; and he should normally act as the spokesman of Government on financial and economic questions. His office should not be separate from, but should actually form part of, the central Secretariat. As an officer of the Secretariat, he will work under the general direction of, and maintain the closest association with, the Colonial Secretary; but it should be understood that, in his position as an Executive Councillor, he has the right of access to the Governor, and that his advice in regard to all questions of a financial and economic character will not be overruled without reference to the Governor. He should, moreover, have the right of addressing minutes direct to the Governor, provided that they are sent through the Colonial Secretary, who will be entitled to add his comments. This arrangement is not intended in any way to affect the Colonial Secretary's relation to the Governor, or his responsibilities as the Governor's chief adviser. In the Colonies, as in other countries, nearly all the major problems of the Government, if not themselves directly financial and economic in nature, probably involve important financial and economic considerations. The immediate budgetary implications of these problems will fall especially in the sphere of the Financial Secretary. Their more general bearings will remain primarily in the sphere of the Colonial Secretary, as the Governor's principal adviser upon major issues. But it will be a recognised part of the functions of the Financial Secretary to carry out a connected and continuous study of the financial and economic problems of the moment, in their wider bearings; and the Colonial Secretary will look especially to him for guidance and consultation in forming his own judgment upon them.

In view of the importance of the functions entrusted to him, the

Financial Secretary should be placed, in relation to the other officers of the Secretariat, in a position of independent authority, subject only to the Colonial Secretary himself. Some readjustment will therefore require to be considered in cases where the existing establishment provides for a Deputy Colonial Secretary. In such a case, in order to avoid misunderstanding, it would be desirable that the title of 'Deputy Colonial Secretary' should be changed to one of 'Under-Secretary' or 'Chief Assistant Secretary'. It would be for the Governor to decide, upon occasion, which of the two officers should act for the Colonial Secretary in the latter's absence.

Certain changes in organisation will be required in most Colonies if effect is to be given to the principles which have been laid down. It will be apparent in the first place that the responsibility for collecting and accounting for revenue, and for accounting for expenditure, is not included in the duties which should ordinarily be allocated to the Financial Secretary. This work, important as it is, does not in itself normally involve questions of policy, but consists in the application of a policy already embodied in laws and regulations. In these circumstances a separate organisation under an officer who might be styled 'Chief Accountant', or 'Accountant-General', should be formed to undertake that part of the duties of the existing Colonial Treasurer which comprises the responsibility for the control and the supervision of the accounting work of the Government, including the accounting work of any 'self-accounting' Departments. The structure of this organisation should be such that it offers within itself reasonable prospects of promotion. The contact of the Accountant-General's office with the central Secretariat will naturally be by way of the financial branch of the Secretariat, but the Financial Secretary should not be directly responsible for the administration of that office.

· · · · · ·

In the second place, the work of the Financial Secretary will call for abilities not falling short of the highest standard available in the Colonial Service. Moreover, the officer selected for such a position will require qualifications and experience of a nature for which the existing organisation of the public services in the Colonies does not in general provide. Not only should he be acquainted with the principles by which the financial and economic policy of Government should be guided, but he must also be familiar with the general system of administration, and with the actual conditions under which the work of the Government is carried on. He will thus be enabled to determine how far the application of general principles is administratively practicable. This consideration is one of no little importance. Financial and economic, no less than other, policies must be adapted to the limitations necessarily imposed by considerations of practical administration and convenience; and attempts to carry out proposals which, though theoretically sound and desirable, ignore such considerations, may be both costly and dangerous. It is therefore necessary to organise the service in such a way as to provide that officers possessing the requisite ability should have the opportunity to acquire the special experience which will fit them, in due course, to undertake the important responsibilities falling upon a Financial Secretary.

This reasoning leads to the conclusion that the normal field of recruitment for the higher financial staff must inevitably be the Colonial Administrative Service, though the door should never be barred to officers of any branch of the Service who are suitable for this class of work. The posts of Financial Secretary will themselves be 'super-scale' posts in the Colonial Administrative Service, and in order to secure that a succession of trained personnel should be available to fill these posts, as the product of a system designed for the purpose, the officers who will assist the Financial Secretary should normally be selected from members of the Administrative Service. It is not contemplated that officers who are posted to the financial branch of the Secretariat should be retained permanently in that capacity, or that their experience in the branch should necessarily be limited to a specified or to a single occasion. On the contrary, it is an essential feature of the organisation that it should include a definite, though flexible, system of exchange between duties in the financial branch and duties of an administrative character elsewhere. Such a system will serve the double purpose of providing the Financial Secretary continuously with assistants who have recent practical experience of administration and local conditions, and at the same time of creating and maintaining a pool of officers who possess the qualifications and experience required for promotion to senior posts carrying financial duties. Moreover, the principle of interchangeability would apply to the higher no less than to the junior posts. An officer selected for advancement on the financial side should by no means be regarded as having been side-tracked on to a specialised line. On the contrary, experience in financial work cannot fail to be of value to an officer who is to perform the duties of the highest administrative offices; and the possession of this experience should increase the officer's qualifications for promotion to such posts.

. . . . . .

The system described in the preceding paragraphs can be applied in its entirety only in the larger Dependencies. Similar principles, however, should be followed in the smaller Dependencies, so far as circumstances permit. In places where the only Administrative officer is the Colonial Secretary, it will be necessary to consider, in the light of local conditions, whether a reorganisation should be effected in which provision would be made for the creation of an administrative post on the financial side; or whether the existing organisation, in which the Colonial Secretary himself undertakes the responsibilities of a Financial Secretary, should be preserved.

To sum up: an organisation of the nature which has been indicated has certain very definite advantages as compared with the system which is to-day followed in most Colonies. It provides within the central Secretariat for a trained staff charged with the special function of exercising financial and economic control, as distinct from the subsidiary function of accounting for moneys received and spent; it ensures that the financial and economic aspects of Government policy in all its branches are kept constantly under expert review, and that new proposals are not put forward to the Governor for approval without having been fully examined and criticised by officers specially equipped to advise on their financial and economic as well as their political implications. Finally it provides, as part of the ordinary machinery of Government, a means by which the ablest officers in the Service may acquire the experience necessary to deal effectively with those problems of economics and finance which confront us to-day, and which will increasingly demand the best that the Service can give.

January, 1937.

APPENDIX II

SUMMARY OF APPOINTMENTS MADE BY THE SECRETARY OF STATE IN THE YEARS 1921–1936

The figures given under each year in the table below represent the numbers of candidates selected from outside the Colonial Service, irrespective of any promotions and transfers within it. The table does not include appointments filled by competitive examination nor those technical and other appointments which are filled by the Crown Agents for the Colonies.

Class of Appointment	1921	1922	1923	1924	1925	1926	1927	1928
Administrative*	90	18	67	72	85	103	101	153
Educational	43	39	30	43	46	76	64	74
Financial and Customs ...	21	4	12	9	10	20	18	19
Legal	10	3	8	11	12	7	16	14
Police	32	17	14	32	19	30	19	32
Medical	63	41	49	84	129	97	121	85
Agricultural	40	17	16	35	33	30	42	59
Veterinary	9	6	7	5	8	16	9	11
Forestry	25	3	10	20	16	13	11	11
Other Scientific Specialists (Biological, Analytical, etc.)	7	2	2	7	8	2	18	10
Survey and Geological ...	32	9	5	12	15	15	19	27
Other Appointments ...	13	14	12	22	25	15	22	12
	385	173	232	352	406	424	460	507
Agricultural Scholarships	—	—	—	—	16	17	15	20
Veterinary Scholarships	—	—	—	—	—	—	—	—

* Excluding appointments filled by competitive examination (i.e., Cadetships in Ceylon prior to 1935, and Cadetships in Malaya and Hong Kong prior to 1932).

APPENDIX II

Class of Appointment	1929	1930	1931	1932	1933	1934	1935	1936
Administrative*	115	80	20	25	36	44	67	68
Educational	62	65	18	4	1	5	9	9
Financial and Customs ...	15	14	11	3	9	21	22	11
Legal	11	16	8	7	8	9	17	22
Police	33	26	16	2	5	10	14	9
Medical	107	77	35	12	22	31	48	53
Agricultural	42	40	34	4	9	23	14	16
Veterinary	11	6	3	—	3	3	5	5
Forestry	13	14	7	4	6†	3†	9†	6†
Other Scientific Specialists (Biological, Analytical, etc.)	6	8	1	4	4	1	4	7
Survey and Geological ...	17	9	3	—	2	3	7	9
Other Appointments ...	17	23	9	5	7	11	19	22
	449	378	165	70	112	164	235	237
Agricultural Scholarships	22	24	18	14	7	9	8	10
Veterinary Scholarships	—	9	8	4	2	3	3	4

* See note on previous page.

† Actually the Secretary of State selected six Forestry graduates in 1933, three in 1934, eight in 1935 and five in 1936, and arranged for them to undergo post-graduate training at the Imperial Forestry Institute, Oxford, in anticipation of vacancies occurring in the Colonial Forest Service. Arrangements were also made for the temporary employment under the Forestry Commission in Great Britain of any of these candidates for whom appointments might not be available on the termination of the Institute course. All those selected prior to 1936 have been absorbed into the Colonial Forest Service.

APPENDIX III

LIST OF IMPORTANT DATES IN THE HISTORY OF THE COLONIAL SERVICE

1869 First competitive examination for Eastern Cadetships.

1895 Proposal by Mr J. Chamberlain, Secretary of State, for the formation of a single Colonial Service.

1902 Institution of the West African Medical Staff.

1907 Creation of separate Dominions Division in the Colonial Office.

1910 Formation of the Colonial Audit Department.

1911 Introduction of assimilated conditions of service in the Tropical African Dependencies.

1920 Post-War revision of conditions of service.
Reports of expert Committees on Medical, Agricultural and Veterinary services.

1921 Formation of the East African Medical Service.

1924 Report of Stevenson Committee on Pensions.
Institution of Forestry Probationerships.

1925 Separation of Colonial and Dominions Offices.

1926 Appointment of Chief Medical Adviser to the Secretary of State.

1927 Report of Lovat Committee on Agricultural Research and Administration.
First Colonial Office Conference.

1928 Report of Lovat Committee on Agricultural Research.

1929 Appointment of Agricultural Adviser to the Secretary of State.
Report of Lovat Committee on Veterinary Services.

1930 Report of Warren Fisher Committee on System of Appointment.
Second Colonial Office Conference.
Secretary of State's decision to unify the Colonial Service.
Establishment of Personnel Division at the Colonial Office.

1932 Formation of the Colonial Administrative Service.
Introduction of selection system for Eastern Cadetships.

1933 Formation of the Colonial Legal Service.
Issue of revised Colonial Regulations.

1934 Formation of the Colonial Medical Service.
Report of Plymouth Committee on Leave and Passage Conditions.

1935 Formation of the Colonial Forest Service, the Colonial Agricultural Service and the Colonial Veterinary Service.

1936 Report of Watson Committee on Widows' and Orphans' Pensions.

1937 Formation of the Colonial Police Service.

1938 Formation of the Colonial Survey Service, the Colonial Mines Service, the Colonial Geological Survey Service, the Colonial Postal Service and the Colonial Customs Service.

APPENDIX IV

NOTE ON BOOKS

I do not propose to attempt here to give an exhaustive bibliography of publications relating to the Colonial Empire, but rather to suggest some lines of reading which might be followed up by anyone who may wish to make a more detailed study of the questions relating to the Colonial Service which have necessarily been dealt with in outline only in this book.

For a general consideration of the position occupied by the Colonial Empire within the framework of the British Commonwealth, reference may be made to such works as *The British Empire*, by D. C. Somervell (Christophers, 1930), or *Magna Britannia*, by J. Coatman (Cape, 1936). The political structure and the machinery of Colonial government are described in *The Colonial Service*, by Sir Anton Bertram (Cambridge University Press, 1930), and *The Dominions and Colonial Offices*, by Sir George Fiddes (Putnam, 1926), to both of which books frequent reference has been made in the preceding pages.

Reference has also been made, in the footnotes, to the various reports of Committees and other official publications relating to the development of the Colonial Service. Special attention must, however, be directed to the report of the Committee on the System of Appointment (the "Warren Fisher" Committee), a study of which is indispensable to an appreciation of the recent history of the Service. This report is published by the Stationery Office as Cmd. 3554 (1930).

Amongst periodical publications, the semi-official *Dominions Office and Colonial Office List*, which is issued annually, must first be mentioned. It contains descriptive articles on the history, geography, constitution, economic position, etc., of each of the Colonial Dependencies, illustrated by excellent maps; also particulars of the Government staffs of each, and biographical notes of a large number of the officers; a list of the departments and staff of the Colonial Office; a transcript of the Colonial Regulations; and a mass of other valuable information. Various official publications of a more specialised character are issued periodically by the Stationery Office. There are annual reports on the social and economic progress of the peoples of the several Dependencies; the staff lists of the several unified Services (the Colonial Administrative Service List, the Colonial Medical

APPENDIX IV

Service List, etc.); the Economic Survey of the Colonial Empire; and a handbook on the conditions and cost of living in the Colonial Empire, compiled with special reference to the requirements of members of the Colonial Service.

Details of the establishments, salaries and conditions of employment of the main branches of the Service filled from this country are given in the series of Recruitment memoranda, issued by the Colonial Office. The scope of this series has been indicated on p. 216. In addition to the particulars mentioned, each of the memoranda contains a full and up-to-date bibliography, compiled in the Colonial Office Library. Copies of the current memoranda may be obtained free of charge by interested inquirers, on application to the Colonial Office.

These bibliographies run to some seven or eight pages of close print, and as they are so readily available, and, moreover, have the advantage of being constantly revised, there would be little to be gained by attempting here to make a selection from the very considerable number of books now before the public on particular areas or particular aspects of the Colonial problem. It may, however, be useful to note a few works which embody the actual experience of members of the Colonial Service, and give the reader a first-hand impression of what the life and work of the Service are like. Lord Lugard's classical *Dual Mandate in British Tropical Africa*, and Sir Frank Swettenham's *British Malaya*, for example, are authoritative studies of administrative practice and policy in the respective regions with which they deal. Amongst books of reminiscence and description, mention may be made of *Nigerian Days*, by A. C. G. Hastings (Cape, Travellers' Library); *In Days that are Dead* (Murray, 1926), and *Bushwhacking* (Heinemann, 1929), by Sir Hugh Clifford; *From a Colonial Governor's Note Book* (Hutchinson, 1936), and other works by Lt.-Col. Sir Reginald St Johnston; Gilchrist Alexander's *From the Middle Temple to the South Seas* (Murray, 1927), and *Tanganyika Memories* (Blackie, 1936); and a book by an officer's wife, *Kenya Days*, by Mrs M. Aline Buxton (Arnold, 1928). *A Refuge from Civilisation*, by R. Jones-Bateman (Arnold, 1931), contains some light-hearted comments on the work of an administrative officer in Ceylon.

A recent book of major importance to the student of the Colonial Service in action is Miss Margery Perham's *Native Administration in Nigeria* (Oxford University Press, 1937). Another recent publication containing much interesting information regarding the Colonial Services of the nineteenth century is *The Colonial Office*, by Dr Henry L. Hall (Longmans, 1937).

≪ 253 ≫

APPENDIX V

LIST OF GOVERNORSHIPS, ETC., OPEN TO MEMBERS OF THE COLONIAL SERVICE

Dependency	Title of Post	Emoluments		Classifi-cation fc Pensior
		Salary	Allowances	
Aden	Governor and Commander-in-Chief	Rs. 30,000	Rs. 10,000	III
Bahamas	,,	£3000	£300	III
Barbados	,,	£2500	£500	III
British Guiana	,,	£3500	£1500	II
British Honduras	,,	$8720*	$1000 and £300	III
Ceylon	,,	£6000	£2000	I
Cyprus	,,	£3000	£600	II
Falkland Islands	,,	£1500	£350	IV
Fiji	,,	£3600†	£1200†	II
Gambia	,,	£2500	£750	III
Gold Coast	,,	£4500	£1500	I
Hong Kong	,,	£4800	£2200	I
Jamaica	Captain-General and Governor-in-Chief	£5000	£500	I
Kenya	Governor and Commander-in-Chief	£6000‡	£2500	I
Leeward Islands	,,	£2200	£550	IV
Mauritius	,,	Rs. 50,000	Rs. 10,000	II
Nigeria	,,	£6500	£1750	I
Northern Rhodesia	,,	£3000	£1000	II
Nyasaland	,,	£2500	£500	III
Palestine	High Commissioner and Commander-in-Chief	£4500	£1500	I
St Helena	Governor and Commander-in-Chief	£1200	£300	IV
Seychelles	,,	Rs. 16,125	Rs. 3225	IV
Sierra Leone	,,	£3000	£1000	II
Somaliland	,,	£1600	£200	III
Straits Settlements	,,§	£5500	£2500	I
Tanganyika Territory	,,	£4500	£1500	I
Trinidad and Tobago	,,	$16,800‖	£8160	I
Uganda	,,	£3500	£1500	II
Windward Islands	,,	£2100	£400	IV
Zanzibar	British Resident	£2000	£1000	¶

* U.S. dollars.
† Fiji Pounds. Includes emoluments as High Commissioner for Western Pacific.
‡ Includes £1000 as High Commissioner for Transport.
§ Is also High Commissioner for Malay States.   ‖ $1 = 4s. 2d.
¶ Does not rank as a Governor for pension purposes.

February 1938

INDEX

Accountants, employment of, 195–7, 245
Accountants-General, 98, 196, 245
Accounts, Officer of Colonial, 215
Acting Allowances, 120
Aden Colony and Protectorate, xx
Administrative Service, Colonial, description, 128–42
  formation, 74
  qualifications for employment in, 134–5
  recruitment for, 73–4, 135, 216
  training course, 135
Administrative Services, development of, 7–8, 10–12, 18, 25–6
Administrators (West Indian Islands), 141
Advisers to Secretary of State, 214–15
Age limits for entry into Colonial Service, 135, 179, 233
Age of retirement, 114
Agents for the Colonies, Crown (see Crown Agents)
Agreements, engagement of staff on, 107, 192, 194
Agricultural Adviser (Colonial Office), 50, 174, 214
Agricultural Advisory Council, 50, 64, 174
Agricultural Scholarships, 47, 167
Agricultural Service, Colonial, 78, 166–70
Agricultural Services, Committees on, 44, 46–50, 64
  development of, 18, 25, 31, 44–50
Allowances, acting, 120
  children's (Malaya), 120
  duty, 21, 33, 200
  entertainment, 200
  expatriation, 120
  local, 36–7
  passage (Governors'), 201
  residential (Hong Kong), 139
  seniority, 33
  training, 136, 151, 163
  travelling, 120
Amery, Rt. Hon. L. S., 54–5, 226
Ampthill, Lord, 13
Analytical Chemists, employment of, 195

Animal Health (see Veterinary)
Anthropology, 136, 197
Antigua, xx
Appeal to Secretary of State, right of officers to, 66, 97, 108
Appointments, Private Secretary for, 13, 19, 57–8
Appointments Board, Colonial Service, 58, 74, 106, 217
Appointments Department, Colonial Office, 215–17
Archaeology, 197
Attorneys-General, 98, 143–6
Audit Service, Colonial, 175–7

Bahamas, xx, 28, 85
Barbados, xx, 28, 169
Basutoland, Bechuanaland Protectorate (see South Africa High Commission Territories)
Bell, Miss Gertrude, 236
Bell, Sir Hesketh, 28
Bermuda, xx, 113, 184, 199
Bertram, Sir Anton (author of The Colonial Service), xv, 98, 252
Bonus, Cost of Living, 35–6, 38
British Broadcasting Corporation, 14, 127
British East Africa (see Kenya)
British Guiana, xx, 28, 153, 166, 170, 179
British Honduras, xx, 85, 176
British Solomon Islands Protectorate, xx

Cadet Services, Eastern, 7–8, 58, 74, 139
Carnegie Corporation, grants from, 126
Ceylon, xx, 8, 23, 25, 38, 83, 95, 99, 142, 153, 165, 169, 170, 179, 184, 212, 229
Chamberlain, Rt. Hon. Joseph, 8–15, 225
Chemists, employment of, 168, 195
Chief Medical Adviser (Colonial Office), 44, 157–8, 214
Chief Secretaries, 98, 128, 141
Clifford, Sir Hugh, 132, 253
Climate, varieties of in Colonial Empire, xviii, 70, 124

Climatic Addition (pensions), 23
Colonial Administration Summer
School, 127
Colonial Administrative Service, etc.
(see Administrative Service, Colonial, etc.)
Colonial Empire, definition, xvii
growth, 3, 7, 11, 15, 31
Marketing Board, 223
Colonial Office, history, 206–8
interchangeability of staff with
Colonial Service, 137, 220–1
organisation, 9, 12–13, 53–8, 210–
21
Colonial Regulations, 3–5, 6, 86, 93,
108, 122
Colonial Secretaries, 98, 128, 141
Colonial Service, definition of term,
xvi–xvii
numbers of officers included in,
xvii, 230
Colonial Service Department (Co-
lonial Office), 218–19
Commercial undertakings, prohibited
to members of Service, 108
Committees:
Administrative Service, 72–3, 79
Agricultural Services, 44, 46–52,
64
Education (Advisory), 186, 214
Forestry Recruitment, 164
Leave and Passage Conditions, 82–
4
Medical (Advisory), 157
Medical Services, 42–3
Pensions, 24, 39–40
System of Appointment, 55–62
Tropical African Services, 20–1
Unification, 65–8, 71–2
Veterinary Services, 44–5, 51
Widows' and Orphans' Pensions,
81–2
Conference, Colonial Office, 1927,
48; 1930, 63–9
Confidential Reports on Officers, 13,
122–3
Constitutions, Colonial, xxii–xxiv, 95,
98
Consulting Physicians, 106, 118
Corona Club, 13–14, 69, 132
Courses of Instruction, 21, 67, 89,
135–6, 150, 163, 167, 171, 178,
188, 217
Crown Agents for the Colonies, 59,
107, 191, 193–4, 221–3
Crown, tenure of office at pleasure
of, 105–6, 147

Cunliffe-Lister, Rt. Hon. Sir Philip
(Viscount Swinton), 73–4, 203
Currency, 35–6, 111
Customs Service, Colonial, 180–1
Cyprus, xix, xxiii, 28, 84, 134, 139,
153, 165, 170, 172, 185, 195, 197

Death Gratuities, 40, 115
Death Rate (West Africa), 17
Dental Services, 161
Dependencies, definition of, xvii,
xxii
Disciplinary Regulations, 108
District Administration, principles
of, 132–3
Dominica, xx, 28
Dominions and Dependencies, dis-
tinction between, 9
Dominions Office, creation of, 54,
207
Duty Allowance (see Allowances)

East Africa Protectorate (see Kenya)
East African Dependencies, con-
ditions of employment in, 21,
34–7, 80, 116
growth of, 15, 31
Trade and Information Office, 223
East African Medical Service, 43,
77, 225
Eastern Cadetships (see Cadet Ser-
vices)
Economic Department (Colonial
Office), 213
Education in the Colonies, Advisory
Committee on, 186, 214
Education Service, Colonial, 186–
90
Efficiency bars, 32, 138–9, 165, 172
Emoluments, pensionable, 112–13
Empire Cotton Growing Corporation,
170
Engineers, employment of, 182, 191–
4
Entertainment Allowance (see Allow-
ances)
Entomologists, employment of, 168,
173
Examinations, Colonial Adminis-
trative Service Course, 136
Examinations, competitive, 8, 67,
73–4
Examinations, Law and Language,
107, 136
Executive Councils, 98
Expatriation Allowance (see Allow-
ances)

Falkland Islands, xx, 24, 85, 140, 143
Family Passages, 33, 85, 115–17
Federated Malay States (see Malaya)
Fiddes, Sir George, xv, 210, 252
Fiji, xx, xxiv, 24, 28, 112, 139, 153, 172
Financial Adviser (Colonial Office), 39, 215
Financial Secretaries, 98, 130, 243–7
Fisher, Sir Warren, 55, 72
Forest Officers, recruitment of, 31, 45–6, 163–7
Forest Service, Colonial, 78, 162–6
Forestry Institute, Imperial, 46, 78, 163–4
Forestry Scholarships, 164

Gambia Colony and Protectorate, xx, 15, 176, 180
Game Preservation, 197
Geological Survey Service, Colonial, 184–5
Gibraltar, xix, xxiii, 116, 140, 176, 195, 199
Gilbert and Ellice Islands Colony, xx
Gold Coast Colony and Protectorate, xxi, 10, 13, 15, 28, 33, 141–2, 148, 153, 159, 166, 169, 172–3, 180, 184–5, 189, 195, 197
Gore, Rt. Hon. W. Ormsby, 49, 130, 132–3, 162, 230
Governors, xxiii, 5, 93–6, 142, 198–205
Governorships, list of, 255
Gowers, Sir William, 65
Gratuities, Death, 40, 115
    Invaliding after short service, 113
    Reduced Pensions and, 40, 113
Grenada, xx, 28

Heads of Departments, position of in Colonies, 99–100
High Commissioners, xxiii
Hong Kong, xx, 7–8, 83, 111, 113, 116, 117, 134, 139, 142, 146, 153, 158, 172, 173, 177, 179, 184, 189, 195, 212, 221
Honours, 127, 147
Housing, 117

Imperial College of Tropical Agriculture, 47, 167, 170
Imperial Forestry Institute (see Forestry Institute)
Indian Civil Service, 7, 8, 70
Indirect Rule, principles of, 133–4

Injury Pensions, 114
Investments of Officers, rules relating to, 108
'Iraq, xvii, 31
Irvine, Sir James, 164

Jamaica, xx, xxiii, 153, 169, 179, 195
Judges, 114, 143, 146–8
Judicial Committee of Privy Council, 147
Justice, administration of, 143
Justices, Chief, 143, 146–7

Kenya, xxi, 15, 20, 35–7, 88–9, 98, 116, 124, 132, 140, 142, 146, 166, 169, 172, 173, 177, 179, 180, 182, 184, 190–1, 193, 195, 196–7

Labour Departments, 131
Lagos, Colony of, 10, 15
Law Officers in Colonies, 98, 143–7
Leave Regulations, 5, 21–2, 34, 60, 82–6, 115–17
Leeward Islands, xx, 28, 141
Legal Adviser (Colonial Office), 214
Legal Service, Colonial, 76, 143–8
Legislative Councils, xxiii, 98
Lists, Unified Service, 104, 142
Liverpool School of Tropical Medicine, 16, 150
Local Allowances, 36–7
Local Civil Service (Kenya), 88–9
Locally Recruited Officers, employment of, 96–7, 229–30
London School of Tropical Medicine, 16, 150
Lovat, Lord, 47–9
Lugard, Lord, 236, 253

Malaya, xx, xxiii, 7–8, 23, 37–8, 74, 77, 105, 111, 113, 116–17, 134, 139, 141, 142, 145, 146, 152, 153, 159, 160, 165, 166, 169, 170, 172, 173, 177, 178–9, 180–1, 182, 184–5, 189, 190, 194, 195, 196–7, 223, 253
Malayan Civil Service, 7–8, 38, 74, 111, 139, 141
Malayan Information Agency, 223
Malta, xix, xxiii, 3, 84, 140, 199
Mandated Territories, xvi, xix, xxi, 31, 202
Manson, Sir Patrick, 16
Mauritius, xix, xxiv, 3, 23, 28, 95–6, 165, 169, 184, 195
Medical Advisory Committee, 157

INDEX

Medical Service, Colonial, 77, 100, 149–59
Medical Services, development of, 16–17, 43, 149
Meteorological Services, 184
Milner, Lord, 42, 46–7
Mines Service, Colonial, 185

Native Administrations, xxiv, 133–4
Native States, xx, xxiii–xxiv, 105
New Hebrides, xx
Nigeria, xxi, xxiv, 10, 15, 18, 20, 25, 28, 32, 33, 132, 141–2, 146, 153, 159, 166, 169, 172–3, 177, 179–80, 182, 184–5, 190, 193, 195, 196–7, 236, 253–4
Northern Rhodesia, xxi, 31, 116, 124, 160, 169, 172–3, 180, 184, 190
Nursing Services, 159–61
Nyasaland Protectorate, xxi, 15, 36, 169, 172, 185, 190

Overseas Nursing Association, 59, 160
Overseas Service (Kenya), 88–9

Palestine, xix, xxiii, 31, 84, 116, 120, 134, 139, 153, 165, 170, 172, 177, 190, 195, 221
Passages, Governors', 5, 201
  Officers' and Families', 5, 33, 85, 115–16
Passfield, Rt. Hon. Lord, 55, 63–4, 69–72
Patronage, Secretary of State's, 6–7, 9, 28, 57
Pensions, Governors', 202–5
  Officers', 5, 22–4, 29, 39–40, 81, 112–14
  Widows' and Orphans', 22, 81–2, 119–20
Personnel Division (Colonial Office), 56, 64, 72, 81, 215–20
Petition to Secretary of State, right of (see Appeal)
Pim, Sir Alan, report on Kenya, 98, 172
Plantations, Council of Trade and, 206
Plymouth, Lord, 82
Police Service, Colonial, 177–80
Postal Service, Colonial, 181–3
Prisons Service, Colonial (proposed), 180
Private Practice, Medical, 43, 77, 154–6

Private Secretaries, to Secretary of State (see Appointments)
Probation, 107–8
Promotion Bars, 110, 164–5
Promotion, rules relating to, 103, 121–2
Promotions Machinery (Colonial Office), 13, 56–7, 123, 218–19
Provincial Administration, system of, 132–3
Provincial Commissioners, 33, 36–7, 133, 136, 140–1

Quarters, provision of, 117
Quarters, value of for pension purposes, 113

Railway Services, 190–3
Read, Sir Herbert, 44
Recruitment, Director of, 19, 215
  figures relating to, 235, 248–9
  machinery (Colonial Office), 215–17
  problems of, 7–13, 16–19, 21, 26–7, 30–1, 42–52, 54–60, 234–5
Resident Commissioners, 141
Residents, 33, 132–3, 141
Retirement, age of, 114
Rhodesia (see Northern Rhodesia)
Ross, Sir Ronald, 16
Rulers, Native, xxiii
Rupee currency, 35–6, 111–12

St Christopher-Nevis (St Kitts-Nevis), xx, 141
St Helena, xx, 3, 143
St Lucia, xx, 141
St Michael and St George, Order of, 127
St Vincent, xx, 141
Salary Scales, 20–1, 32–8, 80, 109–11, 138–9, 145, 151–3, 160–1, 164–5, 168, 172–3, 176, 179–80, 182–5, 196
Sarawak, Rajah of, Fund for assisting officers in education of children, 126
Scholarships, Agricultural, 47, 166–8, 235
  Forestry, 164
  Veterinary, 51–2, 171–2, 235
Secretariat Organisation in Colonies, 98, 128–31
Secretary of State, History of Office, 206–7
  Powers, etc., 93–7, 121–3, 206
Security of Tenure, 94–6, 108

≪ 258 ≫

Sierra Leone Colony and Protectorate, xx, 3, 141, 166, 169, 180, 185
Solicitors, employment of, 148
Solicitors-General, 4, 98, 146
Solomon Islands (*see* British Solomon Islands Protectorate)
Somaliland Protectorate, xxi, xxiii, 15, 36, 84, 115, 143, 180, 201–2
South Africa High Commission Territories, xvii, 134
Stanley, Sir Herbert, 64
Stephenson, Sir Edward, 177
Stevenson, Lord, 39
Straits Settlements (*see* Malaya)
Sudan, Anglo-Egyptian, xvii, 204
Superannuation (*see* Pensions)
Survey Service, Colonial, 183–4
Swinton, Lord (*see* Cunliffe-Lister)

Tanganyika Territory, xxi, 31, 35, 85, 116, 132, 141, 142, 148, 166, 169, 170, 172, 173, 179–80, 182, 184, 185, 190, 193, 195
Technical Departments, relation with Administration, 132–3
Thomas, Rt. Hon. J. H., 46
Tomlinson, Sir George, 72
Training (*see* Courses of Instruction)
Transfer, liability to, 62, 65, 66–7, 68–9, 74–5, 103, 124
Travelling Allowances, 120
Treasurers, 4, 98, 130, 243–7
Tropical African Services Course, 21
Tropical Diseases, Bureau of Hygiene and, 158
Tropical Medicine, Courses in, 150–1
Schools of, 16, 150–1
Tropical Services Committee, 20
Trusteeship, principle of, xxii–xxiii, 133–4, 224, 232, 237–9

Uganda Protectorate, xxi, xxiv, 15, 20, 28, 35, 85, 116, 132, 140, 166,

169, 172, 173, 180, 182, 184, 185, 189, 191, 195, 197
Under-Secretaries of State, 211
Unified Services, list of, 101
position of in relation to Service as a whole, 96–104, 227–30
Universities, British, courses at, 135–6
recruitment from, 134–5, 232–6
Universities, Colonial, 158, 189

Veterinary Scholarships, 51–2, 171–2, 235
Veterinary Service, Colonial, 170–3
Vital Statistics (West Africa), 17

War, the Great, effect on Colonial Service of, 30–1
"Warren Fisher" Committee, 55–62, 227
Watson, Sir Alfred, 81
West African Dependencies, conditions of employment in, 10–11, 15–17, 19–22, 32–4, 84, 110, 114, 115, 138–9, 151, 160
development of, 13, 18, 25–6
list of, xx–xxi
West African Medical Staff, 16–17, 20, 27–8, 43, 77, 225, 234
West African Nursing Staff, 160
Western Pacific Dependencies, xx, 134, 139, 141
West India Committee, 223
West Indies, xx, xxii, xxiv, 3, 10, 23, 85, 95, 115, 117, 140, 141, 145, 169, 179, 189, 223
Widows' and Orphans' Pensions (*see* Pensions)
Wilson, Brigadier-General Sir Samuel, 54, 172
Windward Islands, xx, 3, 141
Women, employment of, 18, 149, 159–61, 187, 190, 236–7

Zanzibar, xxi, xxiii, 15, 36, 85, 116, 169, 180

Note: Since this map was prepared, the Aden Colony and P

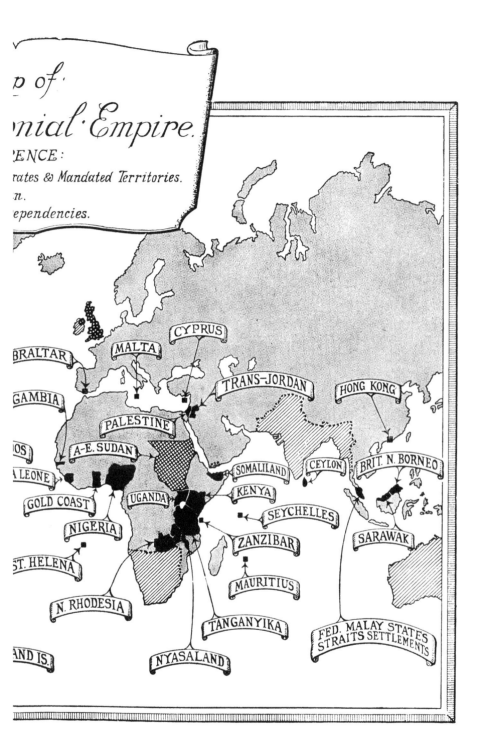

Map of·

nial·Empire.

ENCE:

rates & Mandated Territories.

n.

ependencies.

BRALTAR

MALTA

CYPRUS

GAMBIA

TRANS-JORDAN

HONG KONG

PALESTINE

OS

A-E. SUDAN

LEONE

SOMALILAND

CEYLON

BRIT. N. BORNEO

GOLD COAST

UGANDA

KENYA

NIGERIA

SEYCHELLES

SARAWAK

ZANZIBAR

ST. HELENA

N. RHODESIA

MAURITIUS

TANGANYIKA

FED. MALAY STATES
STRAITS SETTLEMENTS

AND IS.

NYASALAND

Protectorate have been incorporated in the Colonial Empire.

For EU product safety concerns, contact us at Calle de José Abascal, 56–1°, 28003 Madrid, Spain or eugpsr@cambridge.org.

www.ingramcontent.com/pod-product-compliance
Ingram Content Group UK Ltd.
Pitfield, Milton Keynes, MK11 3LW, UK
UKHW010346140625
459647UK00010B/867